keep the international peace made in the winter of 1763. However, as *Borderland Empires* compellingly demonstrates, the imperial adjustments ratified in Paris had far-reaching and in some cases devastating effects on the society and individuals of colonial Florida. Mr. Gold examines their repercussions in this volume, combining judicious appraisal with compassion for the human beings caught in the trammels of imperial policy. *Borderland Empires* is a significant contribution to the history of eighteenth-century colonialism in America. It furnishes in addition insights of contemporary relevance into the implications of international power politics. *Borderland Empires* is a timely and important book. Scholars and students of history will find it absorbing and enlightening; those particularly concerned with the history of Florida and southeastern America, the development of colonialism in America, eighteenth-century international political struggles, and patterns of imperialism will find it of special interest. The book, documented with tables and illustrated with maps, will also interest economists, sociologists, and political scientists. In a general sense, however, this work has broad appeal to all thoughtful individuals concerned with the effects of geopolitics on unique human societies.

Robert L. Gold is Assistant Professor of History at Southern Illinois University. He is a graduate of the University of Iowa, where he took his Ph.D. degree. Equipped with a knowledge of the Spanish language and eighteenth-century Spanish paleology, Mr. Gold has contributed articles and reviews to *The Americas*, the *Florida Historical Quarterly*, and *Hispanic American Historical Review*. He has traveled widely in Mexico and has served on the staff of the University of the Americas in Mexico City.

Borderland Empires in Transition

THE TRIPLE-NATION TRANSFER OF FLORIDA

By Robert L. Gold

Carbondale and Edwardsville

SOUTHERN ILLINOIS UNIVERSITY PRESS

FEFFER & SIMONS, INC.

London and Amsterdam

For Beverly, Kruger, and Rikert

Preface

The transfer of Florida from Franco-Spanish to British control required almost two years of international activity. From February, 1763, to September, 1764, England, France, and Spain acted together and independently to arrange the exchange of colonial rule in Florida. The imperial interchange included the surrender of French Louisiana and Spanish Florida, the transfer of regal and military authority, population movement, and property disposition. The exchange even affected Indian life in the southeastern borderlands. European empires in America were truly in transition after the Treaty of 1763.

In the months that followed the final ratification of the Treaty of Paris, colonial officials of all three nations became involved in the migration and settlement of their subjects. Once the territorial cession was concluded, the movement of population concerned each of the European monarchies. His Catholic Majesty, Charles III, was seriously committed to the obligation of resettling Spanish Floridians in other areas of the Hispanic Indies. George III of England and the Board of Trade were engrossed with the work of planning and settling the recently acquired provinces. In East and West Florida, Englishmen attempted to pacify the inimical Indian tribes. Since somewhat less than one-half of the French Floridians continued their residence under British rule, Louis XV faced the task of supporting the claims of remaining citizens of Mobile and moving other Frenchmen out of Florida.

This study therefore concerns the international transfer of Franco-Spanish Florida and the imperial changes that followed the Treaty of 1763. A three year period, 1763–65, is actually under consideration, although this analysis also includes the relevant history of Florida before and after the era of exchange. In those years

England, France, and Spain eventually adjusted their empires to the cartographic modifications made in Paris. The imperial adjustment was not easily achieved. What happened to the colonies, governments, institutions, and people of Florida after 1763 becomes the subject matter of this manuscript. Although the period under investigation may appear to be arbitrary, it is really quite reasonable and convenient. During those years the rivalry of England, France, and Spain reached a climax in the continuing struggle for the Mississippi Valley and the Florida Gulf Coast. The interval also provides a historical bridge between the First Spanish Period (1565–1763) and the subsequent British Period (1763–84). Since both of these eras have been previously exposed to separate scholarly examination but never before connected historically, perhaps this study will offer some continuity for the history of colonial Florida in the late eighteenth century.

The most important source for this history has been the Stetson Collection of photostated Spanish records obtained from the Archivo General de las Indias in Sevilla, Spain. This famous collection is presently located in the P. K. Yonge Memorial Library of Florida History at the University of Florida in Gainesville, Florida. The library also serves as a depository for an enormous quantity of British, Cuban, French, and other Spanish materials and microfilms. Most of the P. K. Yonge Library's manuscripts relate to the First Spanish Period of Florida history. The bulk of these documents remain in photocopy form, but some of the colonial records have been transcribed and others have been roughly translated. The Archivo General de la Nación, México, the Library of Congress, and the Mark F. Boyd Library of Florida History in Tallahassee, Florida, offered the other significant sources for the research of this study.

FOR THEIR CONCERN with the completion of this work, I should like to acknowledge the invaluable assistance of several friends and colleagues. Initially, I want to express my gratitude to Professor Charles Gibson of the University of Michigan whose constructive criticism, kindly counsel, and suggestions have contributed so significantly to the final form of my manuscript. As a graduate student of Charles Gibson, I shall always be grateful for the guidance of this scholarly and humane historian. I should also like to thank Professor Charles W. Arnade of the University of South Florida for directing me toward the subject and sources of my research; from Charles

Arnade, I learned about the significance of the Spanish periods of Florida history and the availability of research materials at the P. K. Yonge Memorial Library of Florida History. To Professor C. Harvey Gardiner, Professor Thad E. Hall, and Professor Hensley C. Woodbridge of Southern Illinois University, and Professor Donald E. Worcester of Texas Christian University I am indebted for editorial recommendations and careful examination of my manuscript. My special appreciation goes to Librarian Elizabeth Alexander and the staff of the P. K. Yonge Library of Florida History who generously devoted their time and effort to make all their late eighteenth-century papers and collections accessible to me. Thanks are also definitely in order for the consideration offered me by Florida Historian Mark F. Boyd whose Anglo-Spanish sources were especially important to this study. To Margaret L. Chapman, former librarian of the P. K. Yonge Library and now librarian of Special Collections of the University of South Florida, my warm thanks for her encouragement and assistance throughout my research and writing. I particularly want to acknowledge my gratitude to Kenneth H. Beeson, Jr. who continually provided me with his friendship and knowledge of the British Period of Florida history. Mr. William G. Wolff also deserves my appreciation for his necessary proofreading assistance. My principal debt is to my wife, Beverly, upon whom I have relied for months of typing, proofreading, and consolation.

Robert L. Gold

Southern Illinois University
September, 1968

Contents

Illustrations

TABLES

Borderland Empires in Transition

The Triple-Nation Transfer of Florida

1

Spanish Colonial Florida
1513–1763

The Establishment and Early History
of Florida

England assumed legal and sovereign control of Franco-Spanish Florida on February 10, 1763. After more than a century of English imperialism, which assumed the form of southern invasions and guerrilla forays, Great Britain wrested Florida from Spain following the Seven Years' War. The Treaty of Paris concluded the long colonial war. Because a British armada seized Havana, Cuba, in the summer of 1762, the Spanish negotiators reluctantly bartered Florida away in order to retrieve their great treasure terminal of the Indies. Cuba was regained in 1763 after only eleven months of English occupation.

The preliminary articles of peace among Great Britain, France, and Spain were arranged at Fontainebleau on November 3, 1762. Later, on February 10, 1763, signatories of the three countries signed the final treaty of peace. Final ratification followed on February 25. Great Britain, France, and Spain respectively ratified the Treaty of Paris on February 21, 23, and 25, 1763. Less than four months of diplomacy were required to conclude almost two hundred years of Spanish colonial rule in *Tierra Florida*.[1]

The magnificent Aztec civilization of Mexico was still unconquered when Adelantado Juan Ponce de León first sighted the Florida shoreline in 1513. Ponce de León, seeking the legendary island of Bimini, landed on an uncertain floral portion of the peninsula. The new discovery was called "La Florida," and claimed in the name of His Catholic Majesty, the king of Spain. La Florida was without boundary limits. In the middle of the sixteenth century, the crown still considered Quebec to be a part of Florida. In Castile all of North America was called *Tierra Florida,* and somewhat later Spanish Florida was designated as the Atlantic coast area south of the Gulf of St. Lawrence. Actually, this land extended as far to the north and west as military power could support it in the face of later English and French encroachments. Pope Alexander VI's Papal Bull of May 4, 1493, legally granted the crown of Spain "all the Islands and Continents discovered towards the West and South, drawing a line from the North to the South pole, distant one hundred leagues toward the West and South from any of the islands known as the Azores and Cape de Verde Islands." [2] The powers of Europe, however, could not be expected to accept a Papal decision concerning international boundaries for the New World.

Charles I and Philip II initially failed to colonize Florida. In the fifty years that followed the discovery of Florida, Spain entertained only exploratory interest in the tropical colony where gold and silver ores were absent, and where fierce, uncivilized, and uncooperative Indians were too obviously present. The peninsula served as a navigational point on the *carrera* (route) *de las Indias.* For years the treasure-laden *flotas* (fleets) bearing the opulence of the Indies therefore glided past the uncolonized shores of Florida on their way to Europe. Finally, when the Spanish court learned that a colony of French Huguenots had infiltrated the Florida lands in 1564, Spain determined to colonize the peninsula. In the scheme of Spanish colonization was a design to annihilate the unwelcome foreign heretics. The Florida coastal waters were too near the Bahama Channel, New Spain, and the Caribbean to be allowed to remain under the control of any other European power.

Philip II of Spain quickly responded to the occupation of mainland America. In order to protect Spanish territories as well as the convoys of bullion that flowed from Havana through the Florida seas to the Iberian Peninsula, Philip II, on March 20, 1565, agreed to a *capitulación y asiento* (royal contract with specific rights and responsibilities) with Admiral Don Pedro Menéndez de Avilés for the colonization and conquest of Florida. Under the instructions of these orders the French intrusion was destroyed. Although Menéndez squelched the first serious threat to Spanish hegemony in the Indies, numerous other European challenges followed in succeeding years.[3]

Spain retarded but never thwarted the trespasses of England and France in the immense land of La Florida. Spanish conquistadores settled the Americas approximately one hundred years before the other European nations began scrambling for New World colonies. The Spaniards' presumption, however, that all the area north of Ponce de León's landing therefore belonged to the throne of the Catholic kings, was contemptuously ignored by the seafaring states of Europe throughout the colonial period. Iberian claims to the Western Hemisphere were limited by the inevitable passage of time and enervated by numerous political and economic circumstances. The loss of the 1588 Armada, the continuous expenses of the dynastic and religious wars, the erosion of the Spanish colonial machinery, the inflation and monetary devaluation that accompanied the bullion fleets to Spain, and the continuing harassments of the other European powers eventually debilitated Hispanic control of the New World. Inevitably, England, France, and even the Netherlands gradually sliced large pieces of boundless La Florida from the body of Spain's western empire.

Before the end of the sixteenth century, Spain was already beginning to feel pressure on its Florida possessions in America. Initially, foreign pirates besieged the colony in Florida. Corsairs from western Europe habitually hovered in the Gulf streams awaiting the opportunity to loot wayward Spanish galleons. One unusually daring filibuster, Francis Drake, even sacked the town of St. Augustine (San Agustín) in 1586 after a successful year of operations against American shipping.[4]

Locally, the power of the insignificant colony disappeared during the latter part of the sixteenth century. In 1597 an Indian insurrection reduced the actual area of Spanish control to a narrow plot of territory extending around the fringes of the St. Augustine *presidio* and along the northern shores into contemporary southern Georgia. Spaniards ruled a very small portion of La Florida. At the death of Menéndez in 1574, Spain asserted military authority over a wide area of territory northeast of St. Augustine. But continuous contractions decreased Spanish holdings in Florida. Many frontier outposts were abandoned until the Indian uprisings of 1597 left the Spaniards little more than a seaport *presidio* (garrison). Before the beginning of the seventeenth century, St. Augustine was almost obliterated by fire and water. After a fire destroyed most of the wooden town in 1599, an inundating wave seemingly delivered a *coup de grâce* to Spain's sixteenth-century attempts to establish a solid base in Florida.[5]

The colony almost committed suicide in 1602. In an atmosphere darkened by rumors of the British arrival at Roanoke, many Spaniards debated the expense and value of the settlement. The frontier entertained a Cuban *visitador* (inspector) who sojourned in St. Augustine while studying the public testimony for and against the abandonment of the colony. When all the argumentation had been weighed, the crown decided to retain its restricted foothold on the Atlantic coast. Florida therefore survived.[6]

Although Florida continued to represent Spanish territorial strength in eastern North America, the Hispanic position seemed little improved in the early seventeenth century. Similarly, St. Augustine's indigent economy indicated no promise of future progress. Plagued by inept agricultural endeavors, indifferent economic sustenance, and the austere military character of the colony, Florida was indeed a dreary place until the latter part of the century. Nevertheless, Floridians persevered through their impoverished frontier life obeying royal instructions. While their own lives often lacked significance, their existence significantly served the Catholic kings and the Spanish mission to obviate any northern threat to the Caribbean routes of trade. The crown also hoped that the geographic position of Florida would minimize the amount of foreign propaganda and smuggling that might menace the viceroyalty of New Spain.

During the seventeenth century, the kings of Spain expanded their control into the interior of the peninsula. The movement westward to Timucua (central and northeast Florida and southern Georgia), Apalache (the environs of Tallahassee), and northward to Guale (southeastern Georgia) followed the swath of the religious order of St. Francis. Franciscan missionaries arrived in Florida in 1573, succeeding the exhausted Society of Jesus. The Jesuits left Florida in 1572 after five dismal years with the Indians. As the zealous Franciscans foraged for converts through the serpent and insect infested swamps of inland Florida, scattered Indian missions were founded among the Apalache, Timucuan, and Guale peoples. By 1675 the Franciscans achieved their missionary apogee with approximately forty-four centers of conversion and farming. Motivated by pious convictions, the missionaries directed their conversion efforts into the previously hostile areas north and west of the St. Augustine *presidio* and east of Pensacola. Colonization followed the Franciscan missionary organization.[7]

Because the Florida Indians were basically migratory and uncivilized,[8] the mission rather than the *encomienda* became the institutional structure upon which Spanish colonial power rested. The indigenous peoples and territories of Florida were integrated within a system of missions which offered the Spaniards the typical opportunities of expansion, exploitation, and proselytization. But, in Florida, the mission system failed. According to Charles W. Arnade, "The failure of the mission to fulfill its religious, political, and military functions in Florida was the single most important reason for the failure of Florida." [9] While the failure of the "mission" as a colonial institution in Florida may be attributed to Spanish errors, the advent of British attacks on the Franciscan system actually precipitated the end of Spain's control in the interior. Florida contracted in consequence to the reduction of Franciscan authority.

From 1702 to 1704 Governor James Moore of Carolina launched two onslaughts on Spanish Florida. St. Augustine, with its recently constructed Castillo de San Marcos, resisted the first siege, although the residential areas of the town were razed by British and Spanish gunshot. During the second assault the missionary system was irreparably smashed. Moore's troops and Indian allies devastated the Franciscan missions in Apalache and Timucua and dispersed the Indians throughout the peninsula. This crushing blow ended Florida's "golden age" (1672–1704). During those years, Spanish Floridians witnessed the growth of a large population of subject peoples,[10] the evolution of the missionary system, the erection of St. Augustine's *coquina* (shellstone) fortress, and the beginning of commercial agriculture and cattle raising in the territory between the present cities of Gainesville and Tallahassee.[11] In the eighteenth century the *presidio* of St. Augustine continued to obstruct foreign movement along the Gulf Coast and Bahama Channel. But the possibility of future economic or missionary development for Florida apparently passed away with the retiring English army.

Even as Spanish Florida enjoyed its golden epoch, ominous signs indicated that the halcyon days were limited. Eighty years after Drake struck at St. Augustine another British pirate fleet burned and plundered the town in 1668. The results of that attack prompted the Spaniards to build a stone fortress for defense. All nine previous forts had been constructed of wood.[12] Two years later the Spanish community was startled to learn of the English founding of Charles Town, Carolina. The establishment of Charles Town, shown on Map 1, conclusively proved that England was *de facto* ruler of northern or upper La Florida. A coexistence treaty with Great Britain in 1670 virtually conceded that control. The new Carolina colony became England's southern boundary in America. Anglo-Spanish colonial coexistence, however, faced one important legal and political problem: the Carolina charter of 1665 included St. Augustine and the northern portion of Spanish Florida.

Rapacious raids, skirmishes, wars, and the collapse of the Guale missionary attempts in Georgia followed the birth of the British colony. The Guale Indians, who experienced an ascetic life of paternalism, prayer, and toil under the Franciscans, were easily seduced into rum and weapon-bearing alliances with the British colonists. By 1686 the Georgia missionaries migrated southward. The Franciscans abandoned such missionary centers as Santa Catalina de Guale and San Felipe, and Anglo-Indian forces attacked and eventually eradicated all other remaining missions. The plight of the Guale missions was only a prelude to the punishment that the Franciscan system would feel during Queen Anne's War.[13]

Eighteenth-Century Florida

Governor James Moore besieged St. Augustine in 1702. Unable to breach the defenses of the Castillo de San Marcos, the Carolina governor raised his siege, leaving a burned city behind his withdrawal from Florida. One year later in December, 1703, he returned and stormed the Apalache and Timucua mission villages. Thereafter missionary activities were generally discontinued in Florida, although the Franciscans made some later attempts to resuscitate the religious complex.[14]

The departure of Moore permitted the Spaniards to rebuild St. Augustine on the foundations of the razed city. Once again buildings and dwellings were reshaped out of the stark remains south and west of the impregnable Castillo de San Marcos. By 1718, Spanish Floridians established the frontier outpost, San Marcos de Apalache, to defend the western Gulf Coast and the Mississippi Valley. The hinterlands of the interior, however, were never again secure under Spanish rule. Similar to the late sixteenth and early seventeenth centuries, the colony persevered as an almost isolated seaport *presidio* with frontier stations north and west of St. Augustine. Until 1763 British intrusions and Indian hostilities persisted, making life in St. Augustine extremely precarious. The *presidio* also suffered from Spain's apathetic support which often permitted the *situado* (subsidy) payments to lapse years behind the garrison's everyday needs. Since the agrarian program of San Agustín was unproductive, the delays in subsidy payment forced the Florida governors to direct

1   Spanish Florida, 1670–1763

a credit economy which was founded upon the purchase of expensive and sometimes spoiled Cuban provisions at usurious interest charges.[15] As a consequence, Spanish Florida only "existed" in the eighteenth century.

At the juncture of the seventeenth and eighteenth centuries, Spain grappled with foreign usurpers in West Florida and the lower Mississippi Valley. La Salle's Mississippi claims and Iberville's settlement at Mobile seriously threatened New Spain and the Hispanic Caribbean. The actual existence of French Louisiana appalled Florida Spaniards. Enemy occupation of those territories would have permitted invading forces to assault the heartland of the Spanish colonial empire through the Gulf of Mexico. When English ambitions to the lower Mississippi Valley abated temporarily because of Indian problems in Carolina, the French challenge to the Gulf Coast became Spain's primary concern. In order to protect that threshold to Spanish America, the Spaniards established new Texas missions and returned to Pensacola Bay, previously discovered by Tristan de Luna. The Pensacola *presidio,* founded in 1699 by the naval commander, Andrés de Arriola, was called San Carlos de Antonio.[16]

Spain warded off French attacks at Pensacola until 1718–19, when a ground and naval offensive captured the coastal garrison. The seizure of Spanish Pensacola occurred in the same months as the founding of New Orleans. France occupied Pensacola for only four years. After expelling the French aggressors, first in battle and then by treaty (1723), the Spaniards reconstructed their military station on Santa Rosa Island. A hurricane in 1754, however, washed the island post into the sea. After the drowning of Santa Rosa another settlement was established near the present site of Pensacola. This *presidio* survived precariously through the last years of the First Spanish Period because of the assistance of the St. Augustine government and the attentive viceregal authorities of New Spain. Pensacola thereafter partially blocked French and English military thrusts into the Mississippi Valley and the Gulf of Mexico.[17] French Louisiana, however, inevitably limited Spanish power in Florida.

During the years that followed Moore's attack, the English colonists continued their southern advance into Florida. They were seeking a strategic base from which to wage their battle for the Mississippi basin and the Ohio River Valley. By 1721 Great Britain had stationed a fortress as far south as the Altamaha River. Five years later a guerrilla sortie descended southward from the new fort. When General James Oglethorpe received the Georgia grant in 1732–33, he improved his military position by the placement of fortresses on Amelia, Cumberland, Fort George, and St. Simon Islands. Except for the latter station, all of Oglethorpe's "defenses" were installed on the Atlantic coast south of Georgia. As British colonization proceeded toward the St. John's River, the Spaniards became increasingly cognizant of the possibility of a major engagement with England.[18]

The War of Jenkins' Ear (1739–43) provided Oglethorpe with the necessary pretext to invade Florida.[19] Since Hispanic defenses outside of St. Augustine were inadequate, the Oglethorpe army swiftly invaded the St. John's River Valley in January, 1740. The frontier outposts of Picolata and San Francisco de Pupo were quickly overrun and the Negro troops at Fort Mosa[20] capitulated in May. Once again the Castillo de San Marcos repulsed an organized English attack. Except for frightening the civilian population and ineffectually splintering the Castillo's bastions with cannonading, the Oglethorpe campaign was a military failure. When the conflict developed into a lengthy siege, the tired British soldiers retired north to Georgia. A subsequent English assault two years later met with similar frustration.[21]

In the era between Oglethorpe's withdrawal and 1763, the Spaniards determined to strengthen their positions south of the St. John's River. Consequently, the forts at Pupo and Picolata were reconstructed and a Mosa line of defense was erected north of San Agustín. Spanish Floridians placed another stone installation, the Fuerte de Matanzas, on the southern perimeter of the St. Augustine defenses. Charles III of Spain also ordered additional improvements for the Castillo de San Marcos; the cost of building and renovating the ponderous fortress totaled more than 30,000,000 pesos.[22]

Since the War of Jenkins' Ear evolved into the European War of the Austrian Succession, the conflict between Spanish Florida and English Georgia continued in the forties. The mid-century struggles lasted from 1739 to 1748. Even after the Peace of Aix-la-Chapelle ostensibly ended hostilities in August, 1748, guerrilla movements on the border were renewed in the mid-fifties. Anglo-Spanish tension over the "debatable lands" was aggravated by an illegal settlement of English malcontents and fugitives at New Hanover. The outlaw antics of this colony, located between the Altamaha and Satillo Rivers, distressed both Spanish and English settlers.[23]

The Seven Years' War or French and Indian War as it was called in America finally terminated any pretense of Spanish hegemony in Florida. The treaties of 1763 legally climaxed Spain's long struggle with England and France for North American colonies. Prior to 1763, Spain had already lost eastern America north of latitude 31° and southwestern America west of the Perdido River. French Louisiana east of the Mississippi River and English America above St. Augustine existed as *de facto* evidence of the Spanish retreat from North America. At the Paris conferences Spain was forced to acknowledge the territorial loss of the debated extremes of La Florida, along with the loss of the Florida peninsula itself. After the ratification of the Treaty of Paris, Spain's power in Florida was reduced to arranging the imperial transfer of the old colony from Spanish to British control. For France the treaty ended French rule in Canada and all of North America east of the Mississippi River.

2
The 1763 Treaty of Paris

The Diplomatic Background
of the February 10, 1763, Treaty of Paris

Franco-Spanish rivalry in North America was arrested in the last stages of the Seven Years' War. When the death of Ferdinand VI of Spain resulted in the coronation of Charles III, Spain's neutral policy in the four-year war was altered. The English colonies almost immediately earned the new monarch's suspicions because their Mississippi Valley and Louisiana designs endangered the strategic areas bordering the Gulf of Mexico. Continuous British contraband trade with the Hispanic Indies, of course, always angered the Spanish crown. Great Britain's threat to the Spanish Caribbean via Florida also concerned Charles III of Spain. Occupied with those apprehensions, the Spanish king in 1759–61 sought to acquire Louisiana from France "by some means of exchange." [1]

The French negotiators, however, were only willing to cede Louisiana to Spain if His Catholic Majesty would either enter the European struggle as an ally or loan France the necessary capital to continue the military contest. Those terms proved to be unsatisfactory to the Spanish court, but a Franco-Spanish defensive alliance followed those negotiations on August 15, 1761. The union of 1761 reestablished the Bourbon family compact which united France and Spain in 1737 and 1743. Once again the compact allied the Bourbon monarchies and mutually guaranteed the possessions of each ally. Charles III logically feared that the fall of the French empire in America might be followed by increased English aggression against the Spanish Indies. According to later treaty stipulations, Spain was required to wage war on England on or before May 1, 1762, if France and Britain were still involved in a military conflict at that

13

time. Two treaties were actually prepared by Marqués de Grimaldi and the French minister Étienne François Choiseul, Duc de Praslin. The alliance of August 15, 1761, asserted defensive friendship, while the treaty of February 4, 1762, specifically bound the participants to offensive action against Great Britain. The French diplomat, however, was engaged in duplicity. As Choiseul reestablished the Spanish compact and urged Charles III to declare war against England, his ministry also negotiated with William Pitt to terminate the war.[2]

Spain declared war on England on December 16, 1761, and within eleven months both Havana, Cuba, and the Spanish Philippines capitulated to British military forces. After a two-months siege (July and August, 1762), Spain's Caribbean stronghold at Havana surrendered to Great Britain. In the ignominious engagement one-fifth of the ships-of-the line of the Spanish navy were lost in action. Other losses included 1,882,116 pesos confiscated by the British military forces from the treasury of the Havana Company. The capture of the Philippines cost the Spaniards 4,500,000 pesos, which was the price paid to prevent the English armies from sacking Spanish homes and properties. Such shocking losses astonished the Spaniards, who were already lamenting the numerous reverses that their French ally was suffering.[3]

While France relinquished Canada to English military might early in the war, the West Indies and the French colonies in India and Africa also submitted to the armies of Great Britain. The surrender of French Canada on September 7, 1760, followed the seizure of Guadeloupe and preceded the capitulation of Dominica and Martinique. Great Britain captured Guadeloupe in the spring of 1759 and by January, 1761, Dominica also was under British control. French India fell in 1761. The sea campaigns of 1762 culminated in the seizure of Martinique, the Lesser Antilles Islands —Grenada, St. Lucia, and St. Vincent—and ultimately Spanish Cuba. Defeat seemed to be ever present and everywhere for the Bourbon kings. In this unfortunate situation the only recourse for the Franco-Spanish alliance was to sue for peace.[4]

Discussions for peace began in December, 1761, two months before Spain joined the last phase of the Seven Years' War, and more than a year after Canada surrendered to General Jeffrey Amherst. When those inconclusive conferences were suspended in February, 1762, England seized French Martinique. In the summer of 1762, as the Spanish army suffered humiliation in Portugal and

Cuba, diplomatic negotiations resumed between England and the continental powers.[5]

Spain participated reluctantly in the summer peace talks of 1762. Initially, the wary Spanish government refused to permit the cession of French Louisiana to Great Britain. The Spaniards simply eschewed any suggestion that England and Spain could share the northern and eastern Gulf Coast. Because the international discussions apparently had reached an impasse, France, thoroughly exhausted by the long war effort, contemplated a secret treaty with Great Britain in order to end the costly conflict. France intended to cede Louisiana to England surreptitiously. This clandestine plan was prompted by Spain's insistence that the French government could not alter the international status of the Gulf region without Spanish permission; contemporary Spaniards believed that France possessed sovereignty in the Louisiana territory only under Hispanic patronage. As the disaffection between the continental allies increased, Choiseul was authorized to conceal the cession of Louisiana to England. The capture of Havana removed all necessity for such duplicity.[6]

The Spanish and French possessions in the Caribbean, Gulf of Mexico, and West Indies were seriously jeopardized by British naval power after the fall of Cuba.[7] Cognizant of that colonial situation, the Duke of Bedford—Great Britain's representative at the Paris conferences—could easily afford to demand expensive compensations from the enemy as the price of peace. In the subsequent negotiations Florida or Puerto Rico would be required to repatriate Spanish Cuba. Similarly, southwestern Louisiana was often mentioned as an expected prize of war. Great Britain indeed enjoyed an enviable position in the final stages of the Seven Years' War.

While the Duke of Bedford's diplomatic power was obvious in the French and Spanish capitals, his support at home was split by dissension and debate. Essentially, the question of whether to keep Canada or Guadeloupe as spoils of the war divided the English politicians and incapacitated their foreign ministers. As Secretary of State William Pitt cynically inquired, "Some are for keeping Canada; some Guadeloupe; who will tell me what I shall be hanged for not keeping?"[8] Although the Duke of Bedford and his entourage wanted to keep the French West Indies, Pitt, the followers of George Grenville, and the court's politicians led by the Earl of Bute united in their efforts to acquire Canada. The Bedford opposition argued that the ownership of Canada would enable England to control the entire northeastern seaboard of America. For the preservation of peace, France, of course, would be excluded from all contacts with former colonies, including the Newfoundland fisheries. Without French influence in Canada, many members of parliament hoped for the cessation of the dreaded Indian conflicts. The mercantilists in this camp believed that population increases in the Canadian province would improve British export business.[9]

The Bedfordites pursued an entirely different line of logic in this matter. They averred that the addition of French Canada to the British colonial system in North America would undermine English dominance in the New World. Some of Bedford's supporters even suggested that North American independence would occur sooner if Canada became a colony attached to the already established settlements. William Burke, a relative of the famous political philosopher and statesman, warned that, "By eagerly grasping at extensive territory, we may run the risque, and that perhaps in no very distant period, of losing what we now possess. Canada in French hands binds the North American colonies to Great Britain; it is not necessary to us, and its retention may be dangerous. . . . A neighbor that keeps us in some awe, is not always the worst of neighbors."[10] Others complained that Canada could only offer hides and furs as English imports. The French West Indies, to the contrary, would enrich England with such tropical products as rum, coffee, and sugar cane. The Bedfordites computed the colonial value of foreign settlements according to the older theories of mercantilism, while their rivals insisted that economic rewards would be accrued if business were mutually beneficial to England and the colonies.[11]

The acquisition of Florida elicited other disputes. Certain Englishmen believed that the West Indies and Puerto Rico would be more valuable to Britain than would Canada and Florida. One published cry announced, "Florida was as barren as Bagshot Heath."[12] Another detractor of Florida proclaimed that, "Florida was little more than pine barrens or sandy deserts." John Wilkes, the famous political agitator, jested that Florida could provide peat "to give comfortable fires to our cold, frozen West Indian islands."[13] There were proponents, who expected to reap profits from land speculation, agricultural experiments, and timber enterprises in the old Spanish settlement. One admirer even commented that Florida was "the most precious jewel in His Majesty's American dominions." [14] Actually, Florida remained an unknown and mysterious land to most Englishmen until several descriptions of the new colony were sent to Great Britain during the middle and late sixties.[15]

The Colonial American Stipulations
of the Treaty of Paris

Because of England's advantageous position in America after the seizure of Havana, both France and Spain were anxious to obtain a treaty settlement quickly before suffering any further territorial reductions. Previously, the ambitions of the Pitt ministry in 1761 frightened France and Spain and prevented an earlier peace settlement. Louis XV of France, accepting even an expensive peace, offered all of Louisiana to Charles III to end the costly struggle. The French king hoped Louisiana would serve as a compensation for Spanish support in the final phase of the disastrous Seven Years' War. France assumed that the Hispanic foreign minister would then trade Louisiana for Cuba, while still retaining Florida and Puerto Rico. The French proposition, however, was rejected by England and Spain. Great Britain hoped to own all of Florida and Louisiana east of the Mississippi River. Spain was antagonistic to any plan that would locate English colonies along the Gulf of Mexico or near the Mississippi Delta. By the autumn of 1762 the apparently endless negotiations for peace seemed deadlocked.[16]

In November the French and Spanish plenipotentiaries, frightened by the possibility of renewed war, finally concluded the Preliminary Articles of Peace with Great Britain. The continental powers therefore avoided a diplomatic impasse and any additional consequences of continued war. Ultimately, the allies decided to offer Florida and eastern Louisiana to England. In order to placate the defeated and very disillusioned Spaniards, New Orleans and southwestern Louisiana were secretly delivered into Spanish jurisdiction.[17]

The preliminary acts of the Louisiana cession between France and Spain were concluded at Fontainebleau on November 3, 1762. Spanish ratification followed on November 13, 1762.[18] In the same diplomatic sessions Great Britain, France, and Spain arranged the Preliminary Articles of Peace for the settlement of the Seven Years'

War. The three-power ratification of those articles resulted several days later and the final crown and parliament approval occurred in December, 1762.[19]

Two months later, on February 10, 1763, the actual Treaty of Paris was signed by Great Britain's Duke of Bedford, the French Duc de Praslin, and Marqués de Grimaldi of Spain. The Spanish ratification of the Treaty of Paris on February 25, followed the English and French ratifications, previously secured on February 21 and 23, 1763. The final treaty was published in Madrid on the twenty-first of March after an exchange of ratifications. England, France, and Spain completed the exchange procedures on March 10, 1763.[20]

The colonial provisions of the Paris Treaty finished French ambitions in North America and seriously reduced Spanish power beyond New Spain and southwestern Louisiana. Articles IV and VII required France to surrender northeastern America. France yielded Canada and all the French possessions on the North American mainland east of the Mississippi River to Great Britain, except the city and environs of New Orleans which secretly became Spanish domains. According to Article IV "his most Christian majesty cedes, and guaranties to his said Britannic majesty, in full right, Canada with all its dependencies, as well as the island of Cape Breton, and all the other islands, and coasts, in the gulph and river St. Laurence, and, in general, everything that depends on the said countries." [21] Article VII assigned "the river and port of the Mobile, and everything . . . on the left side of the river Mississippi" [22] to Great Britain.

France, however, continued to enjoy fishing privileges in the Gulf of the St. Lawrence and along certain designated sections of the Newfoundland coast. Article VI also permitted France to retain the tiny islands of St. Pierre and Miquelon as unfortified fishing installations. Although the treaty allowed France a few rights in North America, England demanded the repudiation of all French claims to Nova Scotia, the Island of Cape Breton, and all other territories in the St. Lawrence River and Gulf areas. Free passage on the Mississippi River was guaranteed to both British and French subjects. The West Indies generally remained French with Desirade, Guadeloupe, St. Lucia, Marie-Galante, and Martinique continuing under the flag of France. Only Grenada and the Grenadines became British islands according to Article IX. But Great Britain gained a new Caribbean "sphere of influence" that included St. Vincent, Dominica, and the

Tobago Islands. French inhabitants of ceded lands entertained the choice of continuing their residence under English law which promised religious freedom for Catholic worship or selling their properties to British subjects within the space of eighteen months.[23]

Most Frenchmen obviously regarded "le déplorable traité de Paris" (the deplorable Treaty of Paris) as disastrous. Louis XV remarked, "The peace that we have made is neither good nor glorious; no one is more aware of that than I; but in these unfortunate circumstances, it could not be better." The ruinous Peace of Utrecht (1713) was thus followed by the Treaty of Paris—"plus ruineuse encore et plus honteuse" (more ruinous and more shameful).[24] Thereafter, French America east of the Mississippi River existed only as an island empire.

Article XIX of the Treaty of Paris concerned the restoration of Cuba to Spain. The agreement stated that Cuba would be returned to Spanish control with all of its former powers and possessions— "The king of Great Britain shall restore to Spain all the territory which he has conquered in the island of Cuba."[25] Those British subjects who settled the Hispanic island were permitted eighteen months to conclude their residence. Few Englishmen other than military personnel actually resided in Cuba in 1763. A limited number of British ships with stipulated tonnage would be authorized Spanish passports in order to embark all Englishmen and their possessions from Cuba. The English evacuation of Havana could be completed in only one sailing. Vessels that lingered in Cuban anchorages were subject to boarding, investigation, and cargo confiscation. Spain obviously included the latter stipulation in the treaty in order to discourage smuggling or illegal traffic with the Spanish colonies. The British soldiery departed from the Island of Cuba on July 6, 1763, more than five months after the final ratification of the Treaty of Paris. On July seventh, the government of Carlos III was again formally instituted in Cuba.[26]

Article XX discussed the transfer of Florida to English sovereignty. Great Britain became the new landlord of the St. Augustine *presidio,* Pensacola, and all Spanish territory east and southeast of the Mississippi River. Map 2 indicates the extent of this territory. According to Article XX, "his Catholic majesty cedes and guaranties, in full right, to his Britannic majesty, Florida, with Fort St. Augustin, and the Bay of Pensacola, as well as all that Spain possesses on the continent of North America to the east, or to the southeast of the river Mississippi."[27] In an attempt to entice the population to remain in Florida, the treaty declared that the Spanish inhabitants could continue living under British authority worshiping according to their Roman Catholic practice. Those Spanish subjects who wished to leave Florida were allotted eighteen months to settle their affairs and sell their properties. All property, however, had to be sold to subjects of His Britannic Majesty. The eighteen-month proviso would become effective with the exchange of treaty ratifications. Officially, the period of eighteen months commenced on March 10, 1763. The Spanish crown was conceded the same opportunities as its subjects to carry away movable property, including military equipment and supplies.[28]

The actual transfer of Florida to English control was not accomplished until the summer of 1763. Great Britain waited approximately five months to enter Florida. Although Article XXIV of the Treaty of Paris stated that the effective change of sovereignty could occur three months from the date of final ratification, the first British soldiers arrived in St. Augustine on July 21, 1763.[29]

The English Public Response
to the Paris Treaty of 1763

While the French and Spanish courts and citizenry obviously regretted the colonial losses of Canada, Louisiana, and Florida, British reaction to the final arrangements was especially critical. Generally, political spokesmen contended that their Paris representatives stupidly ruined the British military triumph in the Seven Years' War. Continued French possession of the West Indian Islands particularly angered many Englishmen. The climate of public opinion was no more favorable to French fishing rights in the North American coastal seas. The vitriolic *North Briton* analyzed the treaty with abusive language.

The French king, by a stroke of his pen, has regained what all the power of that nation, and her allies, could never have recovered; and England, once more the dupe of a subtle negociation, has consented to give up very nearly all her conquests, the purchase of such immense public treasure, and the blood of so many noble and brave families. Is it therefore at all surprising, that, on this occasion, the most frantic symptoms of insolent joy and triumph have been remarked in France, and of grief and dejection in England?[30]

A New and Accurate MAP of EAST and WEST FLORIDA, Drawn from the best Authorities.

Other detractors of the Treaty of Paris were equally disparaging in their criticisms. One observer sardonically commented, "It is an old observation that we have generally lost by our heads what we acquired by our swords." [31] Another irritated critic complained that the recent agreement was characteristic of England "whose wars, as a rule, are marked at the outset by unreadiness, and at the conclusion by an inadequate treaty." [32] The vituperative Wilkes sneered, "It was the damn'dest peace for the opposition that ever was made." [33] Lord Shelburne, who called Lord Bute (the architect of the Paris Treaty) the "greatest political coward" he had ever known, feared that the treaty would encourage a new European alliance against England. [34]

Pitt, the fallen prime minister, found himself voicing many of the arguments of the *North Briton* against the continued French presence in the West Indies and North America. It was this imperialist's opinion that the pact only succeeded in improving French trade and the economic position of the American colonies. Since France could produce colonial sugar at lower costs than Great Britain, the "elder" Pitt anticipated that French export sales would seriously damage British business in the American colonies. Pitt's fears were not exaggerated. The disgruntled statesman assumed that the colonies would enjoy the European competition and enthusiastically accept the advantages of future price wars between France and Great Britain. [35]

Certainly, there were advocates of the Treaty of Paris. Benjamin Franklin announced in America that England had fashioned a "glorious peace." [36] This famous American assured everyone that Canada and the other colonies would never ally themselves against Great Britain, which was a consideration that concerned a number of Englishmen. Soothingly, he reasoned, "If they could not agree to unite against the French and Indians, can it reasonably be supposed that there is any danger of their uniting against their own nation, which it is well known they all love much more than they love one another." [37] Other observers expressed their satisfaction with the expansive Atlantic-coast position that England secured from the Paris negotiations. Some Englishmen praised the treaty for the security it offered the southern colonies; southern colonial protection had long been a goal of English foreign policy. [38] A contemporary politician surprisingly asserted: "This has been the most glorious war and the most triumphant peace that England has ever known." [39] Lord Shelburne, president of the Board of Trade in 1763, proudly boasted "The total exclusion of the French from Canada and the Spaniards from Florida gives Great Britain the universal empire of that extended coast." [40] Actually, the Treaty of Paris provided future security for British America, established Great Britain as the most formidable colonial power in the western world, and recognized English thalassocracy in Europe and America.[41]

International Problems Resulting from the Treaty of Paris

During the transfer of Florida from Spanish to British control, two issues inadequately discussed in the Treaty of 1763 confounded the personnel involved in the intercolonial exchange. One of these disputes concerned the tropical *cayos* (keys) south and southwest of the Florida peninsula. The other problem originated from the property sales arranged between the exiled Spaniards and the British land speculators. Both of these situations perplexed the English settlers and their Spanish predecessors for almost the entire period of British rule in Florida.

When Captain John Hedges arrived in San Agustín, Florida, on July 21, 1763, he was handed the keys of the *presidio* by the Spanish governor, Melchor Feliú. Bearing the orders of His Majesty's Britannic government and a copy of the royal *cédula* (edict) of February 24, 1763, Hedges asked to be recognized as a representative of the English crown. Governor Feliú immediately acknowledged Captain Hedges as the official agent of George III. Nine days after Hedges ceremoniously received the keys of the old Spanish city from Provisional Governor Melchor Feliú,[42] Major Francis Ogilvie entered Florida and assumed command of all English forces in St. Augustine. British military government thus inaugurated political authority over Spanish Florida.[43]

Don Juan Elixio de la Puente,[44] commissioned realtor of Charles III, appeared at St. Augustine some nine months later. As agent of the king, he was instructed to dispose of all the Spanish goods and properties remaining in Florida after the mass exodus of 1763–64. Puente's sales dossier included crown possessions as well as the personal goods of the former residents of Florida. According to instructions, he submitted his credentials to the British commander, Major Francis Ogilvie, in order to proceed to the business of his visit.[45] Expecting a perfunctory interview, Puente was surprised to find himself subjected to the interrogations of the British commander. The blunt inquiries concerned the (Los Cayos) Florida Keys. When Ogilvie mentioned the Florida Keys, the wary Puente pretended ignorance of their existence. According to his detailed account, Puente reported, "I unhesitatingly replied to his inquiry that I was ignorant of those previously cited Florida Keys, since I had never before heard of their mention, nor was I aware that they existed; since I am a native of this country and well informed of the territory's geographic jurisdiction, it is obvious that I would know of them if they indeed existed." [46] Ogilvie was not fooled, however, by the Spaniard's evasive reply.

Seeking to ensnare Puente, Ogilvie then asked the Spanish agent what the Keys were called which were located between the Island of Cuba and the southern point of the Florida peninsula, extending east and west along the Bahama Channel. Puente glibly answered the officer's question by explaining that those Keys, known as the Martires and / or Norte de la Havana, had always been integral territories of Cuba. Hearing this response, Ogilvie raised himself from his chair and furiously notified the Spanish representative that the Keys corresponded to British East Florida territory. In the same angry tone the English officer warned Puente that any foreigners attempting to infringe on East Florida's lumber or fishing rights in the Florida Keys would be severely chastised.[47] Ogilvie assured his guest that orders would soon be forthcoming from the king demanding the seizure of all ships discovered tampering with English property on those islands. Although the soldier aimed his threats at the Spaniards, he also intended to prevent the British traders of the Bahama Islands, whom he condemned as "opportunistic rogues," from visiting the Keys for supplies of lumber, fish, and turtles.[48]

Puente politely listened to Ogilvie's outburst, and then repeated his arguments that the lands in question actually belonged to the captaincy general of Cuba. The former St. Augustine resident even insisted that the nearest Martire (Key Biscayne) was located at least two leagues from Boca de Ratones, the southern point of the mainland of Florida. The inaccuracy of his geographic claims probably derived from guile rather than ignorance. The Keys, Puente concluded, therefore could not be included in the cession of Florida that Governor Feliú arranged with the English commissioners. Those international negotiations, the Spanish emissary explained, took place in his own presence.[49]

Ogilvie was not impressed by the Spaniard's geography lesson. He sternly lectured Puente, warning him that more specific orders from his sovereign would authorize the English forces to occupy the Florida Keys. Ogilvie informed the Spanish commissioner that upon receipt such orders would be immediately executed. With that notification the discussion ended as both speakers determined to study the situation with their respective governments.[50]

Puente then devoted his efforts to appointed tasks. But he soon managed to send a bulky packet of papers to the governor of Cuba describing his conference with Ogilvie and disclosing the importance of the Martires to Spanish interests in the Caribbean. According to Puente's meticulous research, Los Cayos offered the Spaniards shipbuilding lumbers such as mahogany, fishing and turtle grounds, and sheltered harbors in the northern Caribbean Sea. Most important, the Keys provided fortress positions along the Bahama Channel. The dedicated Floridian feared that England would employ the islands below Florida for naval bases if Spain allowed them to pass under British jurisdiction. From the accessible chain of wooded isles, the Gulf of Mexico and the Spanish Caribbean would be completely open to English reconnaissance and raiding expeditions. In time of war, of course, the strategic significance of the Keys was only too obvious.[51]

Hoping to catalyze his superiors into immediate action, Puente repeated some of the alarming rumors that had personally reached him during his sojourn in English Florida. One rumor suggested that Great Britain was planning to populate the islands with traders and colonists from America and Bermuda. Another item of hearsay, not calculated to please the royal officials of Havana, revealed that fifty-gun British frigates had been observed among the tiny isles north of Cuba. The crafty Puente even endeavored to excite the Church's interest in the Keys. In the hope that the Catholic Church would exert its influence for the retention of the Keys, he advised the captain general and governor of Cuba that the island Indians were desperately in need of the Holy Sacraments.[52]

Spanish officials in Havana could not heed Puente's advice without instructions from Spain. Although the ownership of the Keys was never diplomatically decided on a *de jure* basis, Great Britain occupied the islands from 1763 to 1784. Spanish ships, however, continued to exploit the resources of the chain of isles off the southern coast of Florida. Even as His Britannic Majesty's surveyor, William de Brahm, prepared to investigate the Florida Keys, vessels from Spanish Cuba and British Bermuda were overtly pursuing their economic missions in the lands and waters south and southwest of the mainland of Florida. James Grant, the first governor of East Florida, issued warnings against such trespassers, but all attempts to stop illegal traffic were futile. Fishing boats from Cuba persistently haunted the reefs of the disputed Keys. Spanish-Indian trade among the Martires and along the Florida coast also prevailed during the British Period.[53]

The Keys were never mentioned in the 1763 Treaty of Paris. Articles XIX and XX only clouded the subject of the Keys with vague language. The Twentieth Article stated that Great Britain would obtain Florida and all the Spanish possessions in North America east and southeast of the Mississippi River and "everything that depends on the said countries, and lands." [54] Cuba, according to the Nineteenth Article, was to be restored to Spain "in the same condition as they (all the Cuban territory and fortresses) were in when conquered by his Britannick majesty's arms." [55] The nebulous meaning of those statements enabled both nations to claim sovereignty over the islands.

The other problem conjured up out of the terms of the Treaty of 1763 concerned Anglo-Spanish property transactions. Article XX definitely stipulated that the Spanish residents of Florida could sell their estates to English subjects within an eighteen-month period. The new colony was settled, however, without particular regard to those treaty regulations. Aspiring to attract settlers to the province, the King's Proclamation of October 7, 1763, announced that the Florida lands would be "granted" to soldiers and citizens. The provincial governors were accordingly empowered to grant property, subject only to royal approval.[56] Since Great Britain hoped to reduce border tensions between the colonists and the midwestern tribes, the Proclamation of 1763 offered generous land grants in Florida to coax frontiersmen away from Indian country in the north. The authors of the October Proclamation hoped to activate the movement of the frontier into the almost empty Florida provinces. The unforgettable Pontiac uprisings of 1762–63 obviously panicked Whitehall officials. Indian grievances were therefore partially satisfied [57] as the royal government opened Florida to future settlement. Northern frontiersmen apparently enjoyed priority over southern speculators, and after 1765 the new settlers in Florida often received grants which included real estate already sold to other British subjects during 1763–64. The property terms of the Treaty of Paris were therefore superseded by the Proclamation of 1763.

Since the British government considered the Spanish property titles to be valueless,[58] George III commanded the Florida governors

> not to admit of any claims which should be made within the province under his government on pretence of purchases, grants, or conveyances from the subjects of Spain, nor to suffer any such claims to be entered on record, excepting such only as having been first presented to his majesty should have received his Royal approbation on a proper examination of them by the crown lawyers in England, nor before such royal approbation should be regularly signified to him.[59]

Those Englishmen who previously purchased land according to the terms of the 1763 treaty were forced to acknowledge the loss of their expended cash as well as their recently acquired property unless they were willing to travel to the British Isles to litigate against the royal government. A trip to England would increase expenses without the certainty of remuneration. Typically, the Spaniards received only small retainers or promises of payment for their estates. Most of the Spanish inhabitants of Florida therefore lost their property and the sales profits that they anticipated because of English policy.[60]

One incensed investor, John Gordon of South Carolina, filed a lengthy complaint with the crown when his real estate petitions were rebuffed in Florida. Gordon procured deeds, testamentaries, notary testimonies, and documents of purchase with the hope that he and his partners would not have to forfeit thousands of acres of territory. Gordon's pleas were never satisfied. The new government of East Florida eventually parceled out his lands to other English grantees.[61] Governor James Grant of East Florida directed the Carolina speculator to seek compensation in Great Britain. His officious remarks on the subject were recorded by John Gordon:

> when application should be made to him (Governor Grant) in council, he would grant the lands in the same manner as if no purchases of them from the Spanish proprietors had ever been made, and that he would not allow any action to be brought against the grantees of such land before any court of law in that province, alleging that the case was not cognizable by any court of justice in America, but that the purchasers who supposed themselves aggrieved must apply to his majesty for redress.[62]

Gordon eventually risked a voyage to England to seek reparations. His case was based upon the Treaty of Paris, which outlined a method of international property disposition; the Spaniards possessed legal rights to sell their estates and Englishmen were legally permitted to buy Florida territory. In his accusation John Gordon irritably reminded his government that the crown never proclaimed a public policy asserting the necessity of "purchase rights" in the Floridas. The Carolinian argued that his purchases deserved royal approbation. Although Gordon's argument appeared to have validity, the British Board of Trade would not recognize his property titles. Finally, the home government of George III—twelve years later—in 1775 agreed to pay the 15,000-pound sterling compensation that Gordon claimed he deserved for his investment, petition, and travel costs.[63]

The Gordon case clearly indicates that Great Britain willfully repudiated the Treaty of Paris within the first year of its promulgation. British policy toward Spanish land transactions was almost immediately arbitrary and unilateral. Although English occupation of the disputed Florida Keys may be interpreted as the consequence of imprecise treaty language, the Gordon case appears to lack legal and international justification. England apparently ignored the Treaty of Paris and illegally altered Anglo-Spanish property arrangements in Florida. British national objectives obviously triumphed over international law. In the same period, France and Spain would follow other illegal routes to avoid the restrictions of the Treaty of 1763.

3

Property Transactions during the Transfer of Empires: East Florida

Spanish Florida's Colonial Land System

Complying with a royal *cédula* of April 10, 1764, Don Juan Elixio de la Puente sailed away from the capital of Cuba carrying a portfolio of real estate records and approximately one hundred property proxies. The credentials he carried empowered the old resident of St. Augustine to sell the properties of his friends and neighbors. Because Puente was perhaps the most esteemed and probably the wealthiest citizen of St. Augustine, he was chosen by the former inhabitants of the community to dispose of their possessions. Royal instructions also included orders to sell the remaining crown properties. On May 7, 1764, Puente arrived in St. Augustine and proceeded to the headquarters of the army commander. After confronting the bellicose Ogilvie with his credentials, the Spaniard finally escaped the English officer's inquisition and continued on his errands.[1]

Since Puente was commissioned under the auspices of the royal government with the powers of attorney from the proprietors of Florida, the Cuban officials assumed that their agent could legally dispose of the colony's real estate. The former citizen of St. Augustine therefore proceeded to Florida with full Spanish authority. When processing the sales of territory to British subjects, orders from Cuba authorized Juan Elixio de la Puente to sell all property as if the transactions included Spanish buyers and sellers. Indeed, such instructions were consistent with the terms of the Treaty of 1763 which only stipulated that all sales would have to be made to subjects of His Britannic Majesty, King George III. Apparently, Spain was transferring colonial domains according to both Spanish and international law.[2]

Florida property, like all other territory in the Hispanic Indies, initially belonged to the crown of Spain. The kings of Castile distributed plots and extensive sections of property, including townships, to deserving private individuals, civil servants, or military personnel. Royal grants were typically offered as perquisites for political or economic service to the crown. Usually, conquerors of specific colonial areas earned certain property rights for their efforts in behalf of the Spanish throne.[3] According to Clarence Haring, land distribution followed a typical pattern of operation. Since the Castilian monarchy possessed legal and "ultimate proprietorship" of all the territories in the Indies, private property could only exist by right of royal grant or concession. In the early years of colonization, the crown commissioned *adelantados* (explorers) and *conquistadores* (conquerors) and later *cabildos* (town councils) to distribute lands and house plots to the Spanish soldiers and communities. Initially, the conquerors of America controlled land apportionment. Viceroys and governors and captain-generals subsequently enjoyed similar powers in conjunction with municipal *cabildos*. Actual occupation of ceded properties was essential for effective ownership. In order to obtain proprietorship, colonial regulations, later reiterated in the *Recopilación de las leyes de las Indias* (codification of all colonial laws and *cédulas*) of 1681, required almost immediate house construction and cultivation as well as continuous residence for a minimum of four years.[4] The kings of Castile intended to grant property concessions which would be utilized and productive.

All unapportioned land was legally segregated as Indian or crown domains. Indian property existed legally under state protection. As Spanish America grew older and more populous, however, the scarcity of fertile lands prompted the settlers to occupy the territory that existed outside the areas of distribution. Covetous eyes soon focused their attention on the sectors of designated reservation. Native proprietorship was then gradually reduced as legal and illegal methods of seizure were employed by avaricious colonists to expropriate the land of the indigenous people. Spaniards typically acquired Indian properties by purchase, frequently fraudulent or coerced, viceregal grant, and employment of *encomienda* or *hacienda* political privilege. Corrupt royal officials often helped dislodge the Indians from their desirable property. Death, depopulation, and relocation accelerated the Spanish acquisition of Indian lands. Spain's ever present debts as well as the increasing Spanish population in the Indies even motivated Philip II and his descendants to sell public lands to private persons.[5] Those public domains which were not granted to individuals or groups frequently served Spanish "intruders" who illegally settled the crown's American realms.

By the middle of the eighteenth century the *audiencias* (colonial court-councils) acquired jurisdiction over untitled properties and so-called conceded lands. Estates possessed by Spaniards before 1700 received consideration as "prescribed properties" and were conceded to their owners. Such parcels of territory could be held indefinitely depending on evidence of continued productivity. Similarly, deeds to crown property earned confirmation if effective utilization could be demonstrated to the officials of the Indies.[6]

Land policy in Florida did not follow the typical Hispanic American pattern. After the death of Don Pedro Menéndez de Avilés, the *situado* (subsidy) rather than the *encomienda* or *repartimiento* became the economic institution which sustained the impecunious colonial attempt in North America. The existence of Florida ultimately cost the crown of Spain more than two centuries of expenses. Because the Menéndez colony suffered misfortunes and failed to achieve agricultural stability, St. Augustine governors did not implement the ordinary agrarian programs adopted in other areas of the Spanish New World. The *situado* consequently became the settlement's fundamental means of support. Such a situation forced the *presidio*, except for brief and separated periods, to import most of its foodstuffs and supplies.[7]

Menéndez and his immediate successor, Hernando de Miranda, both enjoyed the *asiento* privileges that the famous admiral received in March, 1565, by the grace of His Catholic Majesty. According to royal determination, the Menéndez grant initially included twenty-five square leagues of land which he and his successors would possess in perpetuity. The crown's agreement with the *adelantado* instructed him to divide the territory of Florida into *repartimientos* and townships for five hundred settlers. Upon the demise of the old conquistador, Miranda continued to hold the legacy of Menéndez. By the end of the century, however, Philip II had repudiated all property rights to Florida, and the struggling settlement then became a king's colony. Thereafter, St. Augustine colonists futilely begged the crown to confirm the deeds to their lands.[8]

The mission, the military garrison, and the *situado* became the channels through which crown power was effectively exerted in Florida. These institutions enabled the Catholic kings to control

Florida without the employment of landed proprietors. Such a service appealed to the Spanish dynasty, whose financial difficulties had inadvertently assisted the development of a colonial latifundia and its inevitable challenge to monarchial notions of "kingship" and "absolutism." The time and distance that separated the colonies from regal authority contributed to the profundity of that continuing conflict. After the historic climax of the long struggle between the kings of Spain and the landed and clerical aristocracy, the sixteenth-century monarchy sadly observed the growth of a new property class in the Spanish Indies. The threat to absolute power that the latifundia represented was at least eliminated in La Florida with the establishment of a king's colony.[9]

Although the entire province of Florida existed under the control of royal officials, Spanish missionaries intimately supervised everyday life in the hinterlands. Governors and captain generals commanded the St. Augustine *presidio* and its fortified line of defenses, but the Indian village-missions were populous areas of authority and influence for the Franciscan clergy. The crown and Church allied to build a colonial state lacking a powerful latifundia. Without a significant class of *encomenderos,* local interference was minimized.

For the missionaries the colony became a laboratory in which the propagation of Roman Catholicism was experimentally arranged in conjunction with agricultural and Indian community endeavors. Las Casas, the "Apostle of the Indies," certainly would have been pleased to view the Franciscan system that developed in seventeenth-century Florida. Florida's "golden age" evolved from the Franciscan experiment, and the expansion of the missionary complex permitted Spain to control vast lands and a prodigious Indian population. At this time Spanish Florida reached its demographic and geographic limits. Later in 1702, when British marauders descended upon the missionary system, the colony lost all geographic meaning outside the port city of St. Augustine.

Property ownership existed in Spanish Florida. But all titles existed in apparent contradiction to the structure of the colony after the crown abnegated the *capitulación y asiento* of Menéndez. Proprietorship depended fundamentally upon the *Recopilación de leyes de los reynos de las Indias.* When the laws of the Indies were codified in 1680 under the direction of the *Real y Supremo Consejo de las Indias* (Royal and Supreme Council of the Indies), Floridians for the first time could petition the council directly to own lands. Because of previous colonial policy, the successors of Pedro Menéndez de Avilés could only occupy space without the security of titles. Monarchical officials permitted the colonists to utilize the lands, but the Council of the Indies refused or ignored their requests for deeds or the power to grant proprietorships. The granting of property or title, their superiors in Spain haughtily reminded them, was a royal prerogative.[10]

In order to apply for proprietorship, according to the new regulations, all petitioners were required to forfeit *baldías* (uncultivated lands) and *realengas* (royal lands) as well as the *frutas* (products) of these lands. Grants of property or title would not be issued without obedience to those laws. Such conditions infuriated many old colonists. Spanish settlers were unwilling to sacrifice properties that they assumed to be the legal inheritance of their ancestors. Some territory had passed, pursuant to the traditional laws of primogeniture, from the victors of the 1565 French campaign to the protesting landowners of the late seventeenth century. The governors of Florida, therefore, complained quite strenuously about the real estate predicaments they confronted with their unhappy colonists. Attempts to enforce the conditions that the Council of the Indies demanded before distributing property to Florida settlers were neither popular nor successful. Hoping to stabilize the situation, the governors requested temporary deeds for occupied areas until land petitions could be processed.[11]

Some of the commotion produced by the *Recopilación* was related to the constant clamoring of St. Augustine governors seeking permission to grant proprietorships. They wanted the same authority that the sixteenth-century governors had been privileged to possess. Powers of land distribution, nevertheless, remained in the office of the *Consejo de las Indias*. The council was extremely reluctant to allow control of colonial proprietorship to exist at the *presidio* level of administration. The unfortunate effects of latifundia power in other parts of the empire probably motivated the royal government to deny the petitions of the Florida governors. Consequently, the powerful Council of the Indies retained all authority to distribute uncultivated territory in Florida. Governors frequently granted land illegally in the "name of the king," but such grants were only valid in St. Augustine. Discrepancies between theory and practice were as evident in Florida as elsewhere in the Spanish empire in America. The governors of San Agustín continued to be frustrated in their plans to secure land grant licenses from the crown.[12]

When land petitions finally earned approval, property was dispensed to individuals in *peonias* and *caballerias,* depending on the social status of the grantees. Typically, the *peonia* was one-fifth the area of the *caballeria.* A similar sized plot surrounded the residential building of each type of proprietorship. The *caballeria* grant was given to an individual with at least an *escudero* (knight) rank, while low-ranking infantry troopers received *peonia* parcels. *Caballerias* in New Spain usually referred to agricultural territory, and encompassed 609,000 square *varas.*[13] Florida's *caballeria* was tantamount to 10,000 square feet and included five times more arable land and pastures than a *peonia.* The Florida *peonia* consisted of a 5,000 square foot section with sufficient arable land to produce 100 *fanegas*[14] of both wheat and barley and 10 *fanegas* of maize. Adequate pasture was provided for 20 cows, 10 sows, 5 mares, 100 ewes, and 20 goats. A *peonia* also included two *huebras*[15] for vegetable gardening and eight *huebras* of wooded property. In order to hold legal title to a royal grant, occupation was ordered within three months from the issuance of the deed. Another stipulation required the construction of a dwelling in a designated length of time.[16]

Florida property was probably held under a form of the fee simple system. It seems reasonable to suppose that certain property owners were accorded *libre de condición* (unconditional) arrangements. In order to sustain the character of the king's colony in the late sixteenth and seventeenth centuries, however, the Council of the Indies necessarily retained some monarchical reservations over proprietorship. Certainly, the crown was easily able to reserve its commanding position in Florida by simply withholding title from the estates of colonial proprietors. Without crown deeds proprietorship remained continually in jeopardy. Until the royal or absolute title to property was awarded to an individual owner, he could not legally sell, grant, or alter his land. Only a king's deed permitted territorial alienation. Since no other property certificate could prevail over royal title, the Council of the Indies, after 1680, theoretically held Florida's proprietors in an inescapable legal custody.

All domains lacking the crown's official seal were regarded as *realengas.* Any persons or families residing on royal property without some sort of lease or tenant's agreement possessed no legal status of any kind. Actually, such interlopers enjoyed occupation rights. "Illegal settlement" was frequently conceded on the local Florida level, but invalidated at the upper echelons of Spanish administration. Basing their claims on arguments of "time immemorial" occupancy, many unauthorized settlers assumed that they rightfully owned the land that they and their ancestors had colonized historically.[17] Regardless of the particular situation of residence, land tenure of crown property was indeed limited. A governor's whim could disenfranchise any usurper of royal domains without the possibility of legal redress, but little evidence exists of such arbitrary action.

When the British settlers arrived in Florida in 1763–64, all Spanish property, whether titled or not, was offered for sale.[18] A bear market resulted and many Englishmen purchased residential plots and estates at abysmally low prices. Speculators even unknowingly bought illegally occupied property. Two English investors, John Gordon and Jesse Fish, purchased several properties from Spaniards whose claims to their lands were founded on "time immemorial" occupation, and governors' grants "in the name of the king." The Spanish crown's realtor, Don Juan Elixio de la Puente, referred to the St. Augustine property owners as possessing their real estate, "by the legal right of having acquired them, some by their industry and personal labor, and others by inheritance from their ancestors." [19] The British buyers were pleased with their "bargain" acquisitions, and the Spaniards were at least relieved to obtain some remuneration for their homes and lands. Somewhat later in 1764–65, Great Britain reevaluated and altered some of the Anglo-Spanish transactions to accommodate settlement plans for Florida. Buyers and sellers both suffered thereafter as England apparently invalidated international law.

Anglo-Spanish Property Transactions, 1763–1765: East Florida

By January, 1764, the Spaniards had completed their maritime exodus from East and West Florida. More than six hundred people including soldiers, citizens, convicts, and Christianized Indians abandoned Pensacola on September 3, 1763. This group of émigrés sailed with Governor Don Diego Ortiz Parrilla toward a new life in Vera Cruz (Veracruz). From St. Augustine, the last inhabitants of the capital were evacuated in eight crowded transports on January 22, 1764. The governor and captain general of St. Augustine, Colonel Melchor Feliú, dispatched more than 3,100 people to Havana and Campeche in the ten months after the exodus commenced on April 12, 1763. During the evacuation only one ship, the sloop

Nuestra Señora del Rosario, was lost with four persons aboard near the Florida Keys.[20]

Seventy-five Spaniards remained in Florida after the January sailings. One of the citizens of Pensacola stayed to guard the salvage of a grounded Spanish sloop. In St. Augustine nine Spaniards temporarily lingered in the old *presidio* to corral the crown's horses that wandered into the surrounding woods before the final embarkations. Three mounted dragoon troopers, two infantry soldiers, two men of the militia, and one interpreter were selected to search for the lost horses. For unknown reasons one Spanish woman also remained in St. Augustine. Sixty-five other Spaniards remained at Apalache, Florida, until February 20, 1764, when they were finally evacuated to Havana. The Apalache command could not leave Florida until a delayed expedition relieved the frontier outpost.[21] Almost a year after the signing of that Treaty of 1763, Spain made its mass exodus from Florida, and for the next twenty years, England ruled the old colony.

The movement of population was only one part of the Spanish evacuation that perplexed Governor Feliú in St. Augustine. Personal goods, church property, garrison records and provisions, and the crown's military equipment and supplies likewise had to be shipped to the captaincy general of Cuba. Melchor Feliú intended to carry away everything of value. The royal storehouses and the Castillo were emptied of cannons, artillery accessories, shot, small arms, clothing, naval goods, carpentry and masonry tools, iron, and even nails.[22] A launch and two longboats and "other trifles of great bulk but little value" would be sold at the highest possible prices. All goods transported from Florida passed over the infamous sand bar of St. Augustine, responsible for numerous shipwrecks since the sixteenth century. The harbor channel that avoided the treacherous bar only offered six to eight feet of sailing passage, prohibiting the entrance of large vessels into St. Augustine Bay. Launches carried most of the cargo out to ships anchored beyond the *Barra de la Florida.* Repetitive work, loading and unloading the launches, therefore characterized the laborious moving process.[23]

Spanish real estate was not initially sold. Feliú reported that since none of the residents would accept the responsibility of selling the private buildings and properties, someone would have to return to Florida for that purpose. The Cuban authorities were also advised by Governor Feliú that a realtor could probably dispose of the crown's lands. Since the Treaty of Paris did not forbid such sales, the Florida governor ordered appraisals of the royal properties.[24]

Don Juan de Cotilla, *ingeniero ordinario* (ordinary engineer),[25] was one of the assistants sent to Florida to encourage the emigration of colonists and expedite the removal of their possessions. The Spanish officials initially wondered if the Floridians would be willing to abandon their colonial home. Compensation for all losses assured mass migration. When the royal government offered to compensate the Floridians with other property opportunities outside of the peninsula, the Catholic citizenry unanimously agreed to leave the old settlement. Another consideration motivated the exodus of the Spanish colonists. Although the Treaty of 1763 stated that Spaniards could continue the practice of their Roman Catholic faith in British Florida, there was an apprehensive feeling among the settlers, which was confirmed by government propaganda, that Catholics could expect religious prejudice if they remained in Florida. Rumors of such prejudice persuaded many Spaniards to accompany the official evacuation.[26]

Since it was not necessary to convince Floridians to abandon San Agustín, Cotilla devoted most of his attention to property matters. After his arrival on July 23, 1763, Cotilla immediately began calculating real estate values. He worked as quickly as possible in order to provide the colonists with sufficient time to sell their possessions before the stipulated eighteen-month period elapsed. Employing masters of carpentry and masonry as professional advisers, Cotilla prepared detailed inventories and estimates of the *coquina* (shellstone) and wooden houses of St. Augustine. The Spaniards were elated to have Cotilla available as their property assessor, but the new British residents accused the Cuban of satisfying his countrymen with "favourable" evaluations. Before his time-consuming task was completed, Ambrosio Funes Villalpando, Conde de Ricla, the governor of Cuba (1763–66), recalled the engineer to Havana. Although his recall was issued on the second day of November, 1763, Cotilla lingered in Florida throughout the month assisting the desperate proprietors of San Agustín.[27]

The beginning of fortification reconstructions on the island of Cuba finally ended the delayed mission in Florida. A month behind his scheduled departure, Engineer Cotilla in early December boarded one of the evacuation ships for Cuba. His official removal was greeted by disapproving protests from the residents of the old city. The St. Augustine citizenry was then obliged to transfer Cotilla's powers to John Gordon, a Carolina merchant and English land speculator. Since the governor of St. Augustine, Melchor Feliú, expected to be leaving Florida soon, he approved the election of John

Gordon as temporary sales representative for his people. He prophetically warned his people, however, that if they did not obtain the best possible remuneration from their property while Spain still controlled Florida, they would have to expect monetary losses with the advent of British administration.[28]

Ingeniero Voluntario (voluntary engineer) Pablo Castelló assessed public buildings for the crown. Preceding Juan de Cotilla by more than a year, Engineer Castelló voyaged to Florida in 1762. He accompanied Melchor Feliú at the time of the colonel's appointment as provisional governor. Through the efforts of Castelló, the governor's house, the guard corps barracks, the jail, the royal blacksmith, and the royal hospital were measured, inventoried, and appraised. Prior to the cession of Florida, Castelló prepared plans to improve the fortifications of the *presidio,* but the later international agreements eliminated the necessity for their fulfillment. The highly praised Castelló thereafter diligently toiled with Cotilla to estimate the monetary value of St. Augustine's buildings.[29]

Royal officials in Spain hoped that property sales would soon follow house and land appraisals. Although Castelló and Cotilla were employed by the Spanish government to facilitate the disposal of Florida real estate, few houses within the city of St. Augustine were actually sold before the end of the evacuation in January, 1764.[30] Don Juan Elixio de la Puente, the chief officer of royal accounts in Florida, therefore journeyed to St. Augustine as the realtor of Spanish property. Puente's departure orders were dated April 10, 1764, but seventeen days passed before he embarked for Florida.[31] His instructions were quite explicit. The Spanish agent possessed royal permission to dispose of real and personal property. Puente was also authorized to retrieve all remaining assets, provisions, tools, or other valuable articles, which had not been previously sold or traded. If possible, unsold crown belongings could be exchanged for such items as canvas, tackle, nails, and flour. As expected, the royal officials of Cuba required a notary to witness all final sales arranged through the office of their emissary. A detailed report of all his activities was likewise demanded. Finally, the royal authorities strictly commanded Puente to avoid any and all transgressions of the Treaty of 1763.[32]

Puente's immediate, and apparently impossible, duty was to find some means of profitably selling the Spanish buildings. The Floridian soon discovered that property prices had collapsed with the arrival of the English forces. To his dismay, Puente found an

almost inactive land market. As Governor Feliú's last dispatch from
Florida revealed, few interested purchasers were available in St.
Augustine.

In his final communiqué to the Cuban officials, Governor Feliú
blamed the British for the deflation of land values in the old colonial city. The governor readily admitted that the English military
authorities cooperated with his interim government to achieve harmony during the international transfer. But Melchor Feliú casti-
gated the foreign soldiers for stripping wooden sections from the
city's houses in their endless efforts to keep winter fires burning.
Feliú also indicted the military leaders for obstructing property sales
between Spanish and English subjects:

> Major Ogilvie, of the Ninth Regiment, who had recently been
> commissioned Lieutenant Colonel, endeavored during the length of
> my stay to uphold the most perfect harmony. The behavior of his
> troops, however, has not been in agreement with his actions. De-
> spite my continuous appeals they have dismantled the houses, carry-
> ing away the wooden sections for firewood. As a consequence the
> values of the *Presidio* houses have been seriously lessened. The
> delay and inaction with which the English have approached the
> purchasing of the residents' houses is particularly suspicious. I am
> now convinced from the evidence that I have gathered that the lieu-
> tenant governor dissuaded David Martin, a Scotch merchant who is
> the only British Subject showing determination to purchase any of
> the houses, from buying property by giving him certain apprehen-
> sions. Perhaps this is the reason that more houses have not been
> sold; the few that have been sold earned only a fifth or tenth of
> their real value. However, I also believe that the delay of the Lon-
> don court in assigning families to this colony has also been a detri-
> mental factor to the discouraging property sales. . . . The ap-
> pointed governor, Colonel Grant, is expected shortly. They say that
> the governor is accompanied by four hundred families of French
> Huguenots. One hundred other families of the Palatinate have al-
> ready boarded ship for the settlement of this colony that they call
> East Florida.[33]

Even with the advent of another population, rumored to be
arriving soon, Feliú believed that the British government could not
be immediately expected to send multitudes of investors and merchants to Florida. The ex-governor warned his Cuban superiors that
unsold Spanish property would not be absorbed quickly in the
unpopulated province of East Florida. He mentioned the Bar of St.
Augustine as being an insurmountable obstacle to the use of the

capital as an English trading center. The dreaded sand bar, which he asserted was "the worst in the entire North," had already cost Great Britain significant shipping losses. Melchor Feliú also expected Indian problems to limit the population of English Florida. St. Augustine's provisional governor predicted that the incipient increase of native barbarities would discourage settlement in Spain's ex-colony.[34] Obviously, without the possibility of a populous British colonization, the Spanish proprietors never could have hoped for any financial reimbursement for their property.

While Governor Feliú's account offered a number of explanations for the real estate situation, there were at least several other reasons why the Spaniards encountered sales problems. Both Cotilla and Puente, bound by the eighteen-month proviso of the Treaty of Paris, were forced to seek out property markets before an appreciable number of investors arrived in Florida. The expense and extensive time that travel involved in the late eighteenth century obviously limited the number of English settlers in the new province. An army of speculators would not invade an area only generally known to most Europeans. British Americans were very conscious of Florida and indeed those colonists initially streamed into the new provinces.[35]

The earliest occupants of East Florida, except for a few shrewd southern merchants and exporting-house factors, were the English military troops. Few eighteenth-century soldiers, however, could invest in foreign lands. Their meager salaries would not have permitted significant real estate purchases unless they owned commissions or substantial savings. Many soldiers with sufficient money to buy property probably hesitated since they were unsure of the longevity of service in St. Augustine. Other army personnel who could have afforded such investments may not have bought properties because they were hoping for the type of land grant system that the Proclamation of October 7, 1763, soon offered future settlers. Other available investors possibly held similar hopes. News of property opportunities in the King's Proclamation naturally ended investment. Finally, the "high" house appraisals of Cotilla and others probably discouraged prospective buyers from purchase of Florida real estate.[36]

Whatever were the reasons for the poor results, Puente unhappily entertained the same frustrations as his predecessors. He simply could not profitably sell Florida real estate. Eventually the king's agent sought other surreptitious means to dispose of Spanish property. Puente's most important transaction concerned the transfer of the majority of St. Augustine's houses and lots to Jesse Fish, a factor of the Walton Exporting Company of New York. Fish served the Walton Company's interests in St. Augustine for at least nine years prior to the British occupancy of Florida.[37]

On July 24 and 27, 1764, the Spanish realtor delivered the unsold private properties of the St. Augustine *presidio* to Jesse Fish in two separate, but confidential, agreements. Less than two months (forty-five days) of the sales period remained when the real estate pacts were signed. According to the written contract, Fish agreed to sell the unsold properties for the Spanish proprietors even after the eighteen-month deadline, September 10, 1764. The text of the transaction clearly stated "that the aforesaid deeds or contracts of sale were made in confidence, and for the purpose of securing to the legitimate owners the right therein, which they were about to lose under the provisions of the twentieth article of the preliminaries for peace." [38] In order to evade the limits imposed by the Treaty of 1763, Puente transferred realty powers for the Spanish possessions to Mr. Jesse Fish of St. Augustine, "the houses and lots, which, up to the present, have not been sold for want of purchasers, for which reason they have been sold or passed over in confidence to Jesse Fish, a vassal of his Britannic Majesty, giving him only for the precise formality of the case a deed of sale." [39] The Walton Company factor thus became the agent-trustee-owner of approximately 200 properties in St. Augustine.[40]

Fish promised in the confidential transaction to obtain the highest possible prices for the properties in his charge. He also pledged to remit the profits with a punctual account of all sales to the former owners. All estates were signed over to Fish at extremely nominal prices without the necessity of a binding down-payment. According to the international contract, St. Augustine buildings and lands brought a total "low" price of 6,169 pesos. The houses and lots north of the governor's mansion, approximately in the center of the town, west of the plaza, were valued at 3,701 pesos. St. Augustine properties south of that central landmark were estimated to be worth 2,468 pesos. Don Juan Elixio de la Puente also concluded property contracts with Jesse Fish for a portion of the Church lands. Fish "purchased" the Tolomato stone church, situated two leagues north of the *presidio,* as well as the walls of the unfinished Church of St. Augustine for an additional two hundred pesos.[41]

John Gordon acquired the remainder of the Church estates in

another Puente transaction similar to the Fish contract. Gordon's pact with the Spanish agent was likewise concluded during July, 1764. The South Carolinian's acquisitions included the Convent of St. Francis, the Church of Our Lady of the Milk, and the Episcopal building. On July 2, 1764, John Gordon signed his name to a Spanish agreement which stated:

> I acknowledge to have received from John Joseph Elijah Puente an instrument in my favor, of the convent of St. Francis, for the sum of one thousand five hundred dollars (pesos) cash, and likewise another document of the same class for the church of our Lady of the Milk, for three hundred dollars (pesos), both in this place; notwithstanding which I offer and promise to sell and dispose of said convent and church to the best possible advantage for and on account of their proprietors, and remit the proceeds to the above mentioned Puente or pay it over to his order.[42]

Two and one-half weeks later, on July 20, 1764, the Englishman acquired title to the Episcopal house. These properties were sold or entrusted to Gordon for 2,800 pesos,[43] but Great Britain annulled the sale less than a year after the financial arrangements had been settled. According to English administrative opinion, the Church lands were an integral part of Spanish royal domains. Great Britain recognized that the Spanish crown's right of eminent domain was evident in the *patronato real* (royal patronage) relationship of Church and state. Church property therefore became crown property as Spain abandoned Florida. Since the Treaty of 1763 transferred the colony to British control, all royal territories including the Church estates escheated to the throne of George III. Spanish Church property subsequently served the king's Florida provinces. Under crown authority the Convent of St. Francis was renovated to serve as a soldiers' barracks, and the bishop's house was utilized for the religious services of the Anglican Church.[44] Puente's attempt to dispose of Church properties in private sales thus miscarried.

By September, 1764, Puente finished his official business in Florida. All previous transactions were confirmed, and several new sales were either authorized or executed by Puente's personal efforts. Investors, other than Fish and Gordon, purchased assorted quantities of real estate. James Henderson bought thirty houses and lots, including Puente's own house of residence, for approximately 12,300 pesos. The properties of Juan Elixio de la Puente were sold for 7,700 pesos even in the depressed market of 1763–64. With the exception of the Henderson transaction, the other fourteen buyers purchased small parcels of property. Their typical investment earned a house and lot. By 1765 fewer than forty individuals owned all the real estate of St. Augustine.[45] (See Table 1.)

Puente also exchanged or sold the king's barges, pirogues, lumber, stone, and other materials. Spanish livestock was similarly sold

1. St. Augustine's property distribution in 1765

Property Owners	Lots	Major Buildings	Minor Buildings
Bagley	3	4	1
Barton and Kipp	1	24	2
Box	1	2	1
Bullimore	1	1	0
Catherwood	1	1	1
Clements	1	2	0
DeBrahm	1	2	1
Delachoras	1	3	0
Dunnet	1	1	1
Fish	47	156	48
Gordon	4	9	2
Greening	1	3	0
Henderson	14	13	14
Hopkins	1	1	0
Jamison	1	2	0
Jenkin	1	2	2
Johnson	1	1	1
Kipp	7	9	4
Maxwell	1	2	1
Meek	3	4	1
Moore	1	1	0
Nab	1	3	1
Penn	1	1	1
Piles	1	3	0
Prichard	1	3	0
Rainsford	1	2	1
Rochet	1	2	1
Rogers	2	5	0
Sharp	2	2	1
Spanish Crown	5	10	5
Skynner	1	3	0
Thomas	1	4	1
Walton	8	13	7
Walton and Barhop	2	3	0
Williams	1	2	0
Total	121	299	98

SOURCE: Thomas Jefferys' Plan of St. Augustine and surrounding area in 1765. PRO:CO Florida 8, Library of Congress photostat.

or bartered. As instructed, the royal agent procured merchandise, useful supplies, and even money for the Spanish possessions.[46] Juan Elixio de la Puente therefore left St. Augustine knowing his sales mission to Florida was successfully concluded.

The International Significance of the Puente-Fish Transaction

For more than a century and a half the Puente-Fish compact has intrigued and confounded most observers. Few people even understood the transaction in the English Period. From 1763 to 1784, British officials were baffled by the extent of Fish's realty empire and suspicious of its origin and legitimacy. Throughout the nineteenth century, other envious citizens of St. Augustine inquired without satisfaction into the sales of Spanish real estate in 1763. Rumors and questions regarding the opportunism, credulity, and possible conspiracy of the principals involved in the disposal of property have been continually discussed, particularly in this last decade. Many questions remained unanswered. Typically, the most important inquiries have concerned the intended secrecy of the transaction, the incredibly low purchase prices, the absence of any binding payments, and the reasons that the Spanish commissioner unburdened the unsold domains to Jesse Fish. The lucrative opportunities available to Fish after July, 1764, obviously explain the motives of one party in the property transaction. But the intentions of Don Juan Elixio de la Puente in the deal were considerably less apparent. Was Puente a dupe, a plotting conspirator, or only a hurried official trying to arrange the best possible property solution for the émigrés from St. Augustine?

Colonel James Robertson, who was appointed by the British army command in New York to inspect the new provinces, was the first recorded witness to comment wonderingly about the affairs of Jesse Fish. Completely ignorant of the confidential terms of the Puente-Fish transaction, Robertson reported:

> On my arrival at St. Augustine I perceived that Mr. Fish who lived there long as a factor for Mr. Walton, in lieu of the debts due to him by the Spaniards, and from him having an intimate knowledge of the Situation of their affairs, would acquire all the immoveable property belonging to them. Imagining such a monopoly prejudicial to the growth of a new Colony, in order to divide the property I

gave notice of my apprehensions to the Governors Boon and Wright, that the inhabitants of Carolina and Georgia who were most likely to become purchasers might be apprised of the occasion.[47]

Curiously, Robertson assumed that Fish acquired realty opportunities because of unpaid debts. Since Fish acted as sales representative of the Walton Company, Spanish indebtedness would be expected. During the eighteenth century the William Walton Company of New York provided the St. Augustine *presidio* with supplies when the Havana Company in Cuba could not fulfill the *situado* obligations of Spanish Florida. In 1752 the St. Augustine *presidio* owed the Walton Company more than 60,000 pesos, and in 1763 the New York Company claimed debts in excess of 25,000 pesos. But the money owed to Fish cannot be similarly explained. Were the "debts due to him by the Spaniards" personal or company obligations? Company debts could not account for Fish's advantages in purchase of Spanish property. The colonel's second conjecture about Jesse Fish "having an intimate knowledge of the Situation of their affairs" was much more accurate than he would ever realize.[48]

Lacking adequate lodgings for his personnel, Colonel Robertson seemed annoyed by the property situation. In an obviously irritable mood Robertson remarked, "the houses, Churches & Convents in St. Augustine, are all excepting the Governors house Claim'd as private property . . . insomuch that I could hardly find a Spot for a garden to the garrison, & my time not allowing me to enter into a discussion of these Claims, In order to prevent the growth of more, I desired the Spanish Commissary to show the English Engineer what lands were the Kings & to mark them on a Chart which I give you." [49]

The English military commander of St. Augustine almost immediately doubted the authenticity of the property settlement. Major Ogilvie, who had harshly interrogated Puente upon his arrival in St. Augustine, was also suspicious of the July transactions. The rough soldier probably remembered his first unsatisfactory encounter with the Spaniard when he wrote to his superior, Lord Jeffrey Amherst, about provincial affairs in East Florida. After complaining about the continued presence of Spanish people in the province, Ogilvie contemptuously sneered, "they likewise pretend to sell most of the lands." [50] Major Ogilvie apparently presumed the sales were fictitious.

The property situation in St. Augustine was both irksome and suspicious to Ogilvie's successor, Governor James Grant. When the new official assumed administrative command of East Florida in 1764, his complaints paralleled those of his predecessor, Colonel Robertson. To his chagrin, he discovered that most of the property in the old city was ostensibly under private proprietorship. In a letter to the Board of Trade and Plantations, Grant described his predicament and the measures he adopted to solve his problems:

> Upon my Arrival I found every thing was claimed as Private Property except the Governors house & the Hospital; I have declared the Bishop's Palace, The Convent of Franciscans, & all the Churches, to be the King's, also some other Houses about which I have pickt up Information from the Officers who came to take Possession of the Town, for I can learn none from any Body else, as they are all concerned in Purchases.
>
> I do not Admit that any thing is private Property, I Only tell them that, with respect to the Houses, their Titles have not been enquired into, & that therefore the thing is not yet determined, but I have hitherto permitted them to keep Possession.[51]

Almost ten years later, in 1772, Spanish correspondence revealed the story of the transaction. Don Juan Elixio de la Puente disclosed his conception of the real estate agreement in a lengthy dispatch to the governor of Cuba. The ex-Floridian initially explained how he was instructed to sell all St. Augustine property. If worthwhile sales or exchanges could not be accomplished, Conde de Ricla ordered Puente to transfer all unsold estates to an agent who would serve Spain in English Florida. In such circumstances Puente and Fish conducted their negotiations of July, 1764. A secret pact became essential in order to preserve Spanish property rights and to escape the limits of the Twentieth Article of the Treaty of Paris. Finding a depressed and almost inactive real estate market, Puente followed Conde de Ricla's advice. His transactions thereafter obviated the time restrictions of the Treaty of Paris. Of the 298 properties mentioned in Puente's communiqué to the governor of Cuba, only the first 110 had actually been exchanged for merchandise, Negroes, and / or cash. The other 185 private estates plus three Church properties were assigned in strict confidence to Jesse Fish.[52]

The low prices listed for the houses and lots of St. Augustine, Puente explained, were indeed fictitious and intended to convince doubting observers of the sale of Spanish possessions. He obviously hoped that British officials would be beguiled by such a plan. Fish vowed to reward the Spaniards with the highest possible prices when increased population in St. Augustine provided a more favorable market. Puente's evasion of the terms of Article Twenty offered Spanish owners new hope for future sales. The Puente-Fish transaction not only freed the Spanish properties from the immediate threat of confiscation, but also encouraged the former proprietors of St. Augustine to anticipate later profits. Havana officials were also advised that a Spanish agent, Luciano de Herrera,[53] would remain in Florida to receive the sales returns. In the process of real estate payment, all profits would be promptly shipped to Cuba in gold, silver, or notes of exchange. St. Augustine proprietors could then collect their money in the captaincy general of Cuba.[54] Puente apparently contrived the best possible arrangements under the circumstances and orders from Cuba.

The correspondence of Don Juan Elixio de la Puente includes many references of praise for Jesse Fish. The Spanish agent especially appreciated the Englishman's willingness to participate in property transactions which endangered his position with his own monarch, the king of England. His life was actually in jeopardy because of such illegal activities. Puente also praised Jesse Fish for earlier efforts on behalf of the St. Augustine populace. In the autumn of 1762, the Walton Company factor helped Puente supply provisions to the desperate and almost impoverished citizens of St. Augustine. John Gordon also assisted. The conspiring triumvirate clandestinely removed the necessary supplies from British Carolina. Spain and England were still at war in October, 1762, when Fish, Gordon, and Puente carried supplies from Carolina to St. Augustine. Such illicit activities made both British subjects guilty of treason.[55]

The Puente-Fish transaction was clearly an illegal and arbitrary act. While Jesse Fish apparently engaged in treasonous activities for and with the Florida Spaniards, Puente, with the consent of his government, illegally disregarded the terms of the Treaty of Paris. Fish and Puente conspired to extend Spanish proprietorship of Florida real estate. Their pact clearly violated the eighteen-month provision included in Article Twenty,[56] and a secret transaction was essential to the success of their conspiracy. Secrecy obviously protected Spanish property and possibly the life of Jesse Fish. His personal risks were probably compensated by financial advantages in the July agreement. Perhaps, the lack of down-payments and the low prices were the charges Fish demanded for the dangers he faced if the British officials discovered his treason.[57]

When the Spaniards returned to Florida in 1783–84, Fish continued to live comfortably in the Second Spanish Period most probably because of his previous service to the St. Augustine *presidio*. Later the Englishman's holdings in the Second Spanish Period (1783–1821) were jeopardized by claims of former Floridians. At that time Puente's earlier correspondence with the crown was employed to support his case. In all reports the Spanish realtor continually praised Jesse Fish. When the British speculator first encountered difficulties in the defense of his property titles, Juan Elixio de la Puente pleaded his cause to the royal ministers of Charles III.[58] After his activities of 1763–64, Jesse Fish remained highly regarded as a loyal servant of the king of Spain.

The Property Activities
of Jesse Fish and John Gordon

Because the English government of East Florida permitted local house and lot sales, Fish's position must have been relatively secure through the end of the sixties. By 1765 Mr. Fish still owned 204 of the 397 buildings in existence in St. Augustine. Of the 121 empty house lots available in that year, the English realtor possessed 48. His account book indicates that he sold ninety-five separate pieces of real estate by 1770. Altogether, from 1763 to 1770, Jesse Fish disposed of three houses, forty-three lots, and forty-nine houses and lots. He also managed eleven other sales of Spanish goods and materials, which had been left with him by the evacuating Spaniards.[59]

From 1770 to 1774 only one sale was recorded in the speculator's account book. The property agent apparently suffered a sales slump in those years. Other enterprises, however, were sustaining the depressed real estate business. In the seventies his orange industry on Santa Anastasia Island (located across the harbor from St. Augustine) was already producing oranges for export to European markets.[60] In order to exact some profit from the unsold property, Fish probably rented the Spanish houses during his inactive sales years. (See Table 2.)

The Loyalist and Minorcan immigrations of the seventies introduced a real estate boom in the old Spanish city. By the end of the first two years of the American Revolution, Tory refugees were already fleeing from the Thirteen Colonies. Many of the émigrés descended into the Floridas. Succeeding migrations cast more colonists into St. Augustine as the northern war of attrition continued. In the same era another dimension was added to the overcrowded conditions when the Minorcan settlers of Dr. Andrew Turnbull's colony at New Smyrna (seventy-five miles south of St. Augustine) deserted the settlement and swarmed into the capital of East Florida.[61] With the resulting scarcity of housing, real estate was easily and lucratively marketed from 1775 to 1780. In that length of time Jesse Fish sold twenty-two houses and lots, and twenty-one lots lacking improvements. The ingenious realtor also presumably enjoyed a profitable rental business.

Jesse Fish's property register offers a number of interesting facts and statistics regarding his sales activities. Curiously, the account book does not mention the delivery of any proceeds to the previous inhabitants. Although meticulous credit and debit listings are recorded accompanying each owner's name, no evidence exists suggesting that money reached former proprietors of St. Augustine. In 1766 Governor Grant allowed Mr. Fish to voyage to Havana in an English pilot boat ostensibly to settle his financial affairs with the Spanish Floridians. "Mr. Fish who resided here Many Years with the

2. The Spanish property sales of Jesse Fish, 1763–84: total number of sales arranged during the British Period

Year	Houses	Lots	Houses and Lots	Goods and Materials
1763	0	1	5	0
1764	0	3	5	5
1765	0	4	8	2
1766	2	10	6	1
1767	0	10	6	0
1768	0	4	11	1
1769	1	8	8	1
1770	0	3	0	1
1771	0	0	0	0
1772	0	0	0	0
1773	0	0	0	0
1774	0	0	1	0
1775	0	1	2	0
1776	0	5	0	0
1777	0	4	11	2
1778	0	5	6	0
1779	0	0	2	0
1780	0	6	0	0
1781	0	0	0	0
1782	0	0	0	0
1783	0	0	0	0
1784	0	0	0	0
Total	3	64	71	13

SOURCE: The Jesse Fish Account Book. 1763–70, EFP 319.

Spaniards, and who is and always was in great Favor with them, was anxious to get to the Havanah to settle some of his Accounts, and begged of me to allow the Dependence Pilot Boat to carry him over from the Keys which I agreed to, he was at the Havanah for some days." [62] No record of such transactions, however, appears in the Fish accounts.

The Spanish domains grossed nearly 14,000 pesos. Of the total property earnings, Fish claimed more than one-third for various services. He charged the Spaniards approximately 5,000 pesos for legal writings, transfer of accounts, deed processing, and property surveys. In some accounts the service charges equaled the total bill of sale, while in 20 per cent of all transactions, his charges exceeded the selling prices. Typically, Fish's assistance cost the Spaniards 30 per cent of their property proceeds.[63] Fish also possessed more than forty-two acres of territory in the environment immediately surrounding the old colonial city. Almost one-fourth of the area in proximity to St. Augustine was under the proprietorship of Mr. Fish. His claims even embraced the entire island of Santa Anastasia (across the harbor from San Agustín) estimated to contain 10,000 acres of land. Yet, in 1789 he complained to the Spanish minister of justice about the debts he had incurred from the sale of the Spanish property.[64] (See Table 3.)

3. Property distribution for St. Augustine and surrounding areas in 1765

Property Owners	Approximate Acres of Territory
Bagley	21
Edmestor	7
Fish	42
Henderson	37
Jenkin	22
Martin	10
Meek	6
Sharp	13
Walton	19
Total	177

SOURCE: Thomas Jeffery's Plan of St. Augustine and surrounding area in 1765. PRO:CO Florida 8, Library of Congress photostat.

Jesse Fish, whose property interests extended well beyond the area of St. Augustine, joined John Gordon in the purchase of a gargantuan tract of land along the St. Johns River. This territory was located approximately twenty-five miles west of the capital of East Florida. Fish, Gordon, and their associates bought 4,577,280 acres—1,058 square leagues [65]—of real estate on both banks of the St. Johns River. A list of the disputed East Florida properties of Jesse Fish and John Gordon follows: [66]

Abosalla	San Diego
Acuitasiqui	San Geronimo
Arato y Exapile	San Lorenzo y Aramasaca
La Chua	San Matheo
La Nea	San Nicholas
La Rosa del Diabolo	San Onosre y Pirigirigua
Los Corrales y Yquirico	Santa Ana de Alsaja
Pajacara o Agopo	Santa Lucia
Palica	Santo Philipe y Axacu
Picalata	Tampa
Pupo	Tococruz
San Buenaventura	Tocoy
	Yquisay

Several contemporary observers insisted that the speculators acquired as many as 10,000,000 acres. Colonel James Robertson, General Gage's agent in the Floridas, conversed with John Gordon soon after the transaction was completed. On March 8, 1764, Robertson wrote to the general and relayed the details of his conversation with Gordon.

> However on my return to the Continent I found, Mr. Gordon at Charlestown, who show'd me Conveyances that had been made soon after my departure from St. Augustine by the Spaniards to him, and Mr. Fish, the whole amounting to ten millions of Acres, he gave me plans of these purchases, with letters explaining the nature of them, which I have the honor to give you.
> He declared a great desire to avoid obstructing by his purchases any views of His Majestys Ministers, and profess'd a willingness to part with the lands at a very moderate profit to the Crown, he will wait till your pleasure is signify'd to him on this subject after which, he says he can easily procure Setlers to possess them, on advantagious Conditions to himself, he says that a Sum was payd by

the first Grantees to the Spanish treasury in lieu of all dutys, and that these lands consequently are not subject to quit rents.[67]

General Gage apparently had already considered the debated property deal before receipt of the Robertson report. The general viewed the entire enterprise with little sympathy. He believed the Spaniards were selling lands which actually belonged to the Creek Indians. Assuming Creek proprietorship of the territories purchased by the Gordon-Fish partnership, the English military commander expected the transaction to be eventually nullified. In correspondence with Lord Halifax, Gage therefore declared that the land deeds of Gordon and Fish were "far from indubitable." General Gage suggested that the two speculators bought territory only "claimed" but not occupied by Spanish Floridians. Without occupation Gage would not concede ownership. Although the Spaniards asserted property ownership on the basis of sixteenth-century conquest, the Creeks boasted that they more recently re-conquered the same land from Spanish colonists and other Florida Indians. The general liked the logic of the Creek argument.[68]

Accepting the Indian interpretation, Thomas Gage argued that the domains belonged to the Creeks because their warriors in battle achieved a "posterior conquest." Creek tribes actually occupied and controlled most of the territory of Florida outside of the city of St. Augustine. The army commander supported the Indian claim in his letter to Lord Halifax explaining that the Spaniards rarely ventured into the contested lands during the previous colonial period. For years prior to the cession of Florida to Great Britain, death or disappearance awaited any Spanish soldier or citizen who intrepidly stepped into the "savage" interior beyond the protective walls of St. Augustine. General Gage therefore reasoned that the partnership of Fish and Gordon purchased their lands from claimants rather than proprietors.[69]

The first governor of East Florida, James Grant, was also skeptical of the huge territorial sale. In his initial encounter with John Gordon, the governor officially denied all claims to Church property. Several months later, Grant wrote a letter to the Board of Trade ridiculing a second business deal between the Spaniards and John Gordon. His letter of November 22, 1764, defined the Spanish proprietors of St. Augustine as soldiers without significant rank who could never have owned the extensive lands supposedly sold to the Gordon-Fish partnership. Grant concluded, "It therefore is not to be believed that they or their predecessors could have Obtained from his Catholick Majesty Titles and Rights to Ten Million, or indeed to Ten Thousand Acres of this Country, And One cannot conceive any Government to be so defective as to give the permanent Property of a Country to transient People who were liable to be removed to any part of the Spanish Dominions upon a Military Order." [70] Governor Grant's opinions certainly seemed logical.

Four years later, Grant once again discussed the Gordon case in another letter to the Commissioners of Trade and Plantations. The governor continued to be unsympathetic to the East Florida speculators. In 1766 the king in council directed John Gordon to file charges as plaintiff against a crown defended grantee of some of the lands claimed by Gordon, Fish, and others as legally purchased from the previous residents of Florida. The Privy Council advised the king to offer Gordon such a course of legal action so that the Carolinian could test his proprietorship in the English courts. Gordon was reluctant to have his civil case tried in East Florida, where the judges were "to be considered as Partys concerned." Since Gordon refused to bring action against the crown "apprehending he Shall not have a Chance in such Suit," [71] and since he declined to become a defendant in Florida by willfully and voluntarily trespassing on a grantee's property, Governor Grant reported that he would ignore the Carolinian's petitions until a royal judgment decided the matter.[72] Meanwhile, Gordon's "pretended purchases" were distributed to other anxious petitioners in East Florida. The governor's position was explicitly stated in his letter of September 9, 1768, to the Board of Trade.

> I am directed My Lord, by His Majesty's Additional Instructions dated at the Court at St. James's the 23ᵈ day of April 1764, not to admit of any Claims which shall be made to any Lands what ever, within the Province upon pretence of Purchases made of, or Grants or Conveyances from the Subjects of Spain, nor to suffer any such Claims to be enter'd upon Record . . .
> Agreeable to that additional Instruction, the Lands claimed by Mr. Gordon and the other pretended purchasers have been granted away to His Majesty's subjects upon the same footing with other vacant land.[73]

John Gordon waged a long struggle thereafter to win the right to his claims. Initially, he futilely employed written appeals and the intercession of influential London friends. After several years, the

South Carolinian realized that the litigation required his presence in England. Hoping a personal plea would strengthen his case, he resorted to a costly transoceanic voyage in 1772. Gordon's case was not significantly altered by his arrival in Great Britain. The Carolinian continually petitioned for proprietorship using such legal evidence as Spanish titles, English purchase rights, and the stipulations of the Treaty of Paris. He vehemently argued that the purchased lands possessed Spanish titles long before 1763. Neither John Gordon nor the British government probably ever knew the actual state of Spanish proprietorship in Florida. The claimant, however, contended that Spanish titles and the Treaty of Paris entitled him to own his extensive acquisitions. Gordon's written and personal pleas were in vain. The extensive territories which he appraised to be worth 10,000 pounds sterling, were eventually granted to other English subjects. The Carolina investor then waited twelve years to receive remuneration from the crown for his losses and costs of litigation.[74]

In East Florida, England and Spain were both guilty of ignoring the property provisions of the Peace of Paris. Spanish officials sought to evade the limitations of the treaty, while the English government denied land sales permitted by international agreement. The colonial and financial importance of Florida territory motivated former proprietors, speculators, and national states to violate the Treaty of 1763. As East Florida was exchanged from Spanish to British control economic interests simply eclipsed international law.

4

Property Transactions during the Transfer of Empires: West Florida

Anglo-Spanish Property Transactions, 1763–1765

Pensacola was the only significant settlement in Spanish West Florida. The St. Augustine *presidio* maintained a western military post at Apalache, but only a small detachment of soldiers held the little fort. The outposts of Picolata, Pupo, Matanzas, and Mosa surrounded the capital city of Florida. San Miguel de Pensacola existed semi-independently, although authority over the administration of Spanish West Florida was theoretically a power of the governorship of San Agustín.

The Spaniards evacuated the *presidio* of San Miguel de Pensacola under the direction of Governor Don Diego Ortiz Parrilla. Ortiz Parrilla assumed the governorship of Pensacola in October, 1761, replacing Don Miguel Roman de Castilla. Following the same procedure arranged in St. Augustine, the royal officials of Cuba sent two assistants to the governor of Pensacola to expedite the evacuation. Don Joseph Bernet and Don Lázaro Alberja thus journeyed to the western outpost in the summer of 1763. The Cuban governor and captain general assured the population of Pensacola that all costs of the difficult and expensive embarkation would be defrayed by the royal treasury.[1]

In order to facilitate property sales, the older citizens of the town were permitted temporarily to delay their voyage from Pensacola. Parrilla accordingly selected the last scheduled evacuation vessels for their passage abroad. As a further aid to the property owners, the crown's Cuban officials appointed Don Joseph Bernet and Infantry Lieutenant Don Pedro Amoscotigui y Bermudo to appraise and inventory all private property. A master of carpentry and masonry,

55

Joseph Valesques, was given the important assignment of evaluating buildings within and without the old fort's stockade. The assessors, however, found only twenty-eight houses and lots available for appraisal in the small *presidio*. Many of the properties were appraised to be worth less than 300 pesos, although there were estimates as high as 1,500 pesos and as low as 60 pesos.[2]

Lieutenant Colonel Augustin Provost commanding the Sixtieth Royal American Regiment entered Pensacola with 350 troops on August 5, 1763. He regarded the Spanish capital of West Florida as a small village "consisting of about one hundred huts." Presuming that all the buildings inside the stockade belonged to the British crown, Provost only allowed house and lot sales outside the wooden defenses. The dilapidated condition of the fort's quarters and the obvious lack of other lodgings pressured the soldiery into hasty house purchases. British officers, soldiers, and army supply contractors quickly bought the properties immediately surrounding the *presidio*. Spanish émigrés later claimed that the transactions were concluded without final and mutual agreement. As late as April, 1764, the Spanish ambassador to England requested the British government to satisfy the claims of the former proprietors of Pensacola. The Spaniards demanded payment according to their evaluations since prices were never explicitly settled at Pensacola.[3]

Englishmen entering West Florida found a barren country. Land in the environs of Pensacola was generally uncultivated because of its poor quality and the ubiquitous presence of Indians. Speculators, however, hurried to the *presidio* to seize the few plantations and fertile territories that were available. The population of Pensacola resided in the immediate vicinity of the fort because of Indian hostilities. Provost, nevertheless, assumed that the surrounding area remained uncultivated because of Spanish lethargy. Many of the property transactions were completed even before the English troops arrived. With the advent of military government, new proprietors were required to register all land transfers and titles. Registration necessarily preceded the military commandant's approval of purchase, and British officials considered both procedures requisite for proprietorship in West Florida. In the process of land registration, valueless titles were invalidated, although the same deeds were often returned to the original purchasers under later property grants.[4] Great Britain assumed authority over all ownership in West Florida.

The new governments wished to give priority to a system of

small proprietorships. Because of their constant efforts to attract frontiersmen, small farmers, and artisans to the Floridas, the British officials were especially reluctant to permit large land holdings. They feared that an absentee landlord class would develop in Florida if extensive land speculation was not prohibited. Their apprehensions were not exaggerated. The British government realized that the growth of such a class would probably arrest the movement of northern settlers into Florida. Continued population pressure on the Indians north of the Floridas could then be expected with the apprehension of further tension and strife. The possibility of another Pontiac rebellion always concerned colonial officials after 1763. Without the existence of a plantation type of proprietorship, the advisors of George III hoped to alleviate the Indian crisis and establish a successful quit-rent system. In such a property scheme, numerous settlers would be encouraged to enter Florida and acquire land holdings directly from the crown.[5]

Under these circumstances West Florida ultimately prospered as an English province. The population of West Florida actually expanded more rapidly than East Florida as frontiersmen, settlers, and speculators flocked to the new colony for land grants. From 1765 to 1775 the steady influx of immigrants more than trebled the existing European population. Mobile, Natchez, and Pensacola became the prominent centers of what was formerly French Louisiana and Spanish Florida. England's settlement at Natchez became economically and demographically significant in the seventies. The successful development of West Florida seemed to be related to the policies inaugurated after the Proclamation of 1763.[6]

As the crown gradually constructed a system of small proprietorships, the landlords of large holdings suffered. Those Englishmen who owned extensive territory from Spanish sales were especially vulnerable. Many purchasers of Spanish property lost their acquisitions when the British government refused to recognize their titles and transactions. Sixteen such petitions were denied in one meeting of the Council of West Florida on January 24, 1765. The Pensacola council would not declare Spanish deeds to be *ipso facto* valid in proprietorship claims. Local crown councils, rather than individuals, controlled the power of land distribution and adjustment in the new provinces. Individuals naturally continued to hold petition privileges.[7]

In January, 1765, one particularly interesting property claim was presented to the West Florida Council by James Noble. Noble already owned a number of houses and lots in Pensacola. This speculator asserted that an investment company including their royal highnesses Edward, the Duke of York, William, the Duke of Cumberland, the Earl of Bute, the Lord of Mansfield, Augustus Keppel, John Kinnion, Marriot Arbuthnot, Samuel Touchet, John Lindsay, Thomas Horsefall, and himself had purchased landed estates from the Yamasee Indians. The Yamasees departed to Vera Cruz in the Spanish evacuation of 1763, and therefore were not available to substantiate Noble's claims. No evidence exists, however, of such a sale. According to the speculator, his investment group paid 100,000 pesos for the lands. Ultimately, James Noble and his alleged business associates suffered the same frustrations that the Gordon-Fish partnership simultaneously entertained in East Florida. The petition of this West Florida claimant, however, was refused for lack of "sufficient" title evidence.[8]

Anglo-French Property Transactions, 1763–1765

By 1763 all property and proprietorships in Mobile were under the auspices of royal authority. Similar power prevailed in other areas of French Louisiana, east and west of the Mississippi River. Sharing the Spanish interpretation of sovereignty in America, the Bourbon kings possessed ultimate control of colonial land grants and titles. Initially, the successors of Robert Cavelier, Sieur de la Salle, and Pierre le Moyne, Sieur d' Iberville, settled the Mississippi Valley under the patronage of Antoine Crozat, proprietor of Louisiana in 1712. Louis XIV ceded the unproductive but strategically located colony to Crozat for one-fifth rights to all riches and promises of economic development. At the time of Crozat's acquisition, Louisiana included only four tiny settlement-forts. Mobile, Biloxi, Dauphine Island in the Gulf of Mexico, and Ship Island at the mouth of the Mississippi River supported the French claims to the Gulf Coast. Five years later Fort Rosalie at Natchez and Natchitoches were added as French settlements in Louisiana. In 1717 the population of the colony consisted of about seven hundred people.[9]

The crown of France reluctantly regained the colony in 1717 when Crozat petitioned to be released from his contract. Louisiana then passed into the control of the Mississippi Company and the famous credit financier John Law. The Mississippi Company (the

Company of the West) acquired a charter to Louisiana for a period of twenty-five years. As a consequence of the king's charter, the company enjoyed enormous power over almost every aspect of colonial life in Louisiana. Its accomplishments included the founding of New Orleans in 1718 and the recruitment of 7,000 settlers for Louisiana. (See Map 3.) Many of the newcomers soon perished because of disease and the rigors of pioneering. Others deserted the frontier to return to France. Their harrowing experiences in Louisiana had little resemblance to the life of luxuries promised by Law and the company's publicity campaign. The population therefore remained relatively stationary at 5,000 residents.[10]

Eventually, the Company of the West was incorporated with the East India Company to form the Company of the Indies. Sustained by public stock purchases, the new corporation practically owned Louisiana and controlled French trade throughout the world. Speculation and the excessive circulation of valueless paper currency inevitably ruined the Company of the Indies. Once again the crown retrieved Louisiana in 1731. After the colony suffered drought, disease, and Indian massacres, the company abandoned its responsibilities to the monarchy. Thereafter, Louisiana remained a royal colony until the Treaty of Paris.[11]

Privately owned property certainly existed in a crown settlement. The kings of France accepted the state of ownership with the stipulation of royal approval. In Louisiana the monarchy preferred small proprietorships which would be cultivated and improved.

> His Majesty will point out to them with reference to the concessions that some very extensive ones have been granted on which the holders of the concessions have not done any clearing and that he has resolved to remedy an abuse so prejudicial to the progress of the establishment of the country, so that the lands may be made productive. . . . The general policy also concerns them jointly and it embraces three principal objects: the increase of the inhabitants, that of cultivation of the land and that of commerce.[12]

After 1716 extensive territorial cessions were forbidden. French grantees then faced the choice of settling all land or losing uncultivated portions to royal expropriation.[13] Spanish proprietors faced similar threats in the colonial period.

On August 10, 1728, the Company of the Indies instructed all landholders to show evidence of title, limits, and cultivation. French Louisiana like Spanish Florida held many subjects whose claims to

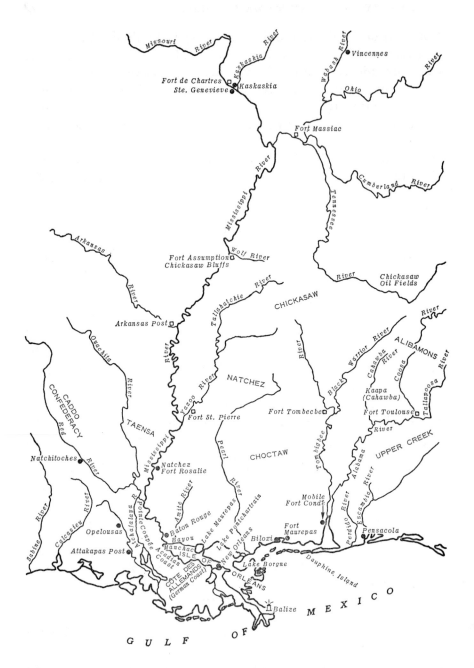

3 French Louisiana, 1699–1763

proprietorship were founded upon occupancy rather than deed. According to the edict of 1728, property without proper title would escheat to the company. Since few settlers risked the required appraisal of their titles, the legality of land possession remained unresolved. The royal officials, Jean Baptiste, Sieur de Bienville, and Edmé Gatlen Salmon, advised the king of the situation in 1733.

> In regard to the concessions, although Sieurs Périer and Salmon caused to be published at two different times the ordinance that they had issued to oblige the inhabitants to report in three months the titles of concession or of acquisition by virtue of which they hold possession there are still some of them who have not complied with it at all. . . . Others have only possession and have made their declarations. It is our opinion that it is advisable to . . . grant titles to them in the name of the King as well as to those who have only possession and to grant an extension of time to those who have not yet presented any titles at all or made any declaration, after which time their lands will be reunited to the domain and granted to others. For that purpose it would be well for his Majesty to issue a decree of his Council which would authorize the Governor and the Commissary General to concede or confirm again or reunite as occasion shall require the tracts of land both of the city and along the river and in the whole extent of the colony.[14]

In 1728 the Company of the Indies was able to obtain the authority to assess a tax of one cent for every acre of territory in the settlement. The company issued other orders for Louisiana. Grants of rich Mississippi Valley property were reduced to twenty acres facing the river unless owners could reveal more acreage under cultivation.[15]

Competition for land in Louisiana never became a serious issue because of the sparse population. The entire colony contained only 4,000 Europeans and 2,020 Negroes in 1744. There were 800 French subjects in New Orleans, 300 settlers in Illinois, and 200 more in Missouri. In what later became British West Florida, 150 Frenchmen lived in Mobile and 8 others occupied Natchez. The latter military station never recovered from the infamous Natchez massacre of 1729–30 when several hundred Frenchmen were captured and killed. No residents were listed for Baton Rouge or Biloxi. The Biloxi region lost its economic meaning as the Mississippi Valley became available as an area of settlement. Approximately twenty years later, in 1763, Mobile's population only included 350 Frenchmen and 98 families.[16] The transfer of French Florida (Louisiana, east of the Mississippi and south of 32° 28′) to British control therefore provided few property problems beyond the city of Mobile.

The Twenty-second and Thirty-fourth Regiments under the command of Major Robert Farmar officially occupied the city of Mobile on October 20, 1763. When Major Farmar arrived in Mobile, he discovered many of the same ramshackled conditions that Provost found in Pensacola. Farmar's troops located even fewer residences than the Pensacola regiment. Because the French population continued to reside in Mobile, unlike the Spanish inhabitants of St. Augustine and Pensacola, the desperate soldiers rented space in foreign homes and converted the town's bake houses into barracks. Frenchmen remaining in West Florida were required to file declarations of loyalty with the British authorities. French subjects of the ceded islands in the Caribbean Sea also received instructions to subscribe to English law if they wished to secure their proprietorships. Frenchmen obtained leases on lands for various periods of tenure provided they abjured French citizenship. Those residents who intended to retain ownership of their houses and lands declared the required oath of allegiance to the English king, George III, in October, 1763. By the second of October, 112 Frenchmen, probably heads-of-families, had offered their required pledges of fidelity. When many of their countrymen decided to follow the French flag to other territories, the local citizens bought up émigré properties with alacrity.[17]

Speculators therefore failed to find the same wealth of property in Mobile previously available in Pensacola. New owners in both Pensacola and Mobile, nevertheless, were ordered to submit deeds to the military government for registry and certification. The patience of investors, whose titles were judged to be invalid, was often rewarded with later grants covering their original purchases. British land policy in Florida frequently seemed to be quite magnanimous in areas or situations where settlement plans were not endangered. In the vicinity of Mobile, Great Britain even permitted French squatters, without titles, to enjoy ownership of lands under cultivation.[18]

Despite such apparent magnanimity there were several French accusations against British policy in West Florida. The acting governor of Louisiana, Jean Jacques Blaise d'Abbadie (1763–65), almost immediately criticized the military occupation of Mobile. On January 10, 1764, the governor complained "after the delivering up of

Mobile to Mr. Farmar, who took possession of it in the name of his Britannic Majesty, this officer issued a captious decree, which is calculated to produce the greatest anxiety in the minds of the French inhabitants." [19] D'Abbadie referred to the required oath of allegiance which he asserted was a violation of the Seventh Article of the Treaty of Paris. The French official objected to the necessity of a loyalty oath for the protection of property rights. Governor d'Abbadie remarked "He (Farmar) requires the French inhabitants to take the oath of allegiance within three months, if they wish to be protected in their property. What right has he to impose any such obligation on these inhabitants, since the treaty grants them a delay of eighteen months to emigrate, if they choose, and since it is stipulated that they shall be, under no pretext, subjected to any restraint whatsoever?" [20] This argument seemed valid and very appropriate.

Other regulations likewise annoyed d'Abbadie. The governor denounced Major Farmar's decision to oblige French residents of Mobile to submit their titles for registry, verification, and approval before allowing real estate sales and disposition. He argued that possession, settlement, and clearing of property entitled a Frenchman to "sufficient title" for transfer to British subjects. Claiming "ownership by occupation" the interim governor related, "on account of the small number of the inhabitants, and of the immense extent of public lands, the mere fact of taking possession and the continuation of it, on permission given to select a tract of land and to clear it of its timber, has always been looked upon as sufficient title." [21] Such claims revealed the chauvinism rather than the logic of Jean d'Abbadie. Nevertheless, Lord Halifax, secretary of state for the Southern Department, later required Governor George Johnstone of West Florida to approve French titles based upon occupation, cultivation, and improvement. Lord Halifax also extended the time limits of the Treaty of 1763 to help the inhabitants of Mobile dispose of their property.

French critics also blamed Great Britain for impeding property transactions between Mobile residents and British subjects in 1763–64. The case of Chevalier Montault de Monberaut supported French complaints. According to Monberaut, Governor George Johnstone of West Florida obstructed the sale of his plantation (Lisloy) in order to obtain the services of the French officer. Monberaut's influence and experience among the surrounding Indians made his recruitment very desirable. In his *Mémoire Justificatif*, Chevalier Montault de Monberaut accused the Florida governor of persuading the customs collector to delay payment after the sale of the planatation was concluded. As the eighteen-month deadline for property disposition approached, the Frenchman faced the prospect of losing his estates if he refused employment with Great Britain. Monberaut therefore served England as deputy superintendent of Indian affairs for British West Florida from December, 1764, to June, 1765. After helping to secure Indian treaties in West Florida, Chevalier Montault de Monberaut was suspended from his superintendency on June 26, 1765. His dismissal occurred amid disputes with Governor Johnstone and Indian Superintendent John Stuart. Threatened with incarceration, the Chevalier de Monberaut fled to New Orleans where he eventually learned of the loss of his properties.[22]

Throughout the period of property transfer, citizens of Mobile reproached Major Robert Farmar for discouraging land transactions. These accusations were accurate. Before his landing at Mobile, Major Farmar notified the French commander, Chevalier Sieur de Ville, "I cannot admit of any Purchases, or sale of real Estates to be Valid that are made before possession is taken by His Britannick Majesty's Troops, and my concent obtained." [23] The English officer also confessed that he advised his subjects "that if they purchase those Houses, and it should appear hereafter that they were the King's property, they should pay Rent to the King for the Houses, and be lyable to be disposses'd." [24] Major Farmar thus disregarded the "spirit" of the Treaty of 1763. Yet, his explanations for such statements appear reasonable. He claimed that his approval of all property sales would prevent French citizens from negotiations in which they might be "disapointed and perhaps deprived of their property without receiving and equivolent for it." [25] Furthermore, Farmar revealed why he deterred Englishmen from purchase of French property.

> I have reason to believe the Officers and French Inhabitants have endeavoured to make a property of everything without the Works that belonged to His Most Christian Majesty, as they do not allow that he had anything without the Works, The Hospital, and Magazine with all the Buildings Thereunto belonging (except one Store House) they pretend was private property. . . . It would appear rather an act of opression in me to seize on those Houses without it was known whether these practices were allowed of, I have therefore inform'd the English Merchants, that if they purchase those Houses, and it should appear hereafter that they were the Kings property,

they should pay Rent to the King for the Houses, and be lyable to be disposses'd.[26]

Property transactions during the transfer of Franco-Spanish Florida to British control appeared to be characterized by illegality and international disregard for the Treaty of Paris. Individual, company, city, and national objectives ultimately superseded the 1763 system of international law. Great Britain and Spain generally accepted the property stipulations of the Treaty of Paris when they did not conflict with particular national goals. English colonial governments conceded the right of real estate exchange among British, French, and Spanish subjects, but they carefully approved only those sales which were congruent with colonization plans for the Floridas. Spain similarly interpreted the treaty in national terms. Agents of Charles III were instructed to comply with the provisions of Article Twenty only to a point where Spanish economic interests seemed to be imperiled. France apparently remained free of illegal real estate activities. But officials, proprietors, and realtors of all three countries became involved in a variety of unlawful conspiracies. The period of imperial transfer therefore featured international violation of the Treaty of Paris.

5

The Official and Demographic Transfer
of Spanish East Florida
to British Control

The St. Augustine Exodus

Only ten months were necessary to complete the evacuation of the Spanish population from St. Augustine. According to previous arrangements, the émigrés were destined for settlement in Cuba and New Spain. From April 12, 1763, to January 21, 1764, a total of 3,103 persons sailed from Florida. In January, 1764, an initial assessment of the exodus indicated that 3,096 people had already embarked, although a later tabulation listed 3,103 Florida exiles. (See Table 4.) A government junta of Governor Melchor Feliú, Esteban de Peña, and Don Juan Elixio de la Puente planned and executed the complicated exodus. Puente was particularly concerned with the movement of his friends and neighbors. His consideration for their comfort resulted in scheduled sailings for complete families, and whenever possible, members of each family departed together with all their belongings. The old Florida resident also loaned his people 14,000 pesos for their transportation and settlement obligations. Puente even deposited 3,100 pesos of his personal funds in the royal treasury as a loan to help finance the costly emigration.[1]

All the *inmigrantes* embarked for Havana, Cuba, except for thirty-four people who eventually moved to San Francisco de Campeche, New Spain. During the entire movement there were only four casualties from the sinking of the sloop *Nuestra Señora del Rosario.* On April 16, 1764, former Governor Melchor Feliú and Don Juan Elixio de la Puente reported that a total of 3,091 people departed from the Plaza of St. Augustine, Fort San Marcos de Apalache, and the towns Nuestra Señora de la Leche, Nuestra Señora de Guadalupe de Tolomato, and Santa Teresa de Gracia Real de Mosa. The statistics of April, 1764, excluded the nine soldiers and citizens left

4. Evacuation statistics, January, 1764: Havana and Campeche

Émigrés	Families	Men	Women	Boys	Girls	Total Number of Individual Evacuees
			Destination: Havana			
St. Augustine military and civilian personnel	364	561	466	442	447	1,916
Catalan Fusileers and families	36	98	36	16	11	161
Canary Islanders	96	89	118	119	99	425
Germans	6	6	10	5	5	26
Christian Indians	19	20	32	18	19	89
Free Negroes	5	10	7	2	4	23
Free Pardos	16	35	27	6	8	76
Convict Laborers	0	38	0	0	0	38
Crown Slaves	0	9	0	0	0	9
Private Slaves	0	83	96	64	57	300
Total	542	949	792	672	650	3,063
			Destination: Campeche			
Military and civilian personnel	3	9	4	8	6	27
Private Slaves	0	3	2	1	0	6
Total	3	12	6	9	6	33
Sum Total	545	961	798	681	656	3,096

SOURCE: Governor Feliú and Don Juan Elixio de la Puente to the governor of Cuba. St. Augustine and Havana, January 22, 1764, and January 27, 1770, MSS, AGI 87–1–5/4, SD 2595.

in St. Augustine to corral the *presidio*'s wandering horses and the four Spaniards who disappeared in the shipwreck of *Nuestra Señora del Rosario*. The remaining Spaniards in St. Augustine, except for Luciano de Herrera, later followed their compatriots to Cuba. Herrera stayed in St. Augustine as the crown's agent to collect money from the sale of Spanish real estate.[2]

Transportation schedules usually conformed to race, rank, and class distinctions. The Spanish creoles of St. Augustine enjoyed first priority over all other civilians. Catalans, Canary Islanders, and German Catholics were regarded as foreigners and therefore received second-class accommodations. Others such as Indians, free mulattoes, and Negroes were often segregated from the Spaniards. Florida settlers from the Canary Islands also typically sailed apart from the other Spanish residents. According to his instructions, Governor Feliú gave precedence to the evacuation of troops, artillery, and the crown's portable goods.[3]

Altogether, 545 families abandoned East Florida. The local Spanish population consisted of 367 families since the Catalan and Canary Island families were listed separately. Colonists from the Canary Islands reached Florida between 1757–61, and by 1763, ninety-six families resided in St. Augustine. Thirty-six families of Catalan Mountain Fusileers arrived in America in 1762 to reinforce the *Presidio de San Agustín* and less than two years later these Spaniards too became statistics in the mass migration. There were also a number of non-Spanish émigrés in the maritime movement to Cuba. Six German families (English colonial exiles), nineteen Christian Indian families, sixteen free *pardo* (mulatto) families, and five free Negro families ultimately sailed with the Spaniards of St. Augustine. Royal and private slaves as well as convicts accompanied their masters out of Florida. Only thirty-four persons including three family units went to Campeche, while 952 men, 794 women, and 1,323 children (673 boys and 650 girls) eventually sailed in family units to Havana. From the capital of Cuba, eight families consisting of forty-three persons later followed the first group to Campeche. With the arrival of the new families from Havana, there was a total of seventy-seven people in San Francisco de Campeche from Florida.[4]

Charles III ordered the Spanish treasury to cover the costs of the evacuation. The bishop of Santiago, Cuba, Don Pedro Agustín Morel y Santa Cruz, financially assisted the royal treasury, however, by paying the travel expenses of seventy-four Floridians. (See Table 5.) Bishop Morel's group consisted of twenty-five women, twelve boys, and thirty-seven girls. While inspecting the parish of St. Augustine in the winter of 1762–63, the Cuban bishop apparently spent diocese funds for the transportation charges of these seventy-four citizens.[5]

The embarkation began early in the spring of 1763. (See Table 6.) On April 12, a fleet of three schooners bearing the bishop's people made the first trip from Florida. In the next nine months forty-four crowded transports would follow the same course through the Bahama Channel toward the Island of Cuba. Almost sixty days elapsed before another human shipment was carried away from port St. Augustine in the sultry month of August. Five schooners with 165 persons departed from Florida on August 3, and fifty-eight evacuees

5. Evacuation statistics, February, 1764: Havana and Campeche

Expense Distribution	Men	Women	Boys	Girls	Totals
Destination: Havana					
Floridians transferred to Cuba at the expense of the bishop of Cuba	0	25	12	37	74
Floridians transferred to Cuba at the expense of His Catholic Majesty	895	760	659	608	2,922
Apalache garrison transferred to Cuba at the expense of His Catholic Majesty	50	8	2	5	65
Total	945	793	673	650	3,061
Destination: Campeche					
Floridians transferred to Campeche at the expense of His Catholic Majesty	13	6	9	6	34
Floridians temporarily remaining in Florida	8	1	0	0	9
Total	21	7	9	6	43
Sum Total	966	800	682	656	3,104

SOURCE: Governor Feliú and Don Juan Elixio de la Puente to Minister Julián de Arriaga. Havana, February 20, and April 16, 1764, MSS, AGI 86–6–6/43, SD 2543.

left on the following day. On the fifth, sixth, and seventh of August, two schooners and three sloops boarded 343 passengers for the Atlantic Ocean voyage to Cuba. Another 141 residents of Florida were emigrated on the tenth of August, and an English packet boat with a cargo of 250 people sailed from the peninsula on August 20, 1763. The exodus continued with the evacuation of 114 émigrés on the twenty-second day of the month. Another British ship, the sloop *Hawk,* packed 104 more Spaniards off to Havana on the thirtieth of August. Finally, a Spanish vessel moved 133 additional Floridians on the last day of the month. By the end of August, the Florida junta in conjunction with the royal officials of Cuba had directed the departure of almost 1,400 inhabitants from St. Augustine. More than one-third of the population of East Florida was carried to the captaincy general of Cuba after five months of preparation and really only one month of scheduled sailings.[6]

6. The evacuation vessels and their passengers, 1763–64

		Departing Point: **St. Augustine** Destination: **Havana**				
		Passengers				
Date of Departure	Ships	Men	Women	Boys	Girls	Totals
1763						
April 12	Unnamed Spanish schooner	0	5	2	3	10
April 12	Unnamed Spanish schooner	0	13	8	27	48
April 12	Unnamed Spanish schooner	0	7	2	7	16
April Total		0	25	12	37	74
August 3	The Schooner Nuestra Señora de Soledad	14	0	0	0	14
August 3	The Schooner Jesus, Mary	11	15	10	9	45
August 3	The Schooner La Candelaria	15	12	4	4	35
August 3	The Schooner San Miguel	4	4	3	2	13
August 3	The Schooner San Francisco de Paula	22	11	12	13	58
August 4	The Sloop Nuestra Señora de Rosario	14	32	9	3	58
August 5	The Schooner La Candelaria	14	12	15	16	57
August 6	The Sloop Nuestra Señora de Rozario	23	1	0	0	24
August 7	The Sloop Nuestra Señora de Regla	20	22	13	13	68
August 7	The Sloop San Antonio	31	39	24	21	115
August 7	The Schooner Nuestra Señora de Dolores	39	21	6	13	79
August 10	The Sloop El Mexandro	60	42	21	18	141
August 20	The English Packet Boat Amitante Sander	55	59	76	60	250

		Departing Point: **St. Augustine** Destination: **Havana**				
Date of Departure	*Ships*	*Passengers*				*Totals*
		Men	*Women*	*Boys*	*Girls*	
1763						
August 22	The Sloop *La Santísima Trinidad*	27	34	25	28	114
August 30	The English Sloop *Hawk*	28	24	29	23	104
August 31	The Sloop *San Francisco Xavier*	45	41	22	25	133
August Total		422	369	269	248	1,308
September 14	The Schooner *Santa Theresa*	21	24	22	15	82
September Total		21	24	22	15	82
October 12	The Sloop *La Santísima Trinidad*	29	33	29	20	111
October 12	The Sloop *La Esperanza*	19	23	22	18	82
October 12	The Sloop *San Juan Baptista*	18	18	14	16	66
October 14	The Sloop *Nuestra Señora de la Luz y Santa Bárbara*	25	21	26	19	91
October 19	The English Sloop *Sally*	24	13	3	3	43
October 27	The Sloop *Santa Ana*	29	26	23	20	98
October 28	The French Sloop *San Antonio*	14	17	26	30	87
October Total		158	151	143	126	578
November 17	The Brigantine *El Firme*	9	12	10	19	50
November 19	The French Sloop *La María*	17	20	20	28	85
November Total		26	32	30	47	135
December 7	The Schooner *Nuestra Señora de la Soledad*	9	4	11	5	29

6. Continued

Date of Departure	Ships	Passengers				Totals
		Men	Women	Boys	Girls	
1763						
December 19	The Brigantine *San Joseph y Nuestra Señora del Rosario*	27	18	23	22	90
December 24	The English Brigantine *Fanny*	7	2	3	0	12
December 24	The English Sloop *Industries*	15	12	16	15	58
December 24	The Sloop *La Santisima Trinidad*	14	21	13	13	61
December 30	The Sloop *Nuestra Señora de la Soledad*	8	6	7	4	25
December Total		80	63	73	59	275
1764						
January 8	The Sloop *La Esperanza*	28	14	18	20	80
January 9	The Sloop *Santa Theresa*	14	7	14	8	43
January 9	The Packet Boat *Nuestra Señora de Begoña*	17	13	11	17	58
January 21	The Sloop *Nuestra Señora de Concepción*	28	21	19	14	82
January 21	The Sloop *La Santisima Trinidad y Nuestra Señora de Concepción*	17	13	18	10	58
January 21	The Schooner *San Judas Thadeo*	35	23	12	16	86
January 21	The Sloop *San Antonio*	13	13	13	13	52
January 21	The Schooner *Nuestra Señora de la Luz y Santa Bárbara*	10	11	7	10	38
January 21	The Schooner *Nuestra Señora de Candelaria*	5	5	6	5	21

Date of Departure	Ships	Passengers				Totals
		Men	*Women*	*Boys*	*Girls*	

Departing Point: St. Augustine
Destination: Havana

1764 January 21	The Schooner *Nuestra Señora de los Dolores*	21	1	4	0	26
January Total		188	121	122	113	544
Total transported from St. Augustine to Havana		895	785	671	645	2,996

Departing Point: St. Augustine and Havana
Destination: Campeche

1763 December 5	The Schooner *San Joseph y las Animas*	3	1	4	2	10
1764 January 23	The English Brigantine *Mary*	10	5	5	4	24
Total transported from St. Augustine and Havana to Campeche		13	6	9	6	34

Departing Point: Apalache
Destination: Havana

1764 February 20	Unnamed vessel	50	8	2	5	65
Total transported from Apalache to Havana		50	8	2	5	65
Total Evacuees		**958**	**799**	**682**	**656**	**3,095**

SOURCE: Governor Feliú and Don Juan Elixio de la Puente to Minister Julián de Arriaga. Havana, April 16, 1764, MS, AGI 86–6–6/43, SD 2543.

During the last days of July, prior to the evacuations of August, 1763, Engineer Juan de Cotilla appeared very pleased to view the incipient sailing preparations for his countrymen. The "total" character of the population exodus away from British East Florida especially delighted him. On the thirty-first of July, ten days after the arrival of Captain John Hedges and British military government, Cotilla smugly reported to the governor of Cuba, Conde de Ricla, "the wills of all our citizens seem generally disposed to evacuation and I expect that Your Excellency will be pleased to command the prompt return of the transport vessels since the arrival of the English governor is imminent. . . . It is obvious that the British are surprised to witness the decision of all our people to emigrate, when they asserted that there would not be enough evacuees to fill one vessel." [7]

Following the movement of sixteen ships and 1,308 Floridians in August there was only one ocean trip to Cuba from August 31 to October 12, 1763. The frequency of September–October northeasters and summer hurricanes probably discouraged sea voyages in the late summer and early autumn. Surely the Spaniards remembered the fate of the treasure flota fifty years earlier (July 31, 1715), when ten ships, more than 1,000 sailors, and $14,000,000 in gold and silver bullion were lost in a storm off the Florida coast. Only 82 Spaniards abandoned Florida on September 14, but three sloops transported 259 persons to Havana almost a month later on October 12, 1763. On October fourteenth, ninety-one Floridians were conducted to Cuba on the sloop *Nuestra Señora de la Luz y Santa Bárbara.* In less than a week, another forty-three people left Florida. Near the end of October, 185 Spaniards journeyed to Havana, on the twenty-seventh and twenty-eighth of that month. The French sloop *San Antonio* served in the evacuation of the last day. [8]

Prior to the winter voyages of December, 1763, and January, 1764, only 135 Floridians were transferred to Cuba in the month of November. The November sailings occurred on the seventeenth and nineteenth. During December a total of 275 people traveled by sea from St. Augustine to Havana, while 544 Spaniards followed the same water route in January. In December three sloops, two brigantines, and a schooner evacuated Spanish citizenry on the seventh, nineteenth, twenty-fourth, and the thirtieth of the month. On Christmas Eve, 1763, the Spaniards employed three vessels of which two were English—the British brig *Fanny* and the sloop *Industries.* [9] Altogether five of His Britannic Majesty's vessels participated in the evacuation of St. Augustine, and these ships transported 467 Spaniards from Florida. Two French sloops were also employed to carry 172 Floridians to Cuba. In the earlier population movements from

Pensacola, four British transports served the Spaniards in September, 1763. Despite historic Habsburg "exclusivism" and Bourbon "mercantilism" foreign ships frequently sailed in Spanish American waters for the crown of Spain. Although the history of the eighteenth century reveals an almost constant state of strife between England and Spain, there is considerable evidence that legal and illegal commercial activity between the English colonies and Spanish Florida continued throughout that century of wars. Because the Havana Company was unable to supply the necessary *situado* merchandise to Florida, the William Walton Company of New York City acquired trade privileges with St. Augustine. The Walton Company, for which Jesse Fish later served as resident factor in San Agustín, secured its trade rights in the middle of the eighteenth century. According to one observer, this New York export company earned about 200,000 pesos a year from Florida contracts until Spain entered the Seven Years' War.[10]

Five sloops, four schooners, and one packet boat completed the St. Augustine evacuation in the first month of 1764. After witnessing the movement of 181 men, women, and children on January 8 and 9, 1764, Governor Feliú and his staff abandoned Florida on the twenty-first of the same month. Other officials and inhabitants accompanied him on a seven-ship convoy which conveyed 363 Floridians to the Island of Cuba.[11] St. Augustine was indeed evacuated and almost empty.

A grand total of 2,996 subjects of Spain were transported down the coast of Florida through the Bahama Channel to the captaincy general of Cuba. The *inmigrantes* included 895 men, 785 women, 671 boys, 645 girls, and apparently even some of the Spanish dead. Feliú explained that "the piety of religion and feminine weakness" obliged him to ship the Spanish deceased to Havana. The governor probably only moved the bodies of people who had recently died. It would be indeed macabre to imagine any other course of action even if influenced by "piety" or femininity. On December 5, 1763, and January 23, 1764, thirty-four other Floridians were carried to Campeche, New Spain. Finally, the sixty-five members of the Apalache garrison eventually sailed from Florida on February 20, 1764. Because British personnel delayed the transfer of that frontier post, the Spanish departure was similarly detained.[12] By the conclusion of the evacuation, 3,061 persons were transferred to Cuba (945 men, 793 women, and 1,323 children), 34 others reached Campeche, 9 Floridians remained in St. Augustine, and 4 Spaniards drowned at sea. Eight of the nine Spanish citizens remaining in St. Augustine were eventually shipped to Havana. The final statistics revealed that Spain evacuated 3,103 persons from East Florida.[13] (See Table 7.)

7. Evacuation statistics, September, 1766: Havana, Cuba

Departing Groups	Number of Families	Men	Women	Children	Total Number of Persons
Spanish Floridians	343	404	458	888	1,750
Spanish officials, clergy, army officers, and soldiers	0	204	0	0	204
Canary Islanders	120	115	122	212	449
Catalans	36	34	36	27	97
German Catholics	6	6	8	11	25
Free Mulattoes	15	32	16	11	59
Free Negroes	5	8	6	6	20
Christian Indians	19	14	32	37	83
Construction Laborers	0	38	0	0	38
Foreigners	?	?	?	?	21
Crown and Private Slaves	?	?	?	?	350
Total	544	855	678	1,192	3,096

SOURCE: Puente to the governor of Cuba. Havana, September 22, 1766, MS, AGI 87–1–5/3, SD 2595.

Almost one-half of the population was composed of military personnel and other people not considered to be Floridians. There were 1,115 of the latter category in the evacuation of Florida including 425 Canary Islanders, 161 Catalans, 26 Germans, 89 Indians, 99 free Negroes and mulattoes, and 315 Negro and mulatto slaves. Another assessment of the St. Augustine exodus, prepared in 1766, indicated that 1,142 non-Floridians left East Florida in 1763. The total of 1766 included 449 Canary Islanders, 97 Catalans, 25 German Catholics, 83 Indians, 79 free Negroes and mulattoes, 21 foreigners, 38 construction laborers, and 350 slaves. Since the *presidio* served an important military mission, the evacuation statistics reveal a military preponderance. One-sixth of the total citizenry was officers and soldiers. Excluding the 85 men of the militia, the garrison of St. Augustine supported 235 infantry soldiers, 90 Mountain Fusileers, 52 mounted dragoons, 39 foot dragoons, 39 artillery troops, and 11 soldiers posted at Fort Mosa.[14]

The Florida Settlement in Cuba

Most of the Florida exiles initially settled in Havana, Cuba. Some of the civilians found temporary housing in the city of Havana. A larger number of émigrés moved to lodgings in the suburb Barrio de Guadalupe, located outside the walls of the port-city. Regla and Guanabacoa, two towns in proximity to Havana, also accommodated the immigrants from Florida. Regla was located directly across the bay from Havana, while Guanabacoa stood only six miles distant from the trade center of the Indies. The civilians and militia temporarily obtained various amounts for subsistence except for those people whose professions and occupations could be continued on the Island of Cuba. Some refugees, however, received nothing. Soon after arrival, the Florida soldiery was incorporated into the reorganized Spanish army of Cuba. The various infantry, artillery, and dragoon units immediately recruited most of the regulars of the St. Augustine *presidio*. Catholic clergy also found new assignments in Cuba or other areas of the Spanish Indies. The able clerical evacuees were quickly assimilated into the appropriate orders and services of the Church.[15]

Several months following their sea journey from Florida, 331 civilians were transferred from Havana to Matanzas, Cuba. These men, women, and children moved during the spring of 1764 after many of the exiles had become acclimated to life in Havana. Once again Floridians changed their residence under crown orders. But the second transfer, unlike the first, conveyed the residents of Florida from an urban seaport to a rural farming milieu. In a region called Ceiba Mocha, the crown established a settlement for the Florida refugees. Ceiba Mocha was an uncultivated inland area located within the jurisdiction of Matanzas, Cuba. A portion of Ceiba Mocha became available for colonization because a local *hacendado*, Don Gerónimo Contreras, voluntarily donated some of his extensive properties to the people of Florida. According to contemporary rumors, Contreras also came from a Florida background. Don Gerónimo Contreras relinquished sufficient territory to provide at least 108 *caballerías* of land for an agrarian community. The new colony was officially entitled San Agustín de la Nueva Florida, although "Ceiba Mocha" continued as the popular name of the area.[16] (See Table 8.)

The governor of Cuba installed seventy-three families on the

8. Florida families located at San Agustín de la Nueva Florida

Colonizers	Families	Men	Women	Children	Total Number of Persons
		Original Settlers			
Spanish Florida Families	13	13	11	32	56
Canary Islanders	43	43	43	111	197
Germans	4	4	4	9	17
Free Negroes	4	4	4	9	17
Free Pardos	9	9	9	26	44
Total	73	73	71	187	331
		Later Arrivals			
Florida Soldiers' Families	9	...	...	...	...
Shore Guard Family	1	...	...	...	...
Canary Islanders	1	...	...	...	...
Total	11				

SOURCE: Puente to the governor of Cuba. Havana, September 22, and 26, 1766, MSS, AGI 87-1-5/3, SD 2595.

uncultivated lands of San Agustín de la Nueva Florida. Thirteen Spanish families, forty-three Canary Island families, four German families, nine free *pardo* families, and four free Negro families moved to Ceiba Mocha. A significant number of "foreign" and native Floridians were separated from the émigré settlement at Havana. Other St. Augustine families later followed their neighbors into Matanzas. Eleven families of servicemen secured royal permission to settle in San Agustín de la Nueva Florida. In 1764, after these colonists arrived, the Contreras territories held a total of eighty-four families. Thereafter, the population decreased during the mid-sixties as many disillusioned settlers sought opportunities elsewhere.[17]

On March 17, 1764, Conde de Ricla composed his instructions concerning the settlement of the émigrés. The governor's orders guaranteed privileges and proprietorship for all Spaniards who had voluntarily abandoned their Florida homes. Each family transferred to Ceiba Mocha at crown expense would be distributed one *caballería* of land from the territory obtained from Contreras. The new settlers were also given one Negro slave and a stipend of sixty pesos for clearing and cultivating their portion of property. Cuban officials bestowed all grants in perpetuity, but grantees were obliged to cultivate their new lands in order to retain possession. The crown likewise ceded estates to free Negroes and mulattoes, although a meticulous segregation policy was implemented during the process (Table 9) of property distribution. Spanish and "colored" settlers

9. The location of the population of San Agustín de la Nueva Florida after 1766

Location in Cuba	Families	Men	Women	Children	Total Number of Men, Women, and Children
Families remaining at Nueva Florida					
Spanish Floridians	2	2	2	4	8
Canary Islanders	9	9	8	25	42
Germans	3	3	2	4	9
Free Negroes	2	2	2	6	10
Families renting farms outside of Nueva Florida					
Canary Islanders	6	6	6	14	26
Free Mulattoes	1	1	1	3	5
Families residing in the city of Matanzas					
Spanish Floridians	1	1	1	4	6
Free Negroes	1	1	1	4	6
Free Mulattoes	4	4	4	9	17
Families returning to the city of Havana					
Spanish Floridians	11	11	9	31	51
Canary Islanders	28	28	28	80	136
Germans	1	1	1	1	3
Free Negroes	2	2	2	1	5
Free Mulattoes	3	3	3	9	15
Total	74	74	70	195	339

SOURCE: Puente to the governor of Cuba. Havana, September 22, and 26, 1766, MSS, AGI 87–1–5/3, SD 2595.

lived in separated communities within Ceiba Mocha. The governor of Cuba, however, instructed Don Simón Rodriguez, lieutenant of the royal exchequer of Matanzas, to allot contiguous *caballerías* to families who requested immediate contact with each other.[18] Although all grants were given in perpetuity and without ownership limits, alienation of Matanzas property required royal approval.

The crown prohibited the sale of granted territory to any outsiders. Proprietorship could only be transferred to other inhabitants of the new settlement with the consent of the governor and captain general of Cuba. According to royal instructions, uncultivated *caballerías* could not be alienated under any conditions.[19]

The governor of Cuba obliged San Agustín residents to repay the loan of 60 pesos as well as 150 more pesos for the Negro slave. A period of nine years was designated for the liquidation of their indebtedness. According to a royal payment schedule, the immigrants paid nothing toward their debt during the first year of settlement. Thereafter, the settlers were instructed to remit annual installments of twenty-six pesos and two reales. Until the repayment of the crown loan, slaves could not be sold since they remained categorized as mortgaged property. Exchange of slaves among citizens of Ceiba Mocha was permitted with certain restrictions. All such dispositions or substitutions required the royal exchequer's consent. The governor of Cuba did not deliver the sixty pesos totally in cash. Nine pesos and two reales were subtracted from the original amount, equivalent to the cost of a routine consignment of agrarian implements.[20]

The Spanish crown also supplied provisions for San Agustín de la Nueva Florida. Those unspoiled foodstuffs and supplies which survived the evacuation of 1763–64 were distributed among the colonists at Ceiba Mocha. Havana officials sent other necessary commodities to the new settlement at the king's prices. In the governor's instructions the treasury received definite orders not to profit from any sales to the struggling Floridians. Only the usual tariffs were attached to goods passing into Nueva Florida. Conde de Ricla even recommended temporary lodgings for the colonists until the completion of house construction in Ceiba Mocha. Matanzas officials were also urged to extend financial help to the new settlers of San Agustín de la Nueva Florida.[21]

The crown asked the local government of Matanzas to assist the new community in every way possible. Officials of the port-city therefore found themselves responsible for the everyday existence of the Florida exiles, a responsibility which became extremely oppressive by 1766. Other efforts were made to accommodate and comfort the colony of immigrants. In order to provide the colonists with adequate time to arrange their affairs and begin the processes of cultivation and construction, Conde de Ricla permitted the settlement two years for development. Thereafter, the governor and captain general of Cuba warned the refugees that the king's patience would be exhausted and the people of Nueva Florida would lose their property and privileges. Their superiors in Havana threatened the settlers with other unpleasant prospects if they allowed their territories to remain uncultivated. Military service or forced labor were mentioned as possible punishments. In conclusion, Conde de Ricla clearly announced that the property and opportunities in Matanzas would be the only charitable awards that the Floridians could expect to receive from their monarch.[22] The king apparently considered the grants in Ceiba Mocha as adequate compensation for the loss of Florida lands.

Within two years of settlement, San Agustín de la Nueva Florida was suffering economic despair. On August 26, 1766, a memorial from 166 heads of Florida families solicited the governor of Cuba for immediate aid and relief. Although the memorial contained the specific requests of the majority of the refugees, the main petition concerned the miserable state of affairs at Ceiba Mocha. Beseeching the captain general for immediate sustenance, the memorial graphically described the hardships and unfortunate history of the community. Only civilians without official employment placed their signatures on the memorial. Those Floridians who served in the Spanish administration and military services, or whose wives and / or daughters received a government allotment were not permitted to sign the petition. The name Don Juan Elixio de la Puente appeared prominently among the signatures on the petition even though the Florida official never became a member of the Matanzas settlement. Puente actually served the memorialists as author of some, if not all, of the documents. He therefore extended his efforts in behalf of his relatives, friends, and neighbors to Nueva Florida. Throughout his life, Don Juan Elixio de la Puente continued to be the ubiquitous spokesman for Florida and the exiled Floridians.[23]

A list of impecunious persons accompanied the memorial as well as a financial accounting of 261 heads-of-family. The latter roster included Spanish Floridians (soldiers, civilians, militia, and invalids), Germans, Canary Islanders, Negroes, and mulattoes, who lacked employment and financial relief or whose only income was a tiny per diem allowance. Many names with inadequate earnings appeared on these refugee lists. Along with those enclosures there existed an Indian census which related the situation of the Florida natives in Cuba. This record indicated that only fifty-three Indians remained alive of the more than eighty who became voluntary émigrés with the Spaniards of St. Augustine. The living Indians received one-half real per diem during their early residence in Cuba.[24]

Former citizens of Florida were especially angry because they no longer qualified for essential government subsidies. Their serious lack of lodgings similarly distressed them, "we have not even been supplied with shacks to protect our bodies from the punishments of weather, and consequently, without housing and sustenance find ourselves obliged to sleep under doorways exposed to inclement conditions." [25] Sickness, starvation, death, or an ignominious life of begging unfortunately became the destiny of the impoverished and unsheltered exiles in Cuba. In September, 1766, Don Juan Elixio de la Puente informed the governor of Cuba that 663 persons of 3,096 total immigrants had already perished in Cuba. Another population census dated January 22, 1764, revealed that 131 of a total of 961 Florida men, over the age of fifteen, died in Cuba during 1763 and 1764. Such a mortality rate for six months would not be astonishing in an environment known to be enduring tropical fever epidemics.[26]

Conspicuous prostitution was another consequence of the miserable living conditions in Cuba. According to the memorialists "some starving young women, lacking food, clothes, lodging and medicines, have forgotten their honor and religious convictions and have arrived at the unfortunate state of prostituting themselves and committing serious sins against God." [27] The petitioners, however, carefully explained that prostitution appeared only among families of humble means. Lack of education and extreme poverty reduced the poorer women to such dishonorable activities. Other less unfortunate females sold their few clothes and valuables or solicited charity alms in order to continue their precarious existence. Life in Cuba included many vicissitudes.

Accusations against the royal treasury were also among the various charges of the Florida *inmigrantes*. The authors of the memorial blamed some of their financial misfortunes on the treasurer who neglected to issue them their salaries for the last months in Florida. They claimed that all the troops of the Plaza de San Agustín were owed considerable sums of salary monies, although the viceroy of New Spain committed sufficient amounts to the royal coffers early in 1764. The Floridians implied that their funds had been embezzled. In a document entitled "Various Obligations of the Plaza of St. Augustine" the émigrés presented a *dotación* (roster) of persons suffering salary arrears. According to their dossier, the treasury even owed former Governor Melchor Feliú 1,560 pesos. Sergeant Major Alonzo de Cárdenas also lacked 960 pesos, and the militia company, including commissioned and noncommissioned officers, still required 348 pesos. Other treasury payment arrears included 5,408 pesos owed to the Church, 13,967 pesos designated for the military department, and 16,972 pesos, which served as *situado* payments for 186 people (widows, orphans, and unmarried girls) at the rate of two reales per day. An unemployment inventory of 166 military and militia personnel was also included among the manuscripts en route to the royal government in Cuba.[28]

Along with their accounts, petitions, and numerous complaints, the memorialists described in detail the laborious attempts they had made to sustain themselves in Matanzas. Many stories of personal survival appeared in the petition of 1766, and such reports were included to support the claims of the suffering inhabitants of Nueva Florida. Their "defensive" argument seemed to be aimed at anonymous Cuban critics. Certain observers apparently accused the exiles of apathy and lethargy in their life at Ceiba Mocha. These charges were denied in a lengthy refutation which also related the reasons for the failure of the colony. The new settlement ultimately collapsed because a majority of the colonists refused to occupy or farm the uncultivated lands of Matanzas.[29]

Many of the settlers eventually abandoned San Agustín de la Nueva Florida. The soldiers and their families retired from the settlement shortly after their arrival, and eleven of the thirteen Floridian families withdrew from their new estates after a very brief residence. Only two Spanish families from Florida continued their agricultural life at Ceiba Mocha. After additional desertions 16 families and 69 persons remained in Nueva Florida of an original total of 73 families and 331 persons.[30] The movement of settlers scattered Floridians throughout Cuba. Seven families of San Agustín de la Nueva Florida moved to rented farm lands outside Ceiba Mocha. Another six families scurried to the city of Matanzas where their men secured jobs paying daily wages. At the port-city of Matanzas, *guadaño* (harbor boat) employment was contracted at the rate of four reales per day. The Florida soldiers and their families retreated to unknown locations, and the last arriving Canary Island family unfortunately perished before movement could be contemplated. All three lives of this family were lost when the assigned slave murdered his master, frightened his pregnant mistress to death, and then abandoned their child to die "lacking the necessities of life." Forty-five other families returned to Havana where they managed to subsist on charity. Only sixty-nine intrepid Floridians struggled on at Ceiba Mocha including thirty-nine children, and ten of those children were born after the evacuation of 1763–64.[31]

The sixteen remaining families of San Agustín de la Nueva Florida resided on their isolated properties located as far as one league from each other throughout the Contreras territories. A local, but distant, river offered the only water for drinking and irrigation. The absence of regular food staples forced the destitute colonists to consume corn, pumpkins, cassava, greens, and sweet potatoes as a daily diet. All their food was the product of hard agricultural labor. The bark shacks that they hastily constructed provided the only available housing. Remaining residents of San Agustín de la Nueva Florida undoubtedly faced a very trying future. According to Puente, these suffering people would have also deserted their desperate situation if they had possessed enough money to escape from Matanzas. Unfortunately, the small population of Ceiba Mocha lacked even the funds to repay their crown loans.[32]

In addition to these disclosures of the miserable conditions in Matanzas, the memorialists presented a detailed critique of the colonial failure in Nueva Florida. Initially, they reminded their government that Florida was historically founded and settled by soldiers of the crown. Few Floridians therefore possessed knowledge of farming procedures. Without agricultural experience, the émigrés asserted, the lands would still have become productive if the people of Florida had been succored with proper support. They complained that such sustenance never seemed to be forthcoming. Lacking habitable lodgings, medicines, physicians, sufficient provisions, water, and other essential necessities, Ceiba Mocha inevitably remained undeveloped. The *caballerías* were uncultivated because the settlers could not even adequately care for themselves and their families. San Agustín also lacked the holy sacraments and indispensable religious supervision.[33]

Since priests were not present in the community, Spaniards unfortunately went to their deaths without the last sacrament. The wretched citizens of San Agustín de la Nueva Florida also confronted a slave rebellion and murder. Because of the distances that typically separated the colonists from each other and from the *guardia civil* (rural police) in Matanzas, some of the recently purchased slaves openly rebelled and attacked their masters. Several Floridians were killed and others wounded on those occasions. According to the memorial of August, 1766, the lack of royal sustenance resulted in a syndrome of deprivation, suffering, and tragedy which overwhelmed the immigrants and ruined the settlement at Ceiba Mocha.[34]

The petitions of the settlers included numerous requests for relief and future opportunities outside of Ceiba Mocha. Indeed, should patriotic soldiers of the crown suffer in San Agustín de la Nueva Florida? Would Ceiba Mocha be the king's reward for three hundred years of royal service? These were the emotional appeals of the Florida memorialists who reminded their superiors that they had willingly abandoned their property, possessions, and beloved homeland only because of the king's requests. The petitioners neglected to mention the offer of "proprietorship" in Cuba as a motive for their voluntary exile. After forsaking the unconquered country of their fathers and ancestors, and after three centuries of fighting to defend the royal colony, the Floridians vigorously asserted that they deserved better treatment from the crown's government in Cuba.[35] Although obviously polemical the memorialist argument was essentially accurate.

In conclusion, the supplicants requested the governor of Cuba to implement the king's orders for their relief and security. They beseeched the Havana government for immediate attention. The favors which they sought were administrative or military employment commensurate with their rank and experience, financial assistance for all old and ill people, per diem for their wives and children, payment of their salaries and other unpaid but requisite monies. For those Floridians who would not be placed in government service, the memorial solicited agricultural lands in the uncultivated and undistributed estates of Barrio de San Antonio. The signatories warned that further delay would exacerbate the already deplorable condition of the Florida refugees.[36] Although the émigrés claimed that their misfortunes were due to unfortunate circumstances, the petition at least implied that administrative incompetence sabotaged the settlement at Ceiba Mocha.

The crown eventually awarded financial assistance to the Floridians in Cuba. Only women, however, were recipients of royal stipends. Refugee women received *la limosna de Florida* (the alms or pension of Florida) if they were wives, widows, or daughters of Floridians at the time of the Treaty of 1763. A *cédula* of 1731 originally established the *limosna* system for the unmarried widows and orphaned daughters of Florida soldiers. In 1770 the latter women received two reales per diem, while all other Florida females qualified for allotments of one real per day. *La limosna de Florida* served the refugee families from 1770 to 1784. After the British Period (1763–84) , Spanish officials devised another subsidy program to entice Floridians in Cuba to return to Florida. The royal *cédula* of March 18, 1791, provided a number of inducements including an expanded and increased pension system. Florida men never enjoyed eligibility for charity income throughout the term of their exile in Cuba. Except for the implementation of *la limosna de Florida* the captaincy general of Cuba apparently ignored many of the demands in the memorial of 1766.[37]

Twenty-six years after the Florida *inmigrantes* petitioned the governor of Cuba for immediate relief, they received acknowledgement in the king's edict of 1791. If they returned to Florida, the royal *cédula* of 1791 promised the settlers land grants, long-term loans of slaves and agricultural implements, and compensation for former estates which were under other proprietorships. The crown offered these alluring opportunities because only 132 exiles had reoccupied St. Augustine by 1786. Once again, as in 1763, the king's ministers assured the Floridians of royal favor for compliance to imperial policy.[38] Unlike the patriots of 1763–64, fewer Floridians after 1791 accepted the offer of their king and emigrated according to official request.

The Official Transfer of East Florida
from Spanish to British Control

Official notice of the Florida provisions of the Treaty of Paris probably reached St. Augustine during the latter part of March or in early April, 1763. St. Augustine's copy of the notice was dated February 24, 1763. The February papers included specific instructions concerning the treaty and the cession of Florida to Great Britain. Instructions from Havana informed Governor Feliú that total evacuation of the *presidio* of St. Augustine was "recommended" by the king of Spain. A royal recommendation actually equaled a royal order. In order to facilitate the crown's plans, the Council of the Indies instructed Melchor Feliú to convince all inhabitants to emigrate to Havana, where they could be given other colonial homes and assignments in Hispanic America. All military personnel and movable possessions were likewise subject to complete evacuation. The crown ordered everything and everybody to be removed to Cuba as quickly as possible at crown expense. Finally, *cédulas* from Havana directed the governor of Florida to deliver up the old colony to authorized English agents.[39]

Actual knowledge of the impending transfer of Florida to Great Britain supposedly arrived on March 16, 1763. On that date, the H.M.S. *Bonetta* sailed into port St. Augustine with an English version of the Preliminary Articles of Peace. The British copy included the three-power ratification of the preliminary agreement of 1762. In the late winter and spring of 1763, published accounts of the same articles were featured in both the *South Carolina Gazette* and the *Georgia Gazette*. The former publication announced the news of Spain's surrender of Florida in the edition dated February 5–12, 1763. Two months later, on April 14, treaty information appeared in the Georgia periodical.[40]

Anglo-Spanish activities to exchange the control of Florida were initiated in the spring of 1763. As early as April 18, the Earl of Egremont (England's secretary of state) notified the secretary of war to send a military contingent to Florida. A token force would be ordered to occupy Florida and arrange the international cession. For similar purposes, the governor of Cuba, Conde de Ricla, sent the Spanish transfer orders of February 24, 1763, to General William Keppel, commander-in-chief of the English forces in Florida. General Keppel then commanded Major Francis Ogilvie to embark the Ninth Regiment for St. Augustine. The British high command also distributed orders to Major Forbes of the Thirty-fifth Regiment and Major Loftus of the Twenty-second Regiment for the occupation of Mobile and Pensacola. These appointments were later altered by General Keppel. Captain John Hedges sailed to St. Augustine, while Lieutenant Colonel Augustin Provost with the Sixtieth Regiment and Major Robert Farmar, commanding the Twenty-second and Thirty-fourth Regiments, were respectively directed to Pensacola and Mobile.[41]

Captain Hedges, bearing the royal *cédula* of February 24, 1763, commanded the first English unit to enter St. Augustine and Spanish Florida. Map 4 depicts the town and harbor at that time. The captain arrived in Florida on July twenty-first with the British First Regiment. His report to the secretary of war stated, "I had the honour to write to you from St Augustine, acquainting your Lordship of my having taken possession of that Town and Fort, with its dependencys."[42] Since Governor Melchor Feliú regarded John Hedges as the official English representative, the soldier was entrusted with the keys of the *presidio*. His superior officer, Major Francis Ogilvie, followed Captain Hedges to Florida on July 30, 1763, and received the archives of St. Augustine from Governor Feliú. The governor of Florida, however, did not yield any *cédulas*, treasury accounts, or other special papers of the Spanish colonial government. According to the provisions of the Treaty of Paris and the royal instructions of December 13, 1763, those records were destined for Cuban depositories.[43] The departure of Melchor Feliú's military government in January, 1764, was actually the last significant act in the Spanish transfer of Florida. The cession of July was followed by the complete evacuation of the population of Florida. Thereafter, British East Florida would lose its military character and become a civilian "crown" colony, although army personnel would always be stationed throughout the province during the years 1763–84.

Since the early colonial period of Pedro Menéndez de Avilés, the *Presidio de San Agustín* was actually governed by military administrations. Menéndez organized a *cabildo* (town council) for St. Augustine in 1571, but it was suspended in the same year and never reinstated. Other attempts to install a *cabildo* in Florida followed as late as 1762. At that time Governor Melchor Feliú claimed that the necessary people to form a Florida *cabildo,* composed of two *alcaldes ordinarios* (magistrates), six *regidores* (councilors), and a *padre de menores* (clergyman), could not be found in St. Augustine. Civilians often held positions of importance in the upper echelons of local government, but the most powerful official in Florida was "governor" and captain general. The military functions of the frontier garrison throughout the First Spanish Period (1565–1763) necessitated final army authority.[44]

The king of Spain selected the governor and captain general, usually from a list of names and credentials (*relaciónes de méritos y servicios*). Selection usually followed recommendations by the Council of the Indies. Appointed captain generals then enjoyed almost complete control of the military, political, socioeconomic, religious, and judicial functions of the colony. A council (junta) composed of the royal officials [the accountant (*contador*) and the treasurer (*tesorero*)], the sergeant major, the infantry captain and lieutenant, three second lieutenants, a military engineer, the auxiliary bishop of Florida, the church curate, and the guardian of the Franciscan convent assisted and advised the governor of Florida. Although the captain general could act independently of the councils,

4 Thomas Jefferys' map of St. Augustine, 1763

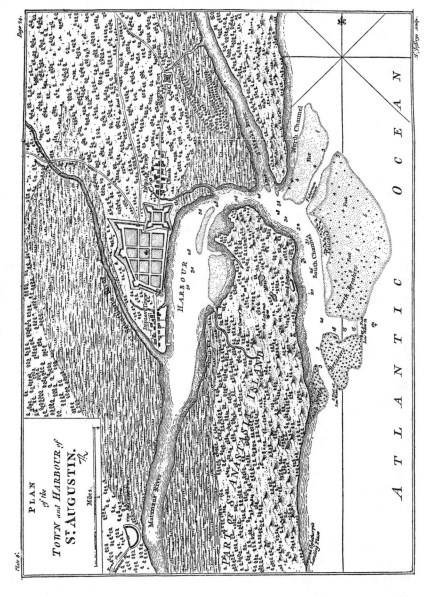

he usually accepted their advice and granted them various powers in order to win their support in disputes with the Council of the Indies. Florida councils typically managed the collection and disbursement of the periodic subsidy (situado). The seemingly absolute authority of the governor and captain general was subject to numerous restraints. Pesquisa, residencia, and visita (forms of inquiry, investigation, and inspection) provided three methods of supervising the office of governor and captain general. The governor also was frequently under the orders of the captain general of Cuba and the viceroy of New Spain. Finally, the continuous arrival of royal cédulas restricted the colonial powers of the governorship and captaincy general of Florida.[45]

Melchor Feliú arrived in Havana on February 3, 1764. Two and one-half months later the ex-governor of Florida filed a detailed résumé of the mass exodus with Council Minister Julián de Arriaga (1754–76) and the Council of the Indies. The communiqué of April 16, 1764, reported a successful evacuation except for the anticipated passage difficulties at the Bar of St. Augustine. Former Governor Feliú commended Captain Hedges and Major Ogilvie on their efforts to achieve harmony between the two nationalities. The dismantling of the houses of St. Augustine by the British soldiery, however, was a frictional episode for which Feliú blamed Ogilvie. Melchor Feliú also criticized Major Ogilvie for attempting to prevent Anglo-Spanish property transactions. Except for those unpleasant instances, Feliú recorded no other complaints of British behavior during the transfer of Florida.[46]

According to Governor Feliú, the Floridians accomplished an orderly evacuation. The captain general of Florida previously warned his colonists to refrain from all controversy with the foreign soldiers. Feliú recognized that international conflict might have easily developed over property disputes. The Spaniards were particularly angry because the British settlers appeared to be ignoring available sales of real estate. Instead, prospective investors apparently awaited later purchase and land-grant opportunities under English rule. Those astute speculators anticipated a better property market to become accessible when Spain's selling period ended, and such expectations were ultimately realized with the Proclamation of 1763. Since the St. Augustine proprietors avoided arguments over property disposition, both Melchor Feliú and Conde de Ricla recognized that the crown probably would offer the Floridians some "favor or compensation" for their losses.[47] Their expectations proved to be accurate. Within a year of the exodus, the Florida exiles received grants in Cuba and New Spain.

While Juan Elixio de la Puente encountered an unexpected debate with Major Ogilvie concerning the Keys, his sales and evacuation missions proceeded without any apparent hindrance from the new government in Florida. The realtors Cotilla and Castelló likewise experienced no English interference as they evaluated and sold Spanish property. Similarly, Don Miguel Krannenbourgh, Don Fernando Cuesta, and Don Bentura Doral completed their embarkation of soldiers, artillery, and military supplies without opposition. Only Don Thomas Sothvel, the naval ensign in charge of seventeen evacuation ships, complained that the English were "impertinent and molest us daily." [48]

A general Spanish consensus therefore indicated that the international transfer proceeded in a calm and cooperative atmosphere. British vessels were even employed in the evacuation. The Spaniards actually congratulated the British commanders for their efforts to maintain harmony between English and Spanish subjects. Later legends insisted that Major Ogilvie's "impolitick behaviour caused all Spaniards to remove to Havanna." Governor Vicente Manuel Zéspedes y Velasco, the first governor of East Florida after the British interlude, condemned Major Ogilvie and military occupation by remarking, "God deliver me from remembering what was practiced then." [49] From the information currently available, it would seem that both those statements inaccurately described the last days of the First Spanish Period. The Spaniards evacuated Florida at the urging of their king, and the movement apparently was concluded without any serious complications.

Although the British soldiers waited anxiously to see the last foreigners exiled from Florida, they made no mention of any altercations with the Spaniards of St. Augustine. Their international contacts with the Spanish citizenry were certainly cordial. Nevertheless, the ever critical Ogilvie offered his views of the Spaniards and their evacuation in his dispatch of January 26, 1764:

The Spanish Governor & all the Spaniards inhabiting this town sail'd from this place on the 21st Inst. & as all the Inhabitants belonging to the Spanish Government here were paid by the King of Spain, if they had an inclination to continued under the British Government, do not believe that by the definitive treaty I could have kept them, their was three or four Merchants but none of them offered to stay, blieve their Clergy had great influence over them, cannot help observing to your Lordships that it's no loss to His Majesty's Government of East Florida, their not staying here as they were the least Industrious People I ever saw, having depended intirly on our Colonies in America for supplies of Provisions, their was no trade or Manufactures of any kind in this Province, & by the Constant War with the Indians their little Capacity to carry it on, they were helm'd in within the lines of St. Augustine excepting two posts Piculata & Apalachia, which were supported by very bad troops, they pretended to sell great tracts of this Country, as the definitive treaty says they have a right to sell their Houses & Estates is too serious an affair for me to determine, do not propose leting these Gentlemen possess any part of them 'till I have His Majesty's & your directions concerning them.[50]

On another occasion, Francis Ogilvie's correspondence with Lord Jeffery Amherst revealed that the commander of the East Florida garrison was impatient to witness the final departure of the inhabitants of St. Augustine. Amherst's replacement, General Thomas Gage, who referred to the lingering Spaniards as "troublesome guests" undoubtedly entertained similar feelings.[51] When English officials discovered the "totality" of the emigration they seemed to want every Spaniard exiled immediately. James Robertson also mentioned Anglo-Spanish housing problems, which produced some concern.

The houses, Churches & Convents in S^t. Augustine, are all excepting the Governors house Claim'd as private property, there being no barracks for Officers, those with the Brittish troops on their arrival, were quarter'd upon the houses of private people, as there were no publick houses to receive them.

Tho this was done by the Spanish Governors Authority and under the direction of a person appointed by him to make the distribution, The Spaniards disliking to have strangers in their familys generally quitted the houses where Officers were quarter'd.

The Spanish Commissary on my arrival presented to me a demand and a complaint on the subject, his demand for the Officers lodging amounted to 180 dollars a week, and he complain'd that the Sale of the houses and the intent of the treaty of peace was disappointed as no Merchants would buy a house where an Officer was quarter'd.

I told the Governor that the Brittish subjects all over America, when the number of troops in their neighborhood could not be contain'd in barracks or publick houses, had Officers and Soldiers quarter'd on them without any expence to the Crown, that the

Spaniards during their stay should not only have the protection of Brittish laws, but meet with all the kindness that as Strangers and friends was their due, but that I could not put the Crown to an expence in their favor which was not allow'd to Brittish Subjects.

I gave notice by a proclamation, that as soon as any person should purchase a house where an Officer was quarter'd that the Officer should remove.[52]

Except for these petty criticisms, the British military authorities succinctly witnessed the exodus from Florida without serious comment. The English soldiery, like their Spanish predecessors, observed an almost uneventful transition period before the final embarkation in January, 1764. The Spanish population simply abandoned St. Augustine as quickly as possible.

The Evacuation of Apalache

Great Britain inadvertently mismanaged the intercolonial exchange at San Marcos de Apalache. Because the officer in charge of relieving that dreary station delayed his arrival, the Apalache population was unable to effect its emigration until February, 1764. Spanish soldiers previously abandoned San Marcos de Apalache late in the Seven Years' War. After the ratification of the Treaty of 1763, a detachment was sent to deliver the small fort to the English forces. Captain Don Bentura Díaz with forty-six infantry troopers and two artillery men arrived from St. Augustine on August 3, 1763. The Spaniards then waited almost seven months for the appearance of the British army. Fifty men and fifteen women and children finally escaped the bleak Apalache outpost, appropriately entitled the "Remote Frontier," on February 20, 1764.[53]

Although the Spaniards at Apalache could not surrender the outpost until February, 1764, the British army ordered Captain John Harries and a company of troops to relieve the Díaz command as early as November, 1763. After a month of sailing, Harries initially arrived in Apalache on November 8, 1763. Captain Harries embarked from St. Augustine with Lieutenant Colonel James Robertson, who was en route to Pensacola on the brig *Hannah*. Without landing at Fort Apalache, Robertson parted company with Harries as the captain visited his new command. Captain Harries, however, only paused at Apalache for a week and then proceeded hastily to Pensacola to confer with Colonel Robertson.[54]

The departure of Harries left the Spanish garrison in a precarious position. Since the English officer neglected to relieve Apalache, he obliged Captain Díaz to remain at the frontier post until Harries returned. Without adequate food and clothing, the Spanish detachment at Apalache barely subsisted. Because Díaz had already dismissed his intended exodus vessels, when the waiting period became prolonged, there were no immediate means of supply available. In November, Captain Díaz petitioned the governor of Cuba for assistance, and Conde de Ricla quickly responded to the requests of his subordinate with a delivery of food and supplies. The Apalache post received a sufficient quantity of stores for four months residence. In his letter to the governor of Cuba, Don Bentura Díaz estimated the state of the garrison's provisions and reported the inadequate condition of his fighting force. The loss of five deserters decreased his contingent to thirty-four soldiers. Díaz also informed his commander in Cuba that he had allowed five Indians to join the Spanish emigration upon the condition that they would become Catholic Christians. While lamenting his unfortunate position, the Spanish captain assured his superior that he would not abandon Apalache. He stated that the flag of Spain would continue to fly until the British troops arrived and were permitted to occupy the post.[55]

By January, 1764, the Díaz command still held the desolate station. According to his report of January 19, 1764, the annoyed officer notified Conde de Ricla that his detachment continued to occupy the outpost because the first English expedition to Apalache feared the local Indians. The Spaniard further charged that such fears negated all courteous attempts to install the British army at San Marcos de Apalache. In corroboration of his charges, Díaz related how his request to commission an English vessel for the evacuation of the Spanish troops to Pensacola had first been granted at a price of 360 pesos, and then later denied. After a reconnaissance of the fort and its environment, Díaz observed, the British commander reversed his decision. Since Captain Harries refused to transport Díaz and his soldiers from Apalache to the Florida Keys, Havana, or Pensacola, and since the Spanish garrison declined to share the fortress temporarily with foreign troops, the English officer voyaged to Pensacola to discuss the situation with Colonel Robertson. Although Díaz would not allow Harries' troops to live together with Spanish soldiers in the barracks, he did offer them the outside casements for temporary housing. He also would have permitted the British commander to place two unarmed guards with military supplies inside the Apalache fort. The absence of English or Spanish translators probably impaired all such complicated negotiations between the two officers. It was apparent to the vexed Spanish captain that Harries would avoid the occupation of Apalache until he could acquire further defenses for the frontier post.[56]

After waiting more than six months to surrender his command, Captain Díaz decided to abandon Apalache without formal ceremony. He, therefore, informed the commander of Pensacola of his intended departure. On January 21, 1764, following repeated requests for the official cession of Apalache, Díaz wrote a letter to Colonel Augustin Provost at Pensacola disclosing his decision to evacuate Florida on February 20, 1764. Díaz informed Provost that he would depart on that date even if British agents of transfer did not present themselves according to their earlier promises. The Spanish officer's patience was understandably exhausted. If military representatives did not appear in Apalache by the twentieth of February to occupy the outpost, Captain Díaz warned his correspondent that he would not be responsible for what might happen at the unguarded garrison. In the course of his correspondence with Colonel Provost, the Spanish commander of Apalache explained why he denied Harries' request to share the fortress with the foreign detachment. Because he was apprehensive of "mischievous results" from the "heedlessness" of the mixed soldiers, Díaz refused to lodge the British troops in the Apalache barracks.[57]

Díaz wrote to Havana on the same day essentially imparting a similar account of the situation to the governor of Cuba. The opinionated officer, however, informed Conde de Ricla that the delays were only insidious attempts to humiliate the Spaniards. Captain Díaz belligerently declared that he would prefer to block the British entry into Apalache because of their supercilious attitude:

Although it may perhaps displease Your Excellency by its asperity, I hope that you will condescend forgiveness of a transgression born of my brooding and chagrin on observing the complete scorn for our nation that these men exhibit, manifest by the reasons and methods which Your Excellency will understand. Even though they offer in their defense reasons which they find best adapted to their excuse, I will undo these with the truth about the events which have transpired through their lack of observance of the good faith expected of officers of honor. I would give, excellent sir, and I would sacrifice my life, not to comply with the terms of my delivery, if it would perpetuate to the Catholic Crown of the King our Lord this limited dominion. I would begin by the extermination of those who now possess it.[58]

Captain Díaz sent another note to Pensacola on January 27, 1764, once against threatening his intended departure. Several days later, Conde de Ricla supported his subordinate's threat in a determined, but courteous, letter to Colonel Robertson. The governor of Cuba advised his English correspondent that a sloop was en route to evacuate the Apalache garrison from Florida. For the sake of harmonious relations, Conde de Ricla said he expected that the British government would arrange to send an official party to release Captain Díaz from command of Apalache.[59]

While the Spaniards were awaiting the British arrival, Captain John Harries unenthusiastically prepared to relieve the Apalache garrison. Harries initially attempted to dissuade his superiors from occupying the isolated outpost. When that plan miscarried, he set about securing the best possible defense weapons, equipment, and supplies for his dismal command. Later, as Harries started on his "inevitable" trip to Apalache, other unexpected circumstances which probably delighted him, further delayed his sailing to the "remote frontier."

Captain Harries specifically described all the unsatisfactory and unattractive features of Apalache soon after his brief sojourn at the Spanish outpost. Because the military station was "so excluded from all correspondence with the other points of the globe," Harries insisted that three or four months of supplies should always be available. The fortress, he related, needed more artillery, cannon swivels, and a reinforced strength of at least seventy rank and file soldiers. Apalache also lacked such significant essentials as wood and water, and those necessities were only found at a distance from the fort. Water sources existed one and one-half miles from the post, and wood was located as far away as three or four miles. In order to acquire those important items, troops had to trek through unfriendly country at the mercy of the Indians. A number of Spaniards were reported to have been slain on such journeys, although the Spanish residents of Apalache supplied the natives with 1,400 gallons of rum, clothing, and provisions annually; they even provided a house near the fort for the indigenous people. Indian gifts would also be demanded of any British detachment that held the isolated post. Captain Harries reported apprehensively that the Indian population, composed of four hundred or five hundred people, would require serious consideration.[60]

Harries continued his negative account by describing the difficulties of piloting ships through the entrance of the port of Apalache. The English captain admitted that the site of the fort was surrounded by rich timber lands, formerly supplying the Spaniards with boat building materials. But the post never developed into a trading center, Harries observed, probably because there was nothing of value to export.[61] Throughout these reports from Pensacola the English officer's reluctance to assume the command of Apalache was always evident. He repeatedly endeavored to discourage the British high command from holding the hinterland outpost. Such phrases as "if you Sir shd be of the opinion the place is of such importance as to be worth keeping it in our possession," and "If yr Excellency is determined to have possession of Apalache" [62] definitely indicated Harries' feelings for his new assignment. Before boarding the Apalache bound vessels in December, 1763, the captain wrote another carping note to Lord Amherst. In this letter the unhappy Harries bemoaned the pain and discomfort of his rupture, the insecurity of his family, the sickness of his soldiers, and the lack of reinforcements, ships, medicines, Indian traders, and interpreters. Even these last pleas failed to influence his superiors and on December 30, 1763, the commander of Apalache found himself at sea en route to his new post.[63]

Six days later Harries' ship, the *Curacoa,* was grounded on a sand bank. Almost ten days were required to dislodge the boat from the bar, and the crew dumped most of the cannons, supplies, and baggage overboard in order to free the stricken vessel. Without stores and with a stripped and disabled ship, the "luckless" Harries returned to Pensacola. The captain probably considered himself "lucky" as a result of the *Curacoa* shipwreck. At least the grounding permitted him to return to Pensacola in time to write one more letter to military headquarters in New York hoping to annul his Apalache mission.[64]

By the seventeenth of January, John Harries once again enjoyed the haven of Pensacola. However, he promised General Thomas Gage, the new commander-in-chief of the British American forces, that another expedition would shortly be outfitted for Apalache. In his next dispatch to General Gage, February 7, 1764, Captain Harries mentioned many of his usual complaints and again requested additional troops and provisions. Harries also reiterated his personal plight: "The welfare of a wife & one only child a daughter, my decline in life being the worst side of fifty, and the misfurtune of a rupture during the siege of Havannah, make me anxious to see Great Britain once more before I dye." [65]

General Gage replied to the Harries memorandums on March 31, 1764. His commentary on the Apalache crisis severely criticized the old officer for his failure to arrange a smooth transfer of the Spanish outpost. Gage asserted that the captain should have relieved the Spaniards at Apalache on the first sailing to Fort San Marcos. If the Spanish garrison had been formally released to British control in November, 1763, Gage reminded his subordinate, then the subsequent losses and misfortunes would have been avoided. The irate general further grumbled that he would not have blamed the Spanish commander if he had simply abandoned Apalache. Regarding the "Savage" menace that Harries prophesied, Gage concluded that San Marcos de Apalache could easily withstand any assault that the Indians might launch in the future. General Gage's vituperative and sarcastic letter stated:

> It is to be wished that you had thought proper to relieve the Spanish Officer on your first going to Apalachi, and the misfortune and Accidents which happened afterwards to your Detachment, would have been avoided. You must certainly have had other Reasons for neglecting that Service when you was upon the Spot & going away for Pensacola than merely your orders not to furnish the Spaniards with Shipping which they only demanded to Pensacola, and which could not in any Shape have been detrimental to the Service. I could not have blamed the Spanish Commandant had He abandoned the Fort, & left you to answer for the Consequences. I hope that this will find you safe Arrived there at last, and that you will have put every thing in the best order. By the Description you have given me of the Fort, it seems Impregnable against all the Savages on the Continent, . . . [66]

The supreme commander of the British army in America notified Captain Harries that reinforcements, medicines, supplies, and military equipment had been secured for his command. Even "Indian" rum was scheduled for shipment to Apalache. Accompanying instructions ordered the Apalache commander to consult with the superintendent of Indian affairs concerning the distribution of gifts to the natives of the area. Harries' request for a European leave was also approved in the general's letter of March thirty-first.[67]

On February 25, 1764, John Harries dispatched a note to General Gage announcing his arrival at Apalache. The February letter obviously did not reach Gage until after his critical review of his subordinate was already on the way to Florida. In May, 1764, General Gage received the notice of the English occupation of San Marcos de Apalache. Responding to the welcome news of the official transfer, the general wrote from New York stating that he was comforted to learn that Harries "had at length relieved the Spanish garrison of Apalachi . . . and had taken possession of that Post." [68]

San Marcos de Apalache experienced transition irregularities because of English sloth in the occupation of the small garrison. The unfortunate delay that annoyed Gage and angered the Spaniards, however, was not motivated by any deliberate policy. Actually, the high command intended to possess Apalache as quickly as possible. General Thomas Gage was obviously angry with the procrastinations of his Apalache commander. Most of the responsibility for impeding the intercolonial transfer belonged to Captain Harries, but circumstantial factors actually detained the formal cession. Fortunately, both Conde de Ricla and General Gage prevented the incident from becoming significant to either Spain or Great Britain. The governor of Cuba soothed his bristling Apalache commander, and politely urged the British authorities to hurry their relief of the San Marcos garrison. General Gage subsequently pressured his subordinate to occupy the outpost. The unpleasant episode at Apalache apparently had no serious repercussions. Relations between England and Spain were strained over numerous issues in the period following the Paris Treaty of 1763, but the Apalache affair probably passed into oblivion following the transfer of Florida to Great Britain.

East Florida passed from Spanish to British rule with few serious problems. The official exchange was easily accomplished except at Apalache where circumstances and a couple of personalities produced some conflict. Anglo-Spanish relations, however, remained cordial as colonial officers of both countries avoided intensification of such local issues. In Florida the two nations seemed determined to maintain the international peace made at Paris. Charles III's decision to evacuate the entire Spanish population undoubtedly aided the imperial transfer. The removal of all the Spaniards relieved some of the stress of the exchange, but resettlement became a catastrophic experience for many of the Florida exiles.

6

The Official Transfer
of Franco-Spanish West Florida
to British Control

The Departure of the Spaniards
from Pensacola

In April, 1763, Conde de Ricla instructed Governor Don Diego
Ortiz Parrilla to surrender San Miguel de Pensacola to representatives of the British government. Ortiz Parrilla was advised that
General William Keppel would soon send a military expedition to
Florida to inaugurate the formal cession. In order to guarantee
international cordiality, the governor of Cuba ordered his subordinate in Pensacola to arrange a polite exchange of command which
would comply with the Treaty of Paris. Any transfer predicaments,
which could not be adjusted by Governor Ortiz Parrilla, would later
receive royal attention. Conde de Ricla's concise memorandum
urged an organized, but swift embarkation of all personnel and
possessions. Nothing valuable could remain in the former colony.
Special efforts were also required of the governor to convince all
Spanish subjects of the advantages of leaving Florida. Don Diego
Ortiz Parrilla obediently notified his people of the opportunities
available for them in New Spain. Following the advice of his superiors in Cuba, he reminded the Pensacola Spaniards that Florida
would no longer provide them with the spiritual message of Catholicism.[1]

Conde de Ricla, realizing the formidable tasks of total evacuation, sent Don Joseph Bernet and Don Lázaro Alberja to Pensacola
in order to assist the governor. The ships of Lieutenant Don Miguel
de Cabrera, who commanded the naval operation, brought Alberja
and Bernet to the seaport *presidio* in the summer of 1763. Since the
king agreed to pay all transportation expenses, the Cubans carried
1,500 pesos to Pensacola. Governor Ortiz Parrilla's new lieutenants

were authorized to expedite the movement of artillery, stores, and troops. If possible, the governor and his aids hoped to remove the population of Pensacola before the advent of British occupation. Even though the Treaty of 1763 provided eighteen months for the national exile, the Spanish officials wanted to escape all contacts with their former enemies. Following royal instructions, Ortiz Parrilla organized a hurried but very orderly exodus according to rank and class.[2]

The crown designated Vera Cruz, New Spain, as the destination for the populace of Pensacola. Under the same priority as the troops of St. Augustine, officers and soldiers were placed first on the emigration lists. The older people, seeking the disposal of their property, initially enjoyed the privilege of late departures. Neither proprietors nor army personnel ever benefited from their position on the transportation schedule since all Pensacolans traveled to Vera Cruz together.[3]

On September 3, 1763, the entire *presidio* of San Miguel de Pensacola boarded eight ships for Vera Cruz. More than 600 persons quit what the English inhabitants later called West Florida. Along with Governor Ortiz Parrilla, his administrative officials, and the 160 military defenders of the port city, there were 118 civilians, 108 Christian Indians, and 105 convicts as well as the garrison families on board the Spanish and British vessels. Altogether, 622 Floridians sailed from Pensacola. Bernet and Alberja were reported to have returned to Havana prior to the September evacuation.[4]

The 108 Catholic Indians who migrated to Vera Cruz with the Spaniards were called Yamasee Apalachinos. After residing for many years near San Miguel de Pensacola, at the pueblos Escambe and Punta Rosa, the Indians were ultimately proselytized by Franciscan missionaries. In 1763 they petitioned Parrilla to join the expedition to Verz Cruz because of their dread of the other Indians in the surrounding area. Apparently some of the other local tribes, particularly the Tallapoosas, sought their extinction. The lives of the Yamasee Apalachinos probably would have been quite precarious if the Spaniards departed leaving them at the mercy of their inimical neighbors. Because of their plaintive entreaties and professed Catholic faith, forty families were permitted to make the sea trip to New Spain.[5]

The Pensacola Indians spent their first fifteen months in Vera Cruz. From the gulf port the Yamasee Apalachinos moved to Old Vera Cruz (La Antigua or Antigua Vera Cruz) [6] in mid-January,

1765. Old Vera Cruz served them briefly as a base of operations and reconnaissance for their future settlement in Tempoala, an area only two and one-half leagues from La Antigua. After less than a month in Antigua Verz Cruz, in February, 1765, the Yamasee Apalachinos moved to Tempoala.[7]

In Tempoala a planned Indian village called San Carlos was established on uncultivated lands near the shores of the Chachalacas River. San Carlos was located about seven leagues from the port of Vera Cruz. Local builders constructed the Indian pueblo around a typical Spanish square with the church situated on the north and a government building located on the south of the plaza. Wooden dwellings for the Florida natives were erected east and west as well as north of the village square. Forests surrounded San Carlos except south of the town where the Río de Chachalacas flowed to the sea.[8]

The Indian population at San Carlos included seventeen men, sixteen women, three boys, and eleven girls. Only forty-seven Yamasee Apalachinos remained alive of the more than one hundred who voluntarily accompanied the Spaniards to Verz Cruz. Of forty families who abandoned Florida on September 3, 1763, only twenty-two survived the sea and land journey from Pensacola to San Carlos. The tiny settlement still existed in 1774.[9]

The evacuation convoy reached Vera Cruz and the protection of Viceroy Marqués de Cruillas late in September, 1763. In a November letter to Minister Julián de Arriaga, Governor Ortiz Parrilla[10] apologized for not emigrating to New Spain at an earlier date. The former governor of Florida explained that because he lacked transport vessels the voyage was delayed until several English ships could be chartered. The *presidio* purchased one frigate with its immense quantity of surplus flour. Employing the fleet of three Spanish ships under the command of Cabrera as personnel carriers, the foreign vessels were available for cargoes of ordinance, military supplies, and provisions. Since the Spaniards anticipated a lengthy transition period at Pensacola, many of those necessities arrived from Vera Cruz only two months earlier, on June 30, 1763. The entire population, except for a group of families and convicts previously routed to Havana with Alberja and Bernet in August, entered New Spain through the port of Vera Cruz. Only one person temporarily remained in Pensacola to guard the cargo of a wrecked vessel. The exiles landed at Vera Cruz obviously expecting opportunities of resettlement in the viceroyalty of New Spain.[11]

The English Military Occupancy
of West Florida

Great Britain moved to occupy West Forida during the month of July, 1763. General Keppel on July 3, 1763, commanded Lieutenant Colonel Provost of the Sixtieth Regiment to relieve the Spanish garrison at Pensacola with his Third Battalion. Provost was instructed to possess Fort San Miguel de Pensacola and all its supporting dependencies. Military administration would govern the area until the colonial office appointed a provincial governor. For "subsistence and unavoidable contingencies," General Keppel authorized the future commander of Pensacola to draw 3,000 pounds sterling and six months of provisions from the deputy quartermaster-general, Lieutenant Colonel Alexander Moneypenny. Such funds would sustain the occupation force until the advent of civilian government. His superior officer also advised Colonel Provost to notify the secretary of state when the intercolonial exchange was completed.[12]

The Third Battalion embarked from Havana on July sixth, and arrived in Pensacola one month later. Complying with Keppel's directions, Colonel Provost delivered his copy of the transfer orders to Governor Ortiz Parrilla. His notice of cession included instructions from Charles III of Spain. Provost then formally requested permission to receive the Pensacola station. (See Map 5.) Ortiz Parrilla immediately approved the colonel's petition, but the British troops were uncomfortably lodged in huts outside the stockade. The Spanish soldiers continued their occupancy of the buildings within the fortress while awaiting a fleet of transports from Havana. When the ships finally reached the Pensacola fort in mid-August further delays detained the Spaniards in West Florida. The English colonel insinuated that "indolence" retarded the final departure of the Spanish population. Provost reported, "but the numerous Stores they had to put on board together with their indolence, even though assisted by the man and war & Troops, detained the Embarkation 'till the 2d of September, & next day they Sailed for Vera Crux."[13]

Anglo-Spanish intercourse at Pensacola was actually minimized to a period of less than one month. In that brief space of time, however, the British army cooperatively accommodated the Spanish evacuation by offering the townspeople certain necessities for the sea voyage to Vera Cruz. The new government not only permitted the

Pensacolans to charter English boats, but also provided the émigrés with water containers and provisions. Although the Spaniards were exceedingly disappointed to learn that their houses and lots within the stockade would be sequestered by the Britannic crown, they offered no protests over the loss of proprietorship. Following royal instructions, Ortiz Parrilla prohibited his people from engaging in any controversies with the foreign soldiers. Similarly, while English officers complained of delays and the delapidated condition of Fort San Miguel de Pensacola, they avoided all offending contacts with the Spaniards.[14] The complaints or criticisms of both national groups were generally extended to their own superiors. Expressions of international antagonism never affected the imperial exchange at Pensacola. The Anglo-Spanish transfers of St. Augustine and Apalache were also conducted without apparent hostility. Spanish Florida thus passed rather quietly into British control.

The new military government of Pensacola immediately assumed the responsibility of improving the fortifications at Fuerte de San Miguel. Pensacola's defenses apparently had been allowed to become completely undependable. Major William Forbes, commander of the Thirty-fifth Regiment, communicated his critical impressions of the Spanish fort on January 30, 1764.

> I arrived here with 35th Regim[t] the 30th of Nov[r] last. The place which is called the Fort consists of about half a Mile of ground in circumference surrounded with a rotten Stockade without a ditch, so defenceless that anyone can step in at pleasure, the Barracks of the Officers and Soldiers are nothing more than miserable bark hutts, without any sort of Fire places or windows, void of every necessary utencil, the Regim[t] at present is so weak that it can scarcely afford the common Guards, the Artillery Officer requests that a few field pieces may be ordered here. . . . I can venture to assure You Sir that this is the real state of the Fort and Garrison I have the Honor to Command. Ever since my arrival here I have had a few men off duty employed under the direction of the Engineer, in making a ditch round the Fort Sixteen foot broad & five foot deep, which when finished I intend to have picketed all round.[15]

The existence of such conditions soon discouraged the occupation forces of West Florida. They persevered, however, and eventually succeeded in making Pensacola a habitable and well-protected military station.

Although officials of both countries cooperated to accomplish a smooth exchange of control in West Florida, the first months follow-

5   Thomas Jefferys' map of Pensacola, 1763

PLAN
of the
HARBOUR and SETTLEMENT
of
PENSACOLA.

ing the evacuation were painful for the new English population. Besides the hard labor of renovating the neglected defenses of Fort San Miguel, the British troops faced the ravages of tropical fevers which struck the residents of Pensacola. "Inveterate Scurvys" were the reported causes of "Mortifications and Death." [16] General Gage later informed Secretary of State Conway that "bilious fevers" killed more than one hundred soldiers at Pensacola. The diseases, which he blamed on heat and confined living quarters, also prostrated numerous civilian inhabitants. Mobile suffered similarly. Major Robert Farmar, commander of the occupation forces at Mobile, reported, "I have notified the Death of two of our Officers; this place is at this season so dreadfully sickly, that I am greatly afraid for many others." [17] Great Britain's entrance into West Florida was unfortunately affected by the horrible fevers, so well known to the Caribbean Islands of Cuba and Jamaica.

The Transfer of Mobile
from French to British Control

In July, 1763, Major Robert Farmar received his orders to occupy Mobile and all the other French lands east of the Mississippi River. As stipulated by the Treaty of 1763, New Orleans was exempted from British seizure. General William Keppel actually issued his instructions on July 19, 1763, but Major Farmar commanding the Twenty-second and Thirty-fourth Regiments failed to take formal possession of Mobile before October 20, 1763. Military delays in occupying the port-city obviously concerned the British colonial officials, who were anxious to own "the gateway to the southwest" with its flourishing fur trade. The Robertson report to General Gage stated that the Indians annually traded 50,000 skins to French traders at the Tombecbe and Alabama forts. Pontiac's uprising in the region of the Great Lakes also influenced England to secure the southern frontier swiftly. Many French officials and residents meanwhile were reluctant to give up Mobile because, unknown to England, their monarch secretly transferred New Orleans and Louisiana —west of the Mississippi River—to Charles III of Spain. The loss of western Louisiana made them unwilling to move from eastern Louisiana. Nevertheless, Duc de Choiseul's instructions succinctly notified the French government at Mobile to greet the agents of Great Britain with gracious consideration. Governor Louis Billouart de Kerlérec of Louisiana (1753–63) complied with his superior's commands in the weeks before his recall to France. French officials were also ordered to "facilitate the evacuation of said posts and country in accordance with the terms of the Definitive Peace Treaty signed in Paris the 10th. of February, last." [18]

English activities to occupy Mobile originated at Jamaica. Provisions for the new military government in Mobile were supplied by that old settlement in the Caribbean Sea. While his fleet waited at anchorage near Jamaica, Major Farmar appointed Captain John Farmar to precede the main convoy of ships to Mobile. Captain Farmar was given command of two small vessels for the mission to Florida. Loaded with three hundred barrels of powder and artillery stores, John Farmar's two ships set sail for Mobile. Upon arrival at the port-city, the army captain delivered his papers to the French governor requesting permission to land and unload the cargo of his vessels. Farmar explained the necessity of landing his freight before the main expedition reached the Florida Gulf Coast. Since the English navy was quite aware that many of their bulky beamed transports would be unable to navigate safely by the sand bars in the shallow harbor, they hoped to use John Farmar's ships to carry equipment and goods from the anchored fleet to the Mobile wharves.[19] The British plan ignored the possibility of French interference.

On September 20, 1763, Major Farmar's supply ships in the convoy of the H.M.S. *Stag* entered the Pensacola waters. Almost immediately, Major Farmar sent a courier to Mobile to learn if the French town had received the international transfer instructions. The major empowered his messenger, Captain John Lind, to act as George III's representative in the exchange of any and all the military and civilian outposts on the east bank of the Mississippi River. Lind's portfolio contained particular recommendations to Captain Pierre Nicolas Annibel Chevalier Sieur de Ville, the commander and lieutenant governor of Mobile. De Ville was advised to forbid all property sales between French and English citizens. Great Britain would not accept land transactions arranged under French law. England actually intended to validate only those transactions which were registered with the British government. Major Farmar also instructed the courier to proceed to New Orleans if Mobile was not yet in possession of official cession orders. Since Captain de Ville did not possess those necessary documents, John Lind journeyed south and eventually reached New Orleans on September 30. Upon arrival at his destination, Lind delivered his communiques to Governor Kerlérec and his successor, Monsieur Jean Jacques Blaise d'Abbadie.[20]

From New Orleans, Governor Kerlérec issued precise instructions for the transfer of French Florida to Great Britain. Accordingly, he mailed notices to Mobile as well as to the Alabama, Tombecbe, Natchez, and Illinois outposts. Employing the English messenger to contact Major Farmar, Kerlérec sent Captain Lind off to Pensacola with the recommendation that formal occupation of Mobile should not occur until October twenty-fifth. His appeal to delay the exchange seemed reasonable. The French governor explained that such an arrival date would coincide advantageously with future Governor d'Abbadie's landing at Mobile. Major Farmar then would have the immediate opportunity of hearing French advice concerning the organization of the colony extending along the east bank of the Mississippi River. Governor Kerlérec also informed Farmar that Monsieur d'Abbadie would officially cede Fort Condé to him on the day of their meeting.[21] The French governor arranged for Monsieur d'Abbadie to meet Major Farmar at Mobile because of his imminent recall to France. But, before his departure, Monsieur Kerlérec prepared what he thought was a smooth colonial transfer.

> I tell you at the same time, that it is of the utmost consequence for the reciprocal tranquility of the Subjects of the two Monarchs which are under our Subjection that the two Chiefs, English and French arrive at the same time, the Nations may perceive of themselves, all the union, and good understanding that for the present Unites us, and be assured that what I now tell you is from a principle to keep up a good understanding so much to be desired, this is my advice, notwithstanding you are the master to do as you think proper, It is my Duty to comply with the orders, of Mons' Le Duc de Choisuel, and to enter with you into the most minute explanation, in Speaking to you thus, I believe you would not do a miss in putting some little confidence in a Governor who has Governed this Colony eleven years; Mons' Dabbadie imagines he will be at Mobille the 25th of this month, therefore you will see there is no time to be lost recokoning the time that your Officer will take to reach you. Mons' Dabbadie has sent you an explicit copy of a Counsel to be held with the Savages which I am convinced you will approve of, and which I look upon as indispensible.

> The orders for the Evacuation, and the Accession of the English of the Posts of Illinois, Tombekbe, Alibamoux and Natcheres has

been already sent to the different Officers Commanding there, which orders are Original, and conformable to the meaning and Tenor of the sixth Article of the Preliminaries, and the seventh of the definitive Treaty.[22]

Along with additional suggestions regarding the military status and cession of the French posts in Florida, Governor Kerlérec advised his English successor that the artillery of Fort Condé was already evacuated according to royal orders. The movement of the cannon apparently surprised Captain Lind. But the governor calmly revealed that the guns were necessarily removed for employment in other colonial areas. "Capt. John Lind seemed to me greatly surprised that we had already sent away the greatest part of the Artillery from Fort Condé at Mobile, such (Sir) was our orders, and it is our business to obey them, besides we have occasion for them in the different parts which now remains to us of this Colony." [23] The French official also informed Major Farmar that the surrounding Indian nations were persuaded to accept the imperial exchange of Louisiana. In conclusion, Kerlérec even urged Farmar "to give the most punctual orders to your Troops not to make them Drunk, at least to give them as little Liquor as possible." [24]

Major Farmar ignored the abundant advice of his French predecessor, but became furious over d'Abbadie's activities in the new province under his command. For Major Farmar, any French recommendations to English subjects were considered acts of interference. Early in 1764, Farmar wrote a stinging letter to Governor d'Abbadie rebuking him for giving "directions to the Inhabitants of this Government, Contrary to my express orders to them." [25] Farmar then remarked, "I know of no Article in the Treaty of Peace, by which you are Authorized to Act here in a publick Character. . . . I presume if you will reflect a little, it will appear verry evident to you, that no Subject of His Most Christian Majesty, has any right to give orders to the Inhabitants of this Governmt, it being now in the possession of His Britannick Majesty, and under my Command." [26]

In the same letter the English officer protested the surreptitious sale of French boats which Farmar believed to be part of the total possessions ceded to Great Britain by treaty:

by the Seventh Article of the Treaty of Peace, it is expressly said, that the Most Christian King Cedes to His Britannick Majesty, every thing he possesses or Ought to possess on the Left side the River Mississippi (Orleans excepted) Notwithstanding this, you have sold the Boats that formerly belonged to His Most Christian Majesty, and which I am sorry to say, have been Concealed from me, in a manner the most unjustifiable.[27]

Writing to the secretary of war on January 24, 1764, Farmar angrily denounced the French for arson and other insidious enterprises. The French military organization of Mobile was accused of irreparably damaging six cannons and burning their gun carriages before sailing away. These cannons were rendered useless by the removal of their trunnions. Major Farmar probably felt further irked to receive Captain Lind's message revealing how the French army reduced the Mobile defenses during September, 1763. Later, in his report to Secretary of War Welborn Ellis, Major Farmar made particular mention of Kerlérec's movement of artillery and military stores.[28]

Monsieur d'Abbadie defended the removal of artillery in correspondence with Colonel James Robertson. In his letter of December 7, 1763, the governor of Louisiana argued that the cession of 1763 only allowed Great Britain to own the "soil and the structures standing" of the territory east of the Mississippi River. According to Article VII of the Treaty of 1763, Louis XV of France ceded "the river and port of Mobile, and every thing which he possesses or ought to possess, on the left side of the river Mississippi, except the town of New Orleans, and the island in which it is situated"[29] to His Britannic Majesty, George III. D'Abbadie's interpretation appeared reasonable considering the vague language of the treaty. The French official also related in his letter to Robertson that the cannon of Fort Choiseul and Fort Toulouse would remain in place at those installations. Both forts were located far north of Mobile in Indian country. He also promised to leave a few artillery pieces for the British army in Illinois. Monsieur d'Abbadie made these concessions because he recognized the difficulty of supplying arms to the hinterlands of Alabama, Louisiana, and Illinois. The governor advised his English correspondent, however, to inventory all remaining guns in the event that their home governments supported his interpretation of the treaty and required the return of the French equipment.[30]

Anglo-French relations in the transition period were further aggravated by the unfavorable reception that Farmar's vanguard party received in Mobile. Upon requesting permission to empty his two cargo vessels at Mobile before the arrival of the main convoy, Farmar was told that his petition would be sanctioned only under certain conditions. The French commander intended to bargain with the British army. Captain Farmar would be permitted to un-load his ships if he assured Commandant de Ville that the French military evacuation could include twenty-eight barrels of powder located in the magazine of Fort Condé. The ensuing conversations over de Ville's proposal delayed the docking of the two boats, and consequently postponed the landing of the entire English com-mand.[31] The vanguard ships were expected to convey troops, equip-ment, and supplies from the fleet to the French port through the shallow entrance. Meanwhile, according to plan, the heavy trans-ports would have remained anchored outside the harbor at the Bar of Mobile. Because de Ville obstructed the scheduled landing of the two vanguard ships, Major Farmar was obliged to hold his soldiers at sea until his "ferries" appeared at the bar. The British navy initially approached Mobile Harbor on October ninth. Five days later, on the fourteenth of October, the small vessels sailed into view and the ferrying operation commenced. This exhausting and awk-ward work was somewhat reduced on October sixteenth when three of the least bulky vessels of the convoy were able to traverse the treacherous channel waters.[32]

Although the British contingent physically solved the problems of passage into Mobile, the French government continued to delay the final landing. A deputation to Mobile on October eighteenth learned that the French governor wished the soldiers to wait aboard the anchored ships. De Ville wanted to conclude his Indian congress on October twenty-seventh before the advent of British government. Governor d'Abbadie hoped to stall the landing of English soldiers until November 1. The emissaries, including Major Farmar and three other officers, also discovered that no quarters were prepared for their forces. The French commandant, Captain de Ville, claimed he had not anticipated their arrival until the twenty-fifth, the date when former Governor Kerlérec advised the cession parties to meet. Arguing that his army could not healthfully remain aboard ship any longer, Major Farmar finally persuaded the French captain to cede Fort Condé and Mobile five days sooner.[33]

The British commander selected the Grenadiers of John Far-mar's regiments to organize the first landing, and Fort Condé was possessed by those soldiers on October 20, 1763. Since the transports still remained at anchor three leagues from the French town, Far-mar utilized his two ferries and a heavy launch to unload the sea vessels. The transfer of cargo to Mobile proceeded slowly but regu-larly. During the ferrying movement the British regiments apprehensively witnessed the arrival of three thousand local natives. Many of the Indians appeared before the artillery and supplies were secured at Fort Condé. Several thousand indigenous people eventually camped only two miles from the Mobile fort, but the lengthy landing operation and the intercolonial exchange were both accomplished without any interference.[34] A *procès-verbal* acknowledging the cession of French Florida (French "Eastern" Louisiana) [35] to English authority was signed by representatives of His Christian Majesty Louis XV and His Britannic Majesty George III on October 20, 1763. Major Farmar signed as signatory for Great Britain. Captain de Ville and Governor d'Abbadie served as plenipotentiaries for France. In his January letter to the secretary of war, Robert Farmar confirmed the international agreement, and enclosed an inventory of Fort Condé. "Mobille and its Dependencies, and that part of Louisiana Ceded in Consequence of the Seventh Article of the Definitive Treaty of Peace" thus became British possessions.[36]

The French civil and military population departed for New Orleans on October twenty-second. Mobile's garrison included 350 soldiers who defended Fort Condé and the Tombecbe and Alabama posts. The military stations of French Louisiana maintained 100 Swiss troops and 250 national soldiers. Forty families of a total of ninety-eight families remained in Mobile after the French exodus. Major Farmar initially believed that only ten French families would continue in residence at Mobile. More than half of the 350 civilian inhabitants voluntarily embarked from British West Florida to the capital of Louisiana. Although these people abandoned Mobile in October, 1763, they enjoyed the same eighteen-month privilege that the Spanish Floridians possessed by treaty. The departure of so many Frenchmen apparently surprised the British commanders, but ten months later, in August, 1764, the population losses seemed less meaningful. At that time, Robert Farmar remarked, "the French are daily coming to take the Oaths of Allegiance; which has all the appearances of its being shortly a flourishing colony." [37] Surviving Frenchmen were subsequently required to accept laws and regulations of the new government. Major Farmar demanded an oath of allegiance from all those residents who decided to remain in West Florida under His Britannic Majesty.[38]

In order to define the status of the French population in British West Florida, Major Farmar published an explanatory manifesto on October 20, 1763. The manifesto declared that all civil suits would be judged by the military government of Great Britain. French law thereafter was invalidated. The British proclamation, nevertheless, promised the French residents legal protection. Their religious privileges and property rights would be assured according to the 1763 Treaty of Paris. However, the old inhabitants were advised that they would be expected to furnish the foreign troops "with the things they may need and the country produces for which they shall be paid in ready money." [39] The manifesto also exhorted French civilians and English soldiers to live together harmoniously.

Regarding local proprietorship, Farmar insisted that all property titles necessitated official registry, verification, and approval. Before any land could be legally alienated these processes were strictly required. Finally, the British officer ordered all Frenchmen to file a written statement of allegiance to George III of England if they intended to remain in Florida. French citizens were given three months in which to meet their loyalty obligations, and thereafter, they faced dispossession of all proprietorship and deportation. More than one hundred inhabitants took the oath of allegiance to Great Britain by October 2, 1764. All those Frenchmen who complied with the declaration were then allowed to continue living peacefully under English dominion unless they instigated sedition or Indian rebellion. Major Farmar guaranteed all French émigrés their property and personal rights according to the provisions of the Treaty of 1763. "Those among the inhabitants who shall be possessed of an inclination to quit their present abodes and withdraw from this portion of the country, shall be afforded secure and safe transportation of their chattels as provided by the peace treaty." [40]

Soon after the transfer of Fort Condé (Fort Charlotte) the other outposts of French Florida were similarly relieved by British military units. An officer and thirty soldiers of the Thirty-fourth Regiment occupied the Tombecbe post and Fort Choiseul, located north of Mobile on the Tombigbee River. Lieutenant Ford commanded the detachment sent in November, 1763, to receive the cession of Fort Choiseul. The exchange of command was executed quickly and cordially on the twenty-second of November. Ford's report clearly revealed the Anglo-French rapport at Tombecbe.

> The Officers and men were entirely out of provisions, I was requested by the Commandant to let him have one hundred pounds of Pork, and the same quantity of Beef, to serve them on the passage to Mobille, the Commandant has let me have all the Cattle he had here which is four Cows, a Bull, and a Calf, at the same price you

[Farmar] mentioned, at first he did not seem satisfied, until I told him that I was of opinion the French Commandant at Mobille had informed you that was the value; their behaviour to me has been excessive Genteel. I'm sorry it was not in my power to Return it.[41]

Major Farmar deferred the movement of troops to Fort Toulouse. That Alabama fort, constructed in 1714 near the junction of the Coosa and Tallapoosa Rivers, was left unattended because the surrounding Indians objected to its occupation. The English high command could not ignore such objections without confronting hostility and possible war. Woolf King of the Creeks advised Farmar to postpone occupation of Fort Toulouse until the Alabama Indians altered their French attachments. Rather than engage the Florida peoples in a rigorous and unrewarding struggle, the British commanders obeyed native restrictions in order to organize their forces for the impending conflict with the rebellious Indians of Illinois.[42]

Troops of the Thirty-fourth Regiment were also ordered to occupy Biloxi, Natchez, and Dauphine Island. Major Farmar designated a force of fifty or sixty soldiers to take possession of Natchez. A corporal and six privates were stationed at Dauphine Island in the Gulf of Mexico. Since Dauphine Island commanded the Gulf entrance to Mobile Bay, Farmar assigned these few soldiers to the service of a resident pilot who guided British shipping by the channel bar. Along the Gulf Coast, Major Farmar proposed to maintain several outposts from Biloxi to Lake Maurepas. The English officer requested two regiments to defend the coastal stations. According to his suggestions the Anglo-French frontier would be safeguarded when his superiors established a "principal Fort at Biloxi, with small Posts extending along the Lakes Pontchartrain, and Maurepas, to where the River Iberville communicates with the Mississippi, otherwise the French will Command the greatest part of the Indian Trade as it is verry near to them and entirely open." [43] While Robert Farmar deployed the Thirty-fourth Regiment to defend eastern Louisiana, the Twenty-second Regiment proceeded toward the Mississippi River and its mission in the Illinois country.

In 1763–65 Great Britain was concerned with preparations to launch an attack upon the Indian domination of Illinois and the Great Lakes areas. According to military plan, Major Arthur Loftus and approximately 350 troops were scheduled to sail up the Mississippi River to relieve Fort Chartres. At the former French station, Colonel Henry Bouquet and a northern army would be waiting to join the southern force in a combined strike against the Indians. Bouquet hoped to move down the Ohio and Mississippi Rivers to meet the southern flotilla, but the united campaign against Pontiac's rebellion was never realized. Major Loftus' marines were depleted by sickness and desertion and repulsed by the Avoyelles, Choctaw, Ofogoula, and Tunica Indians in the Mississippi Valley. The first riverboat attack upon the Mississippi was actually blocked at Roche à Davion near Pointe Coupée, only 240 miles from New Orleans. A second armed expedition under the command of Major Farmar reached Fort Chartres in December, 1765, two months after the northern forces negotiated their way to the disputed area. In the previous summer a treaty with Pontiac ended Indian resistance and permitted troops to approach the Illinois country in October.[44]

Major Loftus blamed the French officials in New Orleans for the failure of the first expedition to ascend the Mississippi River. Although Monsieur d'Abbadie supported the British assault on Illinois, the Indian ambuscade at Davion's Bluff was charged to French treachery. The governor of Louisiana actually served the English army in several ways. Initially, Major Loftus was permitted to employ New Orleans for a base of operations for the British expedition. D'Abbadie also stationed French soldiers along the lower channel of the river to protect the movement of the fleet (ten boats and two pirogues) upstream. A French interpreter even accompanied Major Arthur Loftus and the Twenty-second Regiment as far north as Pointe Coupée. Finally, the government of New Orleans organized Indian assemblies in an attempt to negotiate a free passage for the English force through the Mississippi Valley. Despite such assistance, Major Loftus accused Governor d'Abbadie of instigating the ambush.[45]

Other English soldiers also implicated French officials in the insidious attack on the Twenty-second Regiment. Captain James Campbell, who visited Pointe Coupée while engaged in a six-month project to cut a channel of the Iberville River into the Mississippi, later corroborated Loftus' accusations. "I discovered some of the Inhabitants of Pointe Coupée using their influence with the Indians and persuading them from entering into Friendship with us, which obliged me to give these People a Warning: That I was well acquainted with how much they were instrumental in encouraging the Savages to attack Major Loftus' Convoy." [46]

Governor George Johnstone, the first governor of English West

Florida, disagreed with the military appraisal of the disaster. George Johnstone applauded Governor d'Abbadie for his assistance and condemned Major Loftus for a "precipitate retreat."

> It was a great Fault in Major Loftus, not to have established himself at Point Iberville, last year, in his precipitate Retreat. The Thing was proposed by Captain Campbell, and agreed to by Major Loftus and the Troops were actually landed. But why he did not continue in the Resolution is as little to be accounted for, as any other part of his Conduct. The sincere Friendship I had cultivated with Mr D'Abbadie and the chearfull Assistance he promised to this Work, was also another Reason for not delaying the Operation 'till I could report Home in which Case the Spaniards will undoubtedly be arrived, and then we may expect every Obstruction.
>
> Mr D'Abbadie is since dead, in whom I have lost a worthy Neighbor, and the English a sincere Friend, as far as was compatible with the Interest of his own Country. From the moment the intended Cession of New Orleans to the Spaniards was publicly notified, he has given me every Information and Assistance in his Power. Monsieur Aubrey, by whom he is succeeded, has likewise favored me with his Friendship; . . .[47]

While the British army planned its maneuver up the Mississippi River, the people of Mobile were enervated by the same fevers that appeared in Pensacola. Mobile actually suffered more severely from tropical disease than Pensacola. In 1763, and again three years later in 1766, yellow fever epidemics struck the city and decimated the population. English plans for the settlement of the region were thereafter temporarily jeopardized. Along with the menace of fever-bearing mosquitoes, the new inhabitants of Mobile confronted inadequate and deteriorated housing facilities. Buildings and lodgings were described as "wanting" doors and / or windows, in "bad repair," and in "ruinous condition." [48] Under these depressing conditions and following the disagreeable colonial exchange, Great Britain began its rule of West Florida.

The official and demographic transfer of Florida from Spanish to British control was successfully and smoothly executed. The royal officials of both countries typically endeavored to maintain a formal, but cooperative relationship during the seven-month period of transition. The intercolonial transfer commenced July 21, 1763, and concluded on February 20, 1764. Although several awkward incidents and certain personality conflicts added tension to the cession of Florida, the Anglo-Spanish exchange of imperial control was generally characterized by a scrupulous regard for the Treaty of Paris. Some of the principals involved in actual cession of areas of Florida entertained attitudes of suspicion, criticism, and even antagonism for their previous enemies, but such feelings were apparently suppressed during the course of the bilateral arrangements of 1763–64. Anglo-Spanish relations in East and West Florida revealed the determination of both countries to avoid international disputes. England and Spain mutually cooperated in Florida continuing the peaceful relationship established by the Treaty of 1763.

On the contrary, relations between England and France were frequently unfriendly during the surrender of Louisiana. The English occupation of Mobile produced several international problems. Anglo-French rapport was obviously impaired by the disputed British movement into Mobile, the procrastination of the French cession, and the contested evacuation of Fort Condé. Continued French residence of Mobile contributed further tension to the intercolonial affairs of England and France in 1763. Although these problems seemed important, especially to the military officers managing the formal transfer of Florida, they were probably forgotten in the post-war period. French "Louisiana" therefore passed controversially with "sound and fury" into British control.

While Spanish officials concluded a relatively tranquil exchange of command, they also organized a complete and orderly emigration. According to *cédulas* from the Council of the Indies, colonial governors evacuated and resettled the entire Spanish population of Florida. Resettlement, unfortunately, became a miserable experience for many of the refugees. Foreign, Negro, and Indian residents of Florida also emigrated voluntarily to Cuba and New Spain and suffered the same fate as the Spanish exiles. Even the many material belongings of the colony and its inhabitants were removed by sea to Havana and Vera Cruz. Only the buildings remained as bleak symbols of Spanish occupation. British imperial control began as the total evacuation emptied Florida of its Hispanic population and possessions.

7

The King's Proclamation
of October 7, 1763

Great Britain's Colonial Provisions
for the New Florida Provinces

Several months before the final evacuation of St. Augustine, George III issued a proclamation for the management of the French and Spanish colonies. The King's Proclamation of October 7, 1763, divided the ceded area of Florida and Louisiana into two administrative provinces. While the new governments of Quebec and Grenada, respectively, organized the vast territory of Canada and the West Indian islands, East Florida and West Florida were formed to govern the southeastern possessions of France and Spain.[1]

East Florida included all the former Spanish domains bordered by the Atlantic Ocean, the Gulf of Mexico, and the Apalachicola River. The northern boundary of East Florida became a drawn line extending eastward from the union of the Apalachicola, Chattahoochee, and Flint Rivers to the ocean entrance of the St. Mary's River. Such a border enlarged the colony of Georgia by the acquisition of the disputed lands located between the Altamaha and St. Mary's Rivers. The geographic limits of West Florida were established by the Apalachicola River, the Gulf of Mexico, the Lakes Pontchartrain and Maurepas, the Mississippi River, and the thirty-first degree north latitude.[2] According to the King's Proclamation, the Floridas possessed the following boundaries:

> The Government of East Florida, bounded to the Westward by the Gulph of Mexico, and the Apalachicola River; to the Northward, by a Line drawn from that Part of the said River where the Chatahouchee and Flint Rivers meet, to the source of St. Mary's River, and by the Course of the said River to the Atlantick Ocean; and to the Eastward and Southward by the Atlantick Ocean, and the

Gulph of Florida, including all Islands within Six Leagues of the Sea Coast.[3]

The Government of West Florida, bounded to the Southward by the Gulph of Mexico, including all Islands within Six Leagues of the Coast, from the River Apalachicola to Lake Pontchartrain; to the Westward by the said Lake, the Lake Maurepas, and the River Missisippi; to the Northward by a Line drawn due East from that Part of the River Missisippi which lies Thirty one Degrees North Latitude, to the River Apalachicola or Chatahouchee, and Eastward by the said River.[4]

As stipulated by the Proclamation of 1763, each of the newly created Florida provinces would be administered by an appointed governor. The gubernatorial appointees, with the "Advice and Consent" of the king's council, were given the authority to summon general assemblies in the same manner as other American colonial governors. Florida governors also held the power, with the consent of the royal council and the general assemblies, "to make, constitute, and ordain Laws, Statutes, and Ordinances for the Publick Peace, Welfare, and Good Government of Our said Colonies, and of the People and Inhabitants thereof, as near as may be agreeable to the Laws of England, and under such Regulations and Restrictions as are used in other Colonies." [5] To insure the maintenance of public justice, the governors were additionally empowered to organize courts of judicature for civil and criminal causes. Furthermore, the colonial decree declared that governors of the Floridas would own sufficient authority to regulate the disposition of all "Lands, Tenements and Hereditaments." British inhabitants of East and West Florida were eligible to obtain proprietorships under the same quitrent system commonly employed in the other American colonies. The king's declaration also announced,

whereas, We are desirous, upon all Occasions, to testify Our Royal Sense and Approbation of the Conduct and Bravery of the Officers and Soldiers of Our Armies, and to reward the same, We do hereby command and impower Our Governors of Our said Three New Colonies, and all other Our Governors of Our several Provinces on the Continent of North America, to grant without Fee or Reward, to such Reduced Officers as have served in North America during the late War, and to such Private Soldiers as have been or shall be disbanded in America, and are actually residing there, and shall personally apply for the same, the following Quantities of

Lands, subject at the Expiration of Ten Years to the same Quit-Rents as other Lands are subject to in the Province within which they are granted, as also subject to the same Conditions of Cultivation and Improvement; . . .[6]

According to the military provisions of the proclamation, field-grade officers enjoyed rights to grants of 5,000 acres. Captains were offered 3,000 acres, while subalterns and staff officers received 2,000 acres. The Proclamation of 1763 permitted noncommissioned officers to acquire 200 acres, and even privates were eligible for grants of 50 acres.[7]

Between 1765 and 1775 approximately 1,650,000 acres of property were granted by the East Florida government. The colonial officials ceded 1,440,000 acres under 114 council orders. Responding to 576 local requests, St. Augustine governors also distributed another 210,700 acres. In West Florida, forty-five grants totaling 350,000 acres were issued from 1763 to 1769. Large property grants required settlement within a ten-year period on the basis of one person for every 100 acres. The West Florida governors also invested 131 grantees with territory pursuant to "family right" privileges. "Family right" provisions enabled Floridians to receive quantities of land according to the number of family members. Heads-of-family were eligible to acquire 100 acres, while other members of the family could each obtain 50 acres of property.[8]

The Privy Council also allotted land grants in the Floridas. These mandamus awards were made in amounts from 4,000 to 20,000 acres. All American colonies included such grants, although the Privy Council issued more orders for proprietorship in East Florida than for the other provinces combined in the years 1764–70. A total of 227 orders for East Florida were processed in Great Britain between 1764 and 1770. In the same period the Privy Council issued only 199 grants for the other American colonies. Altogether, the East Florida awards totaled to almost 2,900,000 acres.[9]

Proprietorship of Florida land required quit-rent payment. Initially, rent was instituted at the rate of two shillings per 100 acres of property, but the crown later demanded one-half penny sterling charges per acre. Private citizens were instructed to begin payments two years from the date of their grants, while soldiers enjoyed a ten-year exemption from such defrayments. Mandamus grants included terms for a quit-rent immunity of five years. According to Beverley Bond, Great Britain never successfully collected such charges during the English occupation of Florida. Because of the sparse settlement of East and West Florida, quit-rent regulations were not seriously enforced.[10]

In order to protect Indian lands and hunting preserves, the king's laws prohibited colonial officials from issuing survey or sales warrants for areas beyond the boundaries of the newly organized provinces. And, "for the present, and until Our further Pleasure be known," similar restrictions were stipulated "for any Lands beyond the Heads or Sources of any of the Rivers which fall into the Atlantick Ocean from the West and North West, or upon any Lands whatever, which, not having been ceded to, or purchased by Us as aforesaid, are reserved to the said Indians, or any of them." [11] All subjects inhabiting the "reserved" areas subsequently received orders to leave the Indian lands. Seeking to prevent frauds, the king's edict forbade private persons from purchasing Indian territory without royal license. Only His Majesty's government thereafter enjoyed the privilege of buying Indian domains. The Proclamation of 1763 clearly justified the new royal powers:

> And whereas great Frauds and Abuses have been committed in purchasing Lands of the Indians, to the great Prejudice of Our Interests, and to the great Dissatisfaction of the said Indians; In order, therefore, to prevent such Irregularities for the future, and to the End that the Indians may be convinced of Our Justice and determined Resolution to remove all reasonable Cause of Discontent, We do, with the Advice of Our Privy Council strictly enjoin and require, that no private Person do presume to make any Purchase from the said Indians or any Lands reserved to the said Indians, within those Parts of Our Colonies where We have thought proper to allow Settlement; but that if, at any Time, any of the said Indians should be inclined to dispose of the said Lands, the same shall be purchased only for Us, in our Name, at some Publick Meeting or Assembly of the said Indians.[12]

Indian trade was likewise submitted to crown supervision. British subjects could no longer negotiate freely with the indigenous peoples. Those who desired to engage in bartering with the Indians were compelled to procure royal licenses. Merchants could continually use trading permits depending upon their respect for the regulations established over Indian affairs. The English colonies were warned that individuals guilty of criminal activities against the Indians and / or infractions of the provisions of the king's proclamation would be apprehended and tried in His Majesty's provincial courts.[13]

The Composition of the Proclamation
of 1763

Great Britain issued the Proclamation of 1763 for several purposes. The October edict organized provinces from the territorial spoils of the Seven Years' War. It also encouraged settlement, especially in the Floridas. But this famous colonial scheme was primarily decreed to propitiate the agitated Indians of America. The midwestern uprising of 1763, usually known as "the conspiracy of Pontiac," made the necessity of an Indian accommodation especially urgent. George III's advisors were quite aware of the reasons for the rebellion. Recognizing that trading abuses and unwelcome infiltrations into hunting grounds infuriated the Indians, the Board of Trade urged the king to proclaim a plan for the protection of his native subjects.[14]

On August 5, 1763, approximately two months before the publication of the Proclamation of 1763, the Board of Trade and Plantations recommended that "a Proclamation be immediately issued by Your Majesty as well on Account of the late Complaints of the Indians, and the actual Disturbances in Consequence, as of Your Majesty's fixed determination to permit no grant of lands nor any settlements to be made within fixed Bounds . . . leaving all that territory within it free for the hunting Grounds of those Indian Nation Subjects of Your Majesty." [15] In September the news from America prompted immediate action on an Indian policy. Since the Illinois country was apparently out of British control, the need for a prompt solution to the situation became generally obvious to the policy-makers in London. The protective "Indian" Proclamation of 1763 was therefore announced.[16]

The king's edict inaugurated a program emphasizing monarchial control of Indian matters. Thereafter, the rights of the American aborigines would be safeguarded by royal government according to written pledges in the Proclamation of October, 1763. Under the leadership of Lord George Halifax (president of the Board of Trade) and Lord Charles Egremont (secretary of state of the Southern Department) colonial planning prior to 1763 developed to a stage where supervision of Indian affairs was considered to be essential. Because of the determination and advice of these officials, George III enacted several protective measures for the natives of British America. Whitehall learned from the war that the general security of America depended upon the protection of Indian rights and lands. The October Proclamation, following the French and Indian War, reflected the British government's recognition of native power and position in America. It also acknowledged the necessity of satisfying Indian demands in order to obtain a lasting peace. The policies of 1763 were obviously promulgated to serve the interests of Indians and English subjects alike.[17]

Plans for an Indian settlement originated in Whitehall before the King's Proclamation of 1763. Halifax managed to invest the royal government with clear authority over all political relations with the Indians, and a superintendency of Indian affairs was subsequently established. With the assistance of the Board of Trade and Plantations, Lord Egremont secured adequate support to forbid colonial governors from settling lands on the Indian frontiers. Recognizing the dangerous proximity of the Indian country to the extremities of the eastern colonies, Egremont hoped that an unoccupied buffer zone might reduce some of the numerous border tensions. Even before 1763, the Allegheny mountain range was considered to be a natural dividing line between the European settlements and the vast hunting reserves in the west. However, the crown's ministers eventually anticipated a gradual diminution of Indian domains on the western side of the mountains. Egremont also adopted a property system which required government approval of all Indian land sales. England's colonial experts were evidently preparing the way for crown control of Indian affairs before 1763. The Proclamation of October 7, 1763, actually culminated those earlier preparations with a commitment of monarchial guardianship for the natives of British America. After 1763, the Indians became wards of the crown.[18]

In 1763, Lord Shelburne (William Petty, and later First Marquis of Landsdowne) succeeded Charles Townshend as president of the Board of Trade. Sharing many of the colonial views of his predecessors, the new president likewise sought to arrange imperial management over the Indians of the Midwest. Shelburne firmly believed that segregation of European and Indian settlements was *sine qua non* to any project of regal control. He suggested the establishment of "defined" boundaries as an effective means to such segregation. A policy including strict boundaries for European settlements also assured the Indians of the inviolability of their hunting areas. The new president of the Board of Trade urged his monarch to monopolize all real estate transactions with the Indians.

Lord Shelburne wanted a temporary moratorium for midwestern settlement until the crown could assume control of all Indian land sales. Although the Proclamation of 1763 clearly prohibited individual and corporative purchase of Indian property, violations of the laws were soon recognized in the period 1768–73.[19]

Shelburne also espoused crown supervision of Indian trade. The president of the Board of Trade believed that commerce should be available to everyone, but securely under military control. His concepts of colonial trade, however, were only partially put into policy. Since the Proclamation of October, 1763, established royal authority over indigenous commerce, licenses became indispensable for all barter with the Indians. But the indiscriminate methods of issuing permits made them almost meaningless. Although official warrants were needed for trade, colonial governors apparently refused few applicants their requests for licenses if the traders satisfied the routine bond and security regulations. As a result of such wanton licensing practices, Indian trade was neither easily confined nor controlled.[20] As exemplified in Spanish America, European law often became incompatible with colonial experience. Under the presidency of Lord Shelburne, the Board of Trade and Plantations continued to exert its influence to increase the crown's powers over Indian relations.

Regarding future expansion, Shelburne hoped to apply a simple plan to westward settlement. Initially, he intended to arrange a "far" western boundary which would open the upper Ohio valley to later colonization. The acquisition of Spanish Florida and Canada provided other unoccupied territories for migrating frontiersmen. Finally, Lord Shelburne expected Great Britain to purchase Indian properties when demand for colonial grants exceeded the available land. As early as June, 1763, Shelburne's encompassing suggestions were submitted to the king for approval and application in the forthcoming proclamation.[21]

Although the proclamation committee experienced some disagreement during its last session, the final declaration essentially represented the consistent planning and compatible thinking of Egremont, Shelburne, and the new president of the Board of Trade and Plantations, Lord Hillsborough. When Shelburne resigned from the presidency of the Board of Trade on September 2, 1763, Wills Hill Hillsborough, Marquis of Downshire, was selected as his replacement. Hillsborough directed the Board of Trade in its last proceedings on the Proclamation of 1763. The October edict actually conformed considerably to Egremont's plans of the previous May. The Allegheny Mountains divided colonial America into two segregated areas, but the upper Ohio valley was not included in the eastern section as advised by Lord Shelburne. Most officials, however, considered the Indian boundary to be only temporary. The Earl of Hillsborough counseled the king to erect permanent borderlines between the indigenous peoples and the British subjects, but his recommendations were ignored. Hillsborough's faith in permanent limits was founded on his conviction that European colonization could be restricted to the eastern seaboard.[22]

The proclamation determined several new colonial policies. Indian domains and trade after October, 1763, were definitely under imperial control. The extension of governmental power over such significant realms of Indian life demonstrated the king's willingness to accept the native peoples as state wards. Protection of the aboriginal people would be maintained thereafter even as the English colonies expanded westward beyond "temporary" boundaries into Indian territory. According to the expectations of the Board of Trade, Great Britain controlled western expansion through purchase of the Indian land.[23]

The recently acquired Floridas were immediately opened for colonization in order to offer speculators and frontiersmen a new direction to explore away from the Indian settlements in the North and West. If Canada and Florida could absorb midwestern colonists, the policy-makers of the sixties believed that Great Britain would be able to keep its subjects within "reach" of royal authority. The colonial office recognized that the isolated settlers of the Midwest might engage in commerce and manufacturing in contradiction to the crown's economic policy. The officials of Whitehall, however, were more concerned with the possibility of Indian war if the English settlements remained in the West. Imperial management of western migration and Indian affairs was subsequently established under the Proclamation of October 7, 1763.[24]

The Tri-State Border Dispute

George III generally employed the Board of Trade's recommendations in the composition of the Proclamation of 1763. The Lords Commissioners of Trade and Plantations, however, accepted Governor Grant's advice on the subject of the northern frontier of East

Florida. Initially, the board proposed a boundary line running from the junction of the Chattahoochee and Flint Rivers to the mouth of the St. John's River. Upon receipt of James Grant's memorial of September, 1763, the Board of Trade approved an extended northern border for East Florida. The new boundary stretched from the circuitous channel of the St. Mary's River to the confluence of the Chattahoochee and Flint Rivers.[25]

Governor James Grant addressed his memorial to Secretary of State Halifax presenting several logical reasons for the use of the St. Mary's River as the northeast boundary of East Florida.

> That as soon as Your memorialist had the Honour to be appointed Governour of East Florida, as he Conceived it to be his Duty, so he made it his immediate Business, to enquire into every Thing that Concern'd the State of that Country -
>
> The first Thing that presented itself to him, were the limits intended for that Province to the North, which he understood was to begin at the Entrance of the River St John, & to run Westward to the Catahouche or Flint River; This Boundary Line he humbly Conceives to be too Confin'd, for the following Reasons.
>
> First, Because of this Division the most Valuable Part of Florida will lose its Name, & be absorbed by Georgia whereby that Valuable Acquisition would become invisible to the Eyes of the World, & Florida would be considered as an inadequate Equivalent for the Havana, & remain that Barren, Broken Sand Bank which it has been eroneously deem'd by the uninform'd Publick.
>
> Secondly, Because this artificial Boundary would be difficult to ascertain in a flat Country, Cover'd with swamps & full of Woods, which of Course would occasion Continual disputes with the neighbouring Province.
>
> Thirdly, Were it even possible to be defined, that Province would be Curtail'd of the Lands which are the most fertile, & most Capable of accomodating Settlers, who might in Time Contribute largely, to the Support and Defence of that Frontier Province, which other ways must always Continue to be a Heavy Burthen upon the Mother Country, the Southern Part of it appearing to be nothing but Barren Lands, and Consequently less fit for Settlement & Cultivation than the Northern Part.
>
> Your Memorialist therefore humbly proposes that the River Catahouche or Flint River, may Continue the Boundary of East Florida to the Westward, and that the River St Mary from its Entrance to its Source, with a West Line from thence to Catahouche or Flint River, may be its Boundary to the North, which natural Line he

Conceives to be more Eligible & Distinct, than any artificial one can be, however marked or describ'd.[26]

The Board of Trade and Plantations confirmed the Grant proposal on September 28, 1763, explaining "we are nevertheless of Opinion, that the Considerations of fixing the Limits by a River, which is a natural Boundary, and that the more southern parts of East Florida are represented to be less fertile, and therefore not so well adapted to Settlement and Cultivation do favour Governor Grant's Proposition." [27] The decision to make the St. Mary's River the northern limit of East Florida settled an old argument between the governments of Georgia and South Carolina. Both colonies previously claimed the crown area south of the Altamaha River and competed for control of the included lands and people. The ensuing colonial struggle to own the disputed territory was not decided conclusively until the formation of the Floridas in 1763.

Carolina's pretension to the contested lands depended upon a 1665 charter which set the twenty-ninth degree north latitude as the southern boundary. Charles II of England granted the extensive charter to Carolina even though the Spanish *presidio* of St. Augustine was situated above the southern limits of the colony. In 1719 South Carolina became a royal province. The crown, once again possessing title to that territory, chartered the debtor and criminal colony of Georgia as an "English" buffer between the Spaniards and the Carolina plantations. A portion of Carolina thereafter became Georgia. The new province was located between the Savannah and Altamaha Rivers and north of the Spanish settlement in Florida. Since George III's government continued to regard the unoccupied area below the Altamaha River as crown property, Georgia and South Carolina competed to include the lands within their respective colonial borders.[28]

In the fifties, the notorious Edmund Gray further confused the struggle for the "borderlands" when he led a band of "criminals, outlaws, and debtors" south of the Altamaha River and founded an illegal settlement. Gray's colony was called New Hanover. The uninvited intrusion obviously disconcerted the governors of Carolina and Georgia. Spanish officials in St. Augustine were likewise frightened to learn of the "foreign invasion." When Spanish Florida discovered the existence of the outlaw colony in 1755–56, an official deputation was sent north to study the situation. Despite their willingness to trade with the gang, the Spaniards ordered the unsavory intruders to abandon the colony.[29]

Fearing that the outlaws might seek foreign protection and inadvertently strengthen the Spanish claim to the territory, Governor Henry Ellis of Georgia vainly tried to appeal to Gray's "English conscience." He ultimately offered the New Hanover settlement a *modus vivendi* existence. The Georgia governor was obviously guilty of extending his authority well beyond the geographic jurisdiction of his government. As soon as the news of these activities reached England, William Pitt and the Board of Trade vigorously remonstrated with Governor Ellis for his indiscretions and ordered the removal of the fugitives from the controversial area. Worrying that Gray's activities might "disturb that peace and friendship which at present so happily subsists between His Majesty and the King of Spain," the English government issued directions for the evacuation of New Hanover on June 10, 1758. Early in 1759 Georgia officials notified the gang to withdraw from the uncharted settlement. Gray's "profligate and refractory" settlers ostensibly abandoned New Hanover in March, 1759, but they soon returned to their previous locality and way of life.[30] In 1761, Governor James Wright, who succeeded Henry Ellis as governor of Georgia, notified the Board of Trade that New Hanover continued to exist contrary to royal orders:

> I think it is my duty to acquaint your lordships that it has very lately come to my knowledge that a set of people who some years ago settled themselves to the southward of the river Altamaha, at a place by them called New Hanover, and who were, in 1759, by His Majesty's command, and in his name, ordered to remove from thence, did only make a show or appearance of so doing, and immediately returned back to their settlements, where they have continued ever since, and yet are. By the best information I can get, these people, in the whole amount to between seventy and eighty men, and are a mixture of runagates from the two Carolinas, Virginia, &c. &c. They are not settled together, but scattered about the country, and on lands at present not within my jurisdiction or authority.[31]

The Gray affair intensified the competition of Carolina and Georgia for the crown lands north of Spanish Florida. South Carolina claimed all the territory south of the Altamaha River to the Spanish border. Meanwhile, Governor Ellis, aware of his superiors' fears of an international struggle over New Hanover, offered to include the area under Georgia jurisdiction and legal protection. The Georgia governor suggested, "that if it were the King's Pleasure to annex these Southern Lands to this Province either expressly, or in general terms, by extending the Jurisdiction of this Government as far as his Majesty's Territorys extended to the South, the irregularities of the Setlers there would be prevented by the operation of Laws." [32] Furthermore, Ellis warned Governor Thomas Boone of South Carolina against any policy which would permit surveys or grants of real estate below the Altamaha River.

Ignoring Ellis and his instructions, Governor Thomas Boone began apportioning large areas of the debated territory. Governor Boone inaugurated his land grant scheme soon after Spain ceded Florida to Great Britain at Paris. By April 5, 1763, Governor Boone had distributed 343,000 acres to less than two hundred South Carolinians. When Governor Wright of Georgia learned of those grants and then discovered that the South Carolina governor had given 160,000 additional acres to other Carolina citizens, he sent a letter of protest to the Lords of Trade and Plantations. [33]

Upon receipt of Wright's complaint, the Board of Trade rebuked the South Carolina governor.

A report having prevailed that you had, with the concurrence of the members of His Majesty's councils in South Carolina, issued orders or warrents for surveying large tracts of land in that part of His Majesty's dominions in America which lies to the south of the river Altamaha, in order to pass grants of such lands, as being within your jurisdiction; and the truth of this report having been confirmed by the copy of a protest or caveat of the Governor of Georgia against making such surveys and grants, which has been communicated to us by the agent of that province, it is our indispensable duty to avail ourselves of the opportunity by a vessel now ready to depart for Charlestown, of expressing to you our surprise and concern that you should have engaged in a measure of this nature so inconsistent with and prejudicial to His Majesty's interests and authority.

The making grants of any part of this country is certainly contrary to the spirit and intention of His late Majesty's orders for the removal of Gray and his adherents from the settlement of New Hanover, and must not only embarrass the execution of what general arrangements may be necessary in consequence of the cession of Florida, but will also interfere with those measures it may be reasonably supposed His Majesty will now pursue to extend the Government of Georgia, and thereby to remove those obstacles and difficulties which that well-regulated colony has so frequently and justly stated to arise out of the narrow limits to which it is confined.

We hope, however, that this letter will reach you time enough to prevent any grants passing in consequence of the surveys; . . . [34]

Boone replied to the Board of Trade on August 17, 1763. He attempted to defend his land grants in terms of Carolina's early charter rights. Although South Carolina's title to the "southern lands" was meticulously argued by Governor Boone, the Georgia claims prevailed. In the Proclamation of 1763, the Board of Trade decided the long standing conflict in favor of Georgia.[35]

On June 8, 1763, the Lords Commissioners of Trade and Plantations presented George III with their recommendations on the Florida boundaries. Since the northern frontier of East Florida was initially established by an artificial line extending from the St. John's River to the meeting point of the Chattahoochee and Flint Rivers, Georgia obtained all the land from that boundary to the Altamaha River.[36] As a result of the "existence" of East Florida, Georgia was enlarged by more than one-third its original size. The Georgia governor only enjoyed his colony's victory over South Carolina for a couple of months, however, before the Board of Trade approved Grant's proposal of September, 1763. Even after the changes inspired by James Grant were included in the Proclamation of 1763, Georgia gained substantial increases of real estate.

The Proclamation of 1763 finally concluded the borderland controversy between South Carolina and Georgia. The limits of South Carolina remained unchanged. However, Georgia significantly augmented its property holdings with the acquisition of the territory between the Altamaha and St. Mary's Rivers. Benefiting from Governor Grant's intercession with the Board of Trade, East Florida secured the St. Mary's River boundary and the agriculturally rich areas south of that sea channel.[37]

The northern boundary of West Florida was also extended in 1764. As consequences of the changes, the new frontier coincided with the 32° 28′ north latitude line and enclosed Natchez within the limits of West Florida. Earlier borders on the thirty-first parallel were located south of the site of Natchez. The Board of Trade approved the enlargement of West Florida in the spring of 1764 after receiving Governor George Johnstone's recommendations during the previous summer. Once again Florida increased in size at the expense of Georgia.[38] Map 6 indicates the boundary changes between Florida and Georgia.

6 Boundaries of British East and West Florida in 1763

As British officials busily arranged the future limits of East and West Florida, their government inaugurated a publicity program to encourage the settlement of the provinces. Florida propaganda thereafter appeared in numerous papers and periodicals. Stressing the healthful climate, ubiquitous resources, and fertile domains of the Floridas, the new governors and the London ministers offered colonists generous land-grant opportunities.[39] Such enticements were proposed to satisfy English settlers and prevent Indian aggression. The colonial office hoped to draw the frontier away from the Allegheny Indian country and toward the almost empty Florida colonies. The southward movement of the frontiersmen was then expected to insure peaceful coexistence with the western Indians and the economic development of the peninsula provinces. Many colonial plans depended upon the successful colonization of the ceded lands. With the formation of East and West Florida, royal officials were able to organize internal affairs in the new colonies, introduce English institutions, and pacify the unfriendly Indians.

8

The Religious Transformation
of Florida, 1763–1765

The Departure of Spanish Catholicism
from Florida

The Roman Catholic Church of Spanish Florida concluded ten months of movement on January 21, 1764. Accompanying Governor Feliú and his staff, the remaining personnel of the Parochial Church of St. Augustine, the Convent of St. Francis, and the resident brotherhoods boarded the last boats heading for Havana. Every one of the seven ships in the convoy was crowded with people and possessions. The parish priest, Don Juan Joseph Solana, and the acting chief-sacristan sailed among the last 350 persons to leave San Agustín. One vessel transported the Church's belongings to Cuba. All the movable property, including altars, ornaments, and other sacred valuables, were conveyed from Florida aboard the schooner *Nuestra Señora de la Luz y Santa Bárbara*. This ship also carried fifteen volumes of parish records containing the vital statistics of the old colony from 1594 to 1763. The crown similarly relieved Pensacola and Apalache of their religious possessions. Apalache's holy articles reached Havana aboard the schooner *San Joseph y las Animas*. According to a previous agreement with Charles III, the transportation expenses were defrayed by the royal treasury.[1]

The shipment of Church possessions appeared in Cuba in early February, 1764. Soon after the arrival of the religious objects, Don Pedro Agustín Morel y Santa Cruz, Reverend Bishop of Santiago, Cuba, and the Province of Florida, issued an edict ordering an inventory of Church valuables. On February 6, 1764, the bishop ordered a complete listing and evaluation of everything from Florida. All goods and paraphernalia were stored in the hall of the Parish Church of Havana under the surveillance of Don Blas Salazar, assistant-sacristan of St. Augustine. These temporary quarters served the exiled Church until the inventory of March, 1764. The stewards of the various *cofradías* (brotherhoods) guarded their own belongings. But the depository general of the ecclesiastical court was given charge of all the gold and silver pieces of the Florida Church.[2]

Clerical agents of Bishop Morel conducted the inventory. A Cuban official, Doctor Juan Monell Tellés, directed the work of assessing the Church possessions with the assistance of the Florida senior-sacristan, Don Simón de Hita y Salazar, and appointed officers of the religious brotherhoods. On the twenty-second of February, Tellés and his staff began the detailed registration and investigation. The team of assessors completed their assignment in approximately five weeks. More than 250 items were listed among the transported goods of the Parish Church of St. Augustine. The inventory included such articles as altars, bells, biers, candlesticks, carpets, icons, tabernacles, and even wooden rattles (noisemaking devices for religious holidays), and white wax. Every individual object was ultimately mentioned and appraised.[3]

Juan Monell Tellés and his associates inventoried the possessions of the Parochial Church along with the belongings of the Convent of St. Francis. The investigators also appraised the religious goods of the confraternities. The six surviving brotherhoods of St. Augustine in 1763 were the Most Holy Christ of the Solitude, the Most Holy Christ of the Holy True Cross, Our Lady of the Milk, Our Lady of Guadalupe, Our Lady of the Rosary (Most Holy Virgin of the Rosary), and Our Lady of the Conception. A seventh confraternity—the Most Holy Sacrament—probably also existed at the time of the evacuation. The first brotherhood functioned under the direction of the Main Parochial Church and the last two confraternities were established for the Convent Church of St. Francis. A royal edict of August 31, 1688, canonized all six of the religious societies of St. Augustine.[4]

The appraisors completed their work on March 30, 1764. Several hundred items were eventually mentioned and described. Records of the entire inventory were subsequently witnessed by the depository general of the ecclesiastical tribunal, the commissioned judge of the inventory, the chief-sacristan of Florida, and a notary of the public.[5]

Later in the same year, the assessors informed Conde de Ricla of the conclusion of their assignment. When Bishop Morel advised the governor that the inventory was finished, Conde de Ricla instructed the office of the Royal Department of Accounts to examine the records. The governor's orders emphasized the importance of determining which gold and silver items actually belonged to the crown. There appeared to be a serious concern over the proprietorship of these precious articles, and the captain general commanded one of his officials to inspect the Florida accounts. Conde de Ricla consequently appointed Marqués Justiz de Santa Ana to serve as the royal accountant for the religious possessions. Marqués Justiz de Santa Ana was required to send his audit to both the bishop of Santiago and the governor and captain general of Cuba.[6]

An investigation regarding the acquisition of the Church valuables accompanied the crown's report. In order to discover which of the accumulated articles belonged to the king, the captaincy general of Cuba requested several Floridians to testify to the "origin and ownership" of the many items listed for the *presidio* of St. Augustine. Cuban officials obviously suspected the Florida clergy of excessive "ownership" claims. Parish Priest Don Juan Joseph Solana, Sacristan Juan Bernardo de Paredes, Royal Treasurer Don Juan Esteban de Peña, Don Juan Elixio de la Puente, and the guardians of the religious brotherhoods were subpoenaed to offer testimony concerning their knowledge of St. Augustine Church possessions. Juan Chrisostomo de Acosta, notary public of the ecclesiastical tribunal, also testified. The court of inquiry commenced its proceedings in January, 1765.[7]

St. Augustine's parish priest was the first witness called for testimony. Father Solana offered his deposition on January 10, 1765. He firmly stated that since beginning his duties as assistant-priest in 1737 he had never witnessed the arrival of any royal delivery of gold or silver valuables destined for the Church of St. Augustine. On the contrary, he claimed that his own parishioners typically supported the financial operation of the Parochial Church. The old *cura* explained that the cost (1,000 pesos) for renovating the hermitage of Our Lady of Solitude (Nuestra Señora de la Soledad) were borne not by the crown, but by the pious citizens of St. Augustine. After the reconstruction, Our Lady of Solitude served San Agustín as parish church.[8]

In the eighteenth century the secular Church occupied dismal quarters in St. Augustine. Governor Manuel Montiano remarked in 1738 that the capacity of the hermitage was so inadequate that many members of the congregation heard mass in the outside street.

Moore's rapacious assault of 1702 destroyed the previous church. Thereafter, the hermitage became the parochial center because only four walls of a new church had been erected. The royal treasury allotted 40,000 pesos for the reconstruction of the devastated building, but St. Augustine spent only 10,687 pesos on the construction of church walls. The remaining funds were expended for relief and military emergencies.[9]

According to the elderly priest, ornaments for pontifical celebrations were acquired when the visiting bishop of Tricale and auxiliary bishop of Cuba arrived in St. Augustine. Auxiliary Bishop Francisco de San Buenaventura Tejada convinced the governor and royal officials to issue a warrant for 100 pesos to cover the expense of their manufacture in St. Augustine. The bishop also arranged for the renovation of the parish church. A new roof and bell-tower were constructed on the recently painted and enlarged building. Other improvements such as a stone sacristy made the church more serviceable to the community.[10]

The Papal Bulls of December 14, 1705, established an auxiliary bishopric for Florida. Since the bishops of Cuba only visited the continent occasionally, the creation of an auxiliary bishopric improved Church administration in the colony. From the sixteenth century to the beginning of the eighteenth century, only two of the twenty-three Cuban bishops ever sojourned in Florida. Auxiliary Bishop Francisco de San Buenaventura Tejada resided in St. Augustine for ten years, 1735–45.[11]

The St. Augustine priest answered his interrogators with additional complaints. Arguing that royal funds never reached the Church or its subsidiary organizations, the old *cura* maintained that the confraternities obtained their only support from current members or from the subscription of local alms. Solana further asserted that the proceeds from rental duties were no longer forthcoming. The Parochial Church previously earned taxes in the amount of nine and one-half per cent, and Father Solana blamed the St. Augustine government for depriving the clergy of that important source of income in the process of tariff collection. The priest unhesitantly criticized the royal officials for their irresponsible financial relationship to the Florida Church. Only the continuous supply of fuel oil for the lamps of the Holy Sacrament was grudgingly credited to the crown of Spain.[12]

Sacristan Juan Bernardo de Paredes served the court as a witness on the following day. The sacristan's testimony broadly substan-

tiated the statements of Father Solana. Paredes testified that the
king contributed two black chasubles and a crimson front-piece to
the Parochial Church of St. Augustine. He also acknowledged the
ornament expenses elicited from the royal officials by the determined bishop of Tricale. Paredes conceded that other sacred paraphernalia reached the Florida colony in 1728 according to crown
instructions. Similarly, the sacristan recalled that a few religious
objects, including a small gold-plated, silver ciborium, arrived without cost from New Spain in the forties. But the church cross and
silver articles, Paredes stated, were purchased from the voluntary
contributions of the parish congregation. Local funds also figured
significantly in the Church's program for building repairs and improvements. The brotherhoods managed their "respectable appearance" because of the consistent support of their own membership. In
conclusion, the senior-sacristan reiterated Juan Solana's charges
against the government for denying the Church its deserved rental
taxes.[13]

Don Juan Elixio de la Puente and Royal Treasurer Don Juan
Esteban de Peña generally corroborated the clergy's testimony. They
both mentioned the significant contributions of Bishop San Buenaventura Tejada in behalf of the impoverished congregation, clergy,
and Church of Florida. In accord with the previous witnesses,
Puente and Peña affirmed that the Church and confraternities of St.
Augustine were financed from local alms, donations, and rental
funds. All the Florida spokesmen asserted that the community supported its Catholic Church. Esteban de Peña, who occupied the post
of royal treasurer from 1742 to 1763, testified that he remembered
no charge to the treasury for items purchased by the parish church
or brotherhoods.[14]

A Cuban official supported the St. Augustine case. The king's
secretary and accountant in Cuba, Joseph Antonio Gelabert, admitted that his records confirmed the testimony of the Florida depo-
nents. Gelabert reported to his superiors that there appeared to be
no evidence that the religious possessions of Florida had been acquired at crown expense. The viceroy of New Spain, he averred,
delivered a ciborium to the St. Augustine *presidio,* but the royal
officials deducted the price of that article from Florida's annual
subsidy. Other sacred objects were requested from the viceroyalty of
New Spain and the costs of their manufacture and shipping were
also charged to St. Augustine. With the conclusion of the investigation, the Church retained ownership of the Florida possessions.[15]

Other property problems also concerned the exiled Church of Florida. While the movable belongings of the St. Augustine parish were passing through the complicated channels of government bureaucracy on their way to eventual Church repossession, the clergy desperately tried to sell its real estate in Florida. The Church simply could not convert buildings and property into specie or any other transferable commodity. A lack of land investors also frustrated any plans to dispose of the real estate profitably. Since the clergy of Florida emigrated before a market was available to absorb the unsold domains, clerical headquarters in Cuba entrusted property transactions to agents of the crown.

Don Juan Elixio de la Puente served as realtor for the Church, the crown, and the private citizens of St. Augustine. He eventually disposed of all the Spanish property. Obeying his instructions to sell everything at the highest possible prices, Puente concluded his assignment for the Catholic Church on July 20, 1764. He completed his transactions only two months prior to the eighteen-month deadline of the Treaty of Paris. The Convent of St. Francis, the Church of Our Lady of the Milk, and the Episcopal house were all transferred to agent-trustee-owner John Gordon in two confidential documents. John Gordon agreed to sell those estates at the highest market figures. All profits from his sales would then be remitted to Puente as realtor for the Florida Catholic Church. Jesse Fish also acquired Church property. The factor of the Walton Exporting Company was invested with similar powers as Gordon when Puente transferred the Tolomato Church and the walls of the unfinished parish church to him in July, 1764. Fish and Gordon relieved the Church of its properties for the modest sum of 3,000 pesos.[16] Soon after these sales, Puente embarked from St. Augustine probably feeling very satisfied over the conclusion of his mission.

Don Juan Elixio de la Puente returned to Havana in September, 1764. The clergy therefore assumed that the disposal of Church property was satisfactorily completed when the crown's agent appeared in Cuba. Within a year of the July agreements, however, the churchmen heard the disappointing news that Great Britain had arbitrarily invalidated their property arrangements. Furthermore, expropriations immediately followed the nullification of their transactions. Since the British authorities considered the Church domains to be crown property, all such estates escheated to His Britannic Majesty. After the seizure of their lands, the Florida clergymen learned to their dismay that the bishop's house would lodge the recusant Anglican Church and the hermitage of Nuestra Señora de la Leche would become an English hospital. The knowledge that the Convent of St. Francis was being utilized as an army barracks likewise appalled the exiled priests.[17]

Other questions regarding Florida Catholicism also perplexed the hierarchy of Spain. Madrid officials of the Church were especially apprehensive of the possibility of Spaniards living in the peninsular colony under Protestantism. More than a year before Great Britain appropriated the Church properties, and approximately a month before the last people abandoned St. Augustine, the Madrid churchmen became concerned about remaining Spaniards in Florida. News of the "total" character of the exodus probably reached Spain in the spring of 1764. Without the reports of Governor Melchor Feliú and Don Juan Elixio de la Puente, the Iberian Church was uncertain of the number of Spanish émigrés. The clergy was understandably obsessed with the dread that numerous Spaniards might continue their residence in English and Episcopal Florida. The Treaty of Paris clearly permitted Spanish Catholics to live in Florida with religious toleration. Catholic Florida, however, ceased to exist in 1764 until the founding of New Smyrna four years later in 1768. Actually, by Christmas Eve of 1763, as the crown and clergy of Spain discussed policy for continuing residents in Florida, only 642 Catholic subjects remained in the colony, and within two months only one Spaniard was left in St. Augustine. When Charles III and the Church of Spain later received statistical information of the mass migration, their interest in English Florida subsequently ended.[18]

Spanish Catholicism abandoned Florida soon after the beginning of the new year of 1764. By the time the Church hierarchy in Spain realized the success of the evacuation, the entire population, including administration and clergy, was resettled in Cuba and New Spain. Except for seventy-seven citizens who moved to Campeche, the civilians, soldiers, and clergy of St. Augustine established residence in Havana and Matanzas, Cuba. Upon arrival, several members of the St. Augustine Church were almost immediately assigned to new positions in the dioceses of Havana. Their congregations again included military personnel. The priest and senior-sacristan of the Main Parochial Church of Florida and the priest of the Pueblo de Gracia Real de Santa Teresa de Mosa continued to serve as clergy at the Fort of Athares.[19] Unfortunately, poor health prevented the chief-sacristan from performing his duties and earning his salary.

The assistant-priest of the Parochial Church was not initially offered a new appointment. Ten Franciscans, including the chaplains of San Marcos de Apalache, also arrived in Cuba seeking reassignment. Those clergymen from the Convent of St. Francis and the Indian towns of Nuestra Señora de la Leche and Nuestra Señora de Guadalupe de Tolomato presumably obtained other missionary assignments within the Spanish Indies. One of the Franciscan priests was known to have moved to Caracas, Venezuela, while two others died in Havana.[20]

The secular clergy of Pensacola apparently voyaged to Vera Cruz with the San Miguel population, although all of the Franciscan missionaries were moved to Cuba. In Mobile, Father Ferdinand, a Capuchin priest, remained in Catholic service after the advent of English administration. He continued in that capacity for eight years, from 1763 to 1771, faithfully performing his duties as resident clergyman. The aging cleric only periodically served his French flock from 1771 to 1773 because parish funds were insufficient to support him permanently in British West Florida. Lacking sustenance for a local priest, the congregation in 1772 even submitted a petition to the English government for a subsidized Catholic clergyman. Although the West Florida council refused to accept fiscal responsibility for French Catholicism, apparently no attempts were made to interrupt the operation of Catholic institutions from 1763 to 1780. Another Capuchin, Father Paul, officiated in Mobile during 1777, but regular Catholic ceremonies were not begun again in West Florida until the return of Spanish control. The Louisiana Spaniards recaptured West Florida in 1780 during the last years of the American War of Independence. Mobile surrendered on March 14, 1780, and British Pensacola was forced to capitulate on May 9, 1780.[21]

Even the Catholic Church suffered losses after abandoning Florida. The clergymen who migrated from Florida to Havana experienced financial distress during their first months in Cuba because the crown did not immediately relinquish their usual stipends. His Catholic Majesty, Charles III, owed the clergy of the Main Parochial Church of St. Augustine, 1,480 pesos in wages. The regular clergy of St. Francis Convent also claimed salary obligations of 1,950 pesos, and other debts included the unpaid wages of the Indian village priests amounting to 675 pesos. Consequently, when Puente and the memorialists of San Agustín de la Nueva Florida implored the governor of Cuba for relief, employment, and salary arrears, the claims of the Florida Church were within the numerous petitions of 1766. Indeed, the Havana officials received many hours of reading material from the Florida memorialists. According to the Memorial of 1766, the royal treasury owed the Catholic Church more than 4,200 pesos. Most of the crown's indebtedness represented unpaid salaries, but many pesos worth of wine, oil, and candle wax were also due the Church of St. Augustine. The religious expenses of oblations and feasts were additionally recorded as unpaid debts of the Spanish treasury. Finally, the Church charged the treasury with per diem arrears for the four female members of the Florida Order of Mercy. A total of 633 pesos was owed to those women who received four reales daily pursuant to the royal *cédula* of January 11, 1761.[22]

The migration of the regular and secular clergy from Florida in 1763–64 actually terminated a century of tribulation for Catholicism. Perhaps the exodus of the Church was anticlimatic. After Moore's attack of 1702 ended the "golden age" of Franciscan Florida, the Church entered a long period of despair and decline. There was never a revival of missionary activity in the eighteenth century, and the clergy ceased to be influential in colonial Florida.

The history of the eighteenth-century Church reveals a succession of misfortunes and failures. Initially, the invasions of 1702–4 irreparably smashed the Franciscan missionary system. From 1705 to the exodus of 1763, the Church of Florida was weakened internally by dissention and harassed externally by Indian hostility and foreign intrigue. Conflict seemed to exist in every sector of Church life. Besides the devastating results of the Moore expedition and other British military excursions in Florida, the Catholic Church suffered from the power struggles of its own clergy. Internal controversy separated the Franciscans into inimical groups of Creoles and *Peninsulares*. Eventually the schism in the order of St. Francis included local governors and even the crown of Spain. Disputes between regular and secular clergy and clerical involvement in the soldiers' mutiny of 1758 also occurred in the last century before Florida was ceded to Great Britain.[23]

In 1715, however, the Franciscans of St. Augustine anticipated a resurgence of missionary activity. When news arrived in Spain that 50,000 natives requested Spanish friendship and protection, a sequel to the "golden age" was envisioned. The king and his council solicited fifty Franciscan volunteers for Florida, but only nineteen missionaries journeyed to San Agustín in the next seven years. The deplorable reputation of Florida obviously impeded all recruitment attempts. Without adequate training in frontier life and without knowledge of Indian languages, many of the neophytes found missionary existence to be a very exasperating experience. A number of the new friars sought excuses to visit Cuba and never returned to Florida. The Creole Franciscans, fearful of losing their control over the missionary system, aggravated the situation by locating their Spanish brothers in undesirable native villages and transferring them frequently after adjustment to alien surroundings. By the forties, both the governor and the king were committed to different sides in the dispute.[24]

During the governorship of Manuel de Montiano (1737–49), Florida officials attempted to arrange a reconciliation between the two religious factions. Governor Montiano and Auxiliary Bishop Buenaventura y Tejada together endeavored to terminate the "civil war" within the Order of St. Francis. Several reforms were proposed which would have separated Creole and Iberian Franciscans, consolidated the Indians into townships, and provided Spanish language education for the indigenous people. One proposal even suggested that the Franciscans should be replaced by Jesuits. All the recommendations were eventually repudiated by the king who wanted preferential assignments for the Franciscans from Spain.[25]

The defection of many Indian tribes to British and French alliances ultimately mitigated the bitter contest between Creole and *Peninsular* factions. With a limited number of Indians available for mission-village life, there was no reason for further conflict. From the middle of the century to 1763, the Franciscan system therefore existed within the peripheral line of outposts encircling St. Augustine. The missionary age had passed away. By the time of the Treaty of Paris, only ten Franciscan clergymen remained in Florida service. Secular priests even managed the administration of the missions and the Convent of St. Francis at the end of the First Spanish Period in Florida.[26]

Discord between regular and secular clergy also existed in the eighteenth century. The tension between the two divisions of the Church evolved from disputes concerning the performance of everyday services for Indian residents of St. Augustine. Both branches of the Church claimed the right to render the sacraments to the local natives. After the regular clergy was initially invested with privileges early in the eighteenth century, secular priests acquired power over Indians and *Mestizos* at mid-century. Thereafter, the Main Parochial Church offered religious rites to all the inhabitants of St. Augustine. By 1763 pedestrian daily service became the only important function of the Florida clergy.[27]

The Treaty of Paris and the transfer of Florida physically ended an era that was already spiritually extinct. Because of the continuous Anglo-Spanish military conflicts, the enmity or indifference of the Indians, and the internecine struggles of the clergy, the Church had lost its missionary significance. For Catholicism, the eighteenth century became a century of retreat, and the Treaty of 1763 concluded sixty years of obvious deterioration. Catholicism, the Spanish Church, and the Spanish Catholic population wearily abandoned Florida in 1763.

The Entrance of Anglicanism into the Floridas

During the period of British occupation, the bishop of London licensed only nine clergymen for religious work in the Floridas. Other unlicensed ministers conducted infrequent Anglican Church services in the twenty years between 1764–84. Schoolmasters also occasionally served in religious capacities for the understaffed clergy. The appointment of Anglican pastors for Florida was arranged through the cooperative efforts of the bishop of London and the Incorporated Society for the Propagation of the Gospel in Foreign Parts. As an advisory organization, this society offered significant financial assistance to the Episcopal Church in America. Although the London bishop and the Gospel Propagation Society jointly examined and recommended the Episcopal candidates, the travel expenses and salaries of the selected clergymen were borne by the treasury. Licensed ministers earned annual stipends of 100 pounds and schoolmasters received a salary of 25 pounds.[28]

Four clergymen and four schoolmasters were initially designated for Florida employment by the Parliament of Great Britain. Upon the recommendation of the Society for the Propagation of the Gospel in Foreign Parts, The Reverend John Forbes became Anglican minister of St. Augustine on May 5, 1764. Soon after his arrival in St. Augustine, John Forbes accepted royal appointment to the governor's council of East Florida. The Reverend Samuel Hart was chosen for the Mobile ecclesiastical post on the same day. Later in the summer of 1764, on July second, William Dawson received his appointment papers for Pensacola. Michael Smith Clerk was subsequently commissioned as clergyman for Apalache after Captain Harries received the Spanish outpost. In the early months of 1765, Jones Read, John Firby, and Enoch Hawksworth were respectively appointed as schoolmasters of Apalache, Pensacola, and St. Augustine. Mobile remained without an English schoolmaster. Although Parliament provided sufficient funds for a fourth schoolmaster, only three teaching positions existed along with the four clerical offices.[29]

Religious facilities in the recently acquired colonies probably proved disappointing to the new clergy. During his first several years in St. Augustine, John Forbes performed Episcopal services in the bishop's house, but the edifice soon became an office building for a number of government employees. The offices of the customs commission, the naval officer, the secretary, the registrar, and the land surveyor were located in the Spanish Episcopal Building. The bishop's house also provided the province of East Florida with council chambers and an assembly room.[30] Later, in the early seventies, a Spanish Church building (La Soledad) on the south side of the plaza was renovated for the Anglican minister. The Episcopal minister called his new center St. Peter's Church. Along with the addition of a wooden spire in 1773, increased financial support enriched St. Peter's with such accessories as a clock and church bells.[31]

In West Florida, after proposing a resolution for the promotion of religion and the restraint of vice and immorality, Governor George Johnstone and the council of Pensacola discussed plans to build a church for their community on January 7, 1765. A public subscription was opened to finance the construction of a church in Pensacola. Governor Johnstone initially contributed 150 pounds to the project from his contingent fund. Future maintenance sums, he hoped, would be acquired from church-pew rentals. The building program of Pensacola, however, was never fulfilled. Throughout the twenty-year period, neither Pensacola nor Mobile managed to erect an edifice for the Church of England despite continuous clerical pleas. Prior to their departure for Florida, John Forbes, William Dawson, and Samuel Hart all petitioned the Board of Trade to arrange housing and church accommodations for their parishes.[32]

Pensacola probably suffered more severely without church facilities than Mobile. Since the population of the French city was composed predominantly of Roman Catholics, who continued to enjoy their own parish center at least until 1773, the civilians of Pensacola probably were more aware of the absence of an Episcopal

Church in their community than the soldiery of Mobile. Yet, even the occupation army complained about the absence of a Protestant church. In August, 1764, Major Farmar petitioned the secretary of war for a regimental clergyman. "I beg to inform you that we have not any Clergymen of the Protestant persuasion in this Garrison, nor any one to Officiate as Chaplain to the Regiment for many Months." [33] Typically, the largest structure in each of the West Florida towns became the center of church and government activities. In 1766 a vivid description of the deficiency of church and state buildings in West Florida was enclosed in a letter to the Board of Trade. To accentuate their construction needs, the authors of the report compared their inadequate and crowded public facilities to the numerous improvements in Spanish Louisiana.

> To see the Fortifications, Churches, Hospitals and Public Buildings, which are everywhere erecting in the Spanish Dominions, since the arrival of Don Antonio de Ulloa whilst nothing is undertaken on our part is extremely mortifying. . . . We have not even any place of Worship for asking the Blessing of Providence on our Endeavours, neither any place for holding the Courts of Justice, nor even the meeting of Assembly, except such changable apartments, as are hired on the Occasions from the Scanty Contingencies of the Province.[34]

Church furniture was particularly in demand throughout Florida. An index of necessary furniture for the several Florida churches, presented to the Lords Commissioners for Trade and Plantations on July 20, 1764, included one large desk Bible, two large prayer books, two surplices, one pulpit cloth and cushion, a linen cloth for the communion table, a pewter flagon, a plate chalice and salver, a brass offering dish, a basson for the font, and two napkins for the communion elements. Estimates of the cost of supplying an adequate number of religious articles to each church approximated sixteen pounds. The Board of Trade soon authorized and financed maximum expenditures of twenty guineas for every church in East and West Florida.[35] Assistance for the Episcopal ministries in the new colonies was also forthcoming from the Incorporated Society for the Propagation of the Gospel in Foreign Parts.

> It is desired also that the Lords Commissioners be acquainted, that this Society in order to Further this excellent design, will send Bibles & Prayer Books for the Churches, and furnish the Mission-

aries & Schoolmasters with small Bibles & prayer-books, and useful pious Tracts to be distributed to the poor as They shall think proper.

The Society beg leave to request one thing of their Lordships, which it is not doubted but They will, of their great goodness readily comply with, viz, that early care may be taken to provide comfortable Houses for the Missionaries to dwell in, and that the kindest assistance may be given them, 'till They are fully settled.[36]

Communion plate was apparently loaned to the provincial churches of Florida. Upon receipt of royal orders, the master of the crown's jewel house produced and delivered the essential plate to the colonial governors of North America. In some instances, the plate, consisting of two flagons, a chalice, one or two patens, and a basin, was donated as a gift to the colonies. East and West Florida, however, borrowed their communion utensils. The treasury usually required the return of these expensive items, often valued at more than eighty pounds, when they were no longer needed. Loans of communion plate, however, did not necessarily include time limits. The crown and the Society for the Propagation of the Gospel cooperated to furnish the Florida clergymen with the appropriate instruments of their profession.[37]

The Propagating Gospel Society of London also sought to obtain special housing and property rights for the Florida missionaries, but British governors only promised to offer them the same opportunities as other subjects of the king. Acreage limits and fee simple arrangements were similar for all settlers. In order to facilitate religious organization in the Floridas, however, Great Britain endeavored to apportion the new provinces into shires, townships, and parishes. According to George III's royal instructions, each parish could establish a ministerial glebe, not exceeding four hundred acres. Grants of two hundred acres were given to schoolmasters during their tenure in Florida.[38] Inevitably, the many recommendations of the Incorporated Society for the Propagation of the Gospel in Foreign Parts irritated the officials of the Board of Trade. The abundant correspondence from the Gospel Propagating Society would have confounded any bureaucratic department. Despite all the generous assistance that the society provided for the clergy, London officials eventually found its constant advice wearying, if not annoying. The numerous letters from this organization must have exasperated the secretaries at Whitehall. In 1765, James Pownall, an officer of the Board of Trade, requested the Society to communicate with the secretary of state for the Southern Department in all future correspondence. Although Pownall thanked the Gospel Propagating Society for all its help, he seemed relieved to notify the Society's secretary of his new correspondent in the Southern Department.[39]

The Reverend John Forbes served in East Florida throughout the British Period, but none of his colleagues remained as long in the new provinces. The first clergymen of West Florida resided only a brief time in their frontier parishes. After approximately a year in Mobile, Samuel Hart migrated to Charleston in 1765 to become the assistant minister of St. Michael's Church. The Reverend Dawson abandoned Pensacola in 1766 and accepted the ministry of St. John's parish in Colleton, South Carolina. Michael Smith Clerk, the clergyman destined for Apalache, apparently never reached Florida or the remote frontier. Instead, Clerk settled in Jamaica where he was given a service warrant by the bishop of London in June, 1764.[40]

Following the departure of Dawson and Hart, the Church of England lacked clerical representation in West Florida from early 1765 to the last months of 1767. During these two years, Dr. Wilkinson, an unlicensed chaplain, performed the religious duties of Mobile. He apparently also served in a similar capacity at Pensacola. With the advent of the Reverend William Gordon, the Anglican Church in Mobile operated continuously from 1767 to 1783. Gordon held his ecclesiastical post in Mobile until England was forced to return the Floridas to Spain. Protestantism reached Natchez in the seventies. In 1772, as Natchez became an important area of colonization, a Congregational minister moved into the Mississippi settlement. Samuel Swayze arrived from New Jersey and initially served the religious needs of the new community.[41]

From 1768 to 1771, Nathaniel Cotton occupied the ministry at Pensacola after William Dawson left for South Carolina. Unfortunately, Cotton died three years later of "dropsy" and other ailments. His successor, George Chapman, declined the Florida appointment because he feared that a man of his age and health would not have "the smallest Chance of living six weeks at Pensacola." [42] In the years that remained, 1771–80, before the Spanish forces of Louisiana Governor Bernardo de Gálvez seized the cities of West Florida, Pensacola possessed no resident minister of the Church of England.[43]

During the British Period, Dr. Andrew Turnbull's agricultural colony at New Smyrna (75 miles south of St. Augustine) enjoyed the religious guidance of both the Episcopal Church of England and the

Roman Catholic Church. The name "New Smyrna" honored the birthplace of Andrew Turnbull's Greek wife. Episcopal Reverend John Fraser conducted the services of his Church in the Greek-Minorcan settlement from 1769 to 1772. John Fraser initially was assigned to Apalache, but he moved from that isolated outpost to the populous indigo plantations of New Smyrna. When Fraser expired in 1772, his Anglican Church duties were first assumed by The Reverend John Leadbeater and later by The Reverend John Kennedy. Since the latter clergyman arrived in America in the late seventies, his Florida tenure lasted only several years.[44]

Catholicism in British New Smyrna

Catholic priests also served the religious needs of the community simultaneously with John Fraser and his Episcopal successors. Urged by Dr. Turnbull, Padre Pedro Camps and his Augustinian assistant, Vicar Bartolomé Casasnovas, accompanied the Minorcan immigration to Florida. With the permission of the Holy See in Rome, the two clerics journeyed to New Smyrna as apostolic missionaries. Because the Minorcans solicited Rome to invest the priests with clerical powers in Florida, each of the clergymen received approval for a three-year assignment in America. From the port of Mahón on the island of Minorca, Father Camps and Vicar Casasnovas embarked for the New World in June, 1768, with more than 1,400 colonists.[45]

Soon after his arrival in New Smyrna, Father Camps attempted to correspond with the governor and the bishop of Havana. His endeavors were almost immediately successful. Employing one of the passing fishing boats to carry his message, the priest communicated with Spanish Cuba in the fall of 1769. In his first confidential note, Pedro Camps asked the Havana authorities to issue him a patent of parochial priest for New Smyrna. Along with that request, Father Camps petitioned the Cuban hierarchy to grant Don Bartolomé Casasnovas the rank of vicar of New Smyrna. The Minorcan *cura* also implored his superiors to send him sufficient holy oil for the exercise of baptism and extreme unction. Pedro Camps explained that his requests were essential for the spiritual health of the many Catholics at New Smyrna. There were more than 1,200 surviving immigrants in the Turnbull settlement. Father Camps finally asked the bishop of Cuba to supply his needs by means of secret deliveries via the fishing vessel routes.[46]

The churchmen of Cuba were extremely suspicious of the letter from New Smyrna. A questioning communication concerning the affair was therefore forwarded to the king of Spain. Since the existence of the Turnbull colony was unknown in Cuba, other state officials also doubted the authenticity of the dispatch. When the correspondence reached the governor of Cuba, he understandably hesitated to consider it worthy of his attention. Governor Conde de Ricla ultimately refused to recognize the legitimacy of the letter or the "pontifical jurisdiction of the pretender." Without instructions from either Charles III or Pope Clement XIV, the colonial officials of Cuba decided to submit the New Smyrna petition to their monarch in Spain.[47]

On August 16, 1771, the crown resolved the inquiries regarding the religious status of New Smyrna. Enclosing a corroborative letter from the bishop of Minorca, Charles III verified the authenticity of the Florida clergy. The letter from the bishop of Minorca dispelled much of the mystery concerning the foreign community in Florida. It revealed the assignments of the two priests and the reasons for secret correspondence. Along with their ignorance of the existence of the colony, the Cuban authorities could not understand the necessity of surreptitious communication with New Smyrna. According to the Treaty of 1763, Great Britain was legally obliged to permit overt Roman Catholic practice in the Floridas. When the Havana clergy learned of English interference in Catholicism on the Island of Minorca, contrary to treaty stipulations, the prelates recognized why the priest insisted upon secret rendezvous with his superiors in Cuba. Pedro Camps obviously anticipated English intrusions in New Smyrna. During the British Period, however, the Catholic Church operated freely in both East and West Florida. Great Britain only required the Church to prepare accounts of its property, revenues, claims, and clerical personnel.[48]

Royal instructions accompanied the Minorcan bishop's letter to Cuba. The *cédula* of August 16, 1771, commanded the government of Cuba to furnish Padre Pedro Camps and Vicar Bartolomé Casasnovas with their requested titles and holy oil. Furthermore, the crown advised the Church officials that precautionary measures should be adopted to preserve the Catholic faith of the Minorcan colony in America. The new governor and captain general of Cuba, Marqués de la Torre (1771–77), promised to dispatch the required

Church titles, two clerical assistants, and three containers of holy oil to New Smyrna. Unfortunately, the governor could not keep all of his promises. When Vicar Casasnovas was forced to leave the colony, Father Camps never secured assistance because of Spain's entry into the American Revolutionary War. Eventually, in the mid-seventies, two Irish priests, Fathers Hassett and O'Reilly, received New World assignments to work in New Smyrna. But their proposed trip to Florida from Havana was arrested by the beginning of war.[49]

On December 3, 1771, more than two years after the Camps petitions were mailed to Havana, Bishop Santiago José Echevarría y Elguezúa wrote to the New Smyrna priests. His letter had an apologetic tone. The bishop initially explained the reason for his delay in replying to their correspondence. Without the approval of higher authorities, he confessed his hesitance to satisfy the entreaties of the Florida clergymen. After receiving the royal *cédula* of August 16, 1771, the bishop announced that all the requests of the Minorcans would be immediately fulfilled. He even expressed his hope that additional clerical powers would soon be conferred upon Father Camps and Vicar Casasnovas.[50]

The New Smyrna priests were also encouraged to continue their conscientious work for the Minorcan settlers. Bishop Echevarría notified his new subordinates that their community could be assured of any assistance required in the future. In order to supply the needs of New Smyrna, the bishop invited his correspondent to send him a detailed report thoroughly describing the religious and socioeconomic conditions of his parish. The bishop of Cuba wished to know the physical state of the new Catholic community, and information was requested concerning the church, its membership, constitution, and material possessions. In the conclusion of his letter to Pedro Camps, Bishop Echevarría once again advised the priest that Cuba would be "always ready" to solve the problems of the parish of New Smyrna.[51]

Later reports from the settlement (via the fishing fleet) revealed that Catholic Minorcans were enjoying the religious privileges of the Treaty of 1763. According to one fisherman's account, New Smyrna possessed a commodious brick church, and the fathers lived in the principal house of the community. The Church of San Pedro was a simple structure containing a high altar and a centrally placed figure of Christ. Statues of St. Anthony and St. Peter also adorned the Minorcan Church. Catholicism therefore seemed to be flourishing in New Smyrna.[52]

Daily prayers were observed in the Church of New Smyrna, although the settlers complained vaguely about the lack of spiritual comforts. Unfortunately, holy oils had to be smuggled into New Smyrna from Havana because Great Britain, fearing treachery from Cuban intercourse with Florida, prohibited commerce and communication between the Spanish Caribbean and the mainland. But Catholic life in Florida was not otherwise affected by British rule. Despite the religious freedom of the Minorcans the Cuban fisherman claimed that the immigrants yearned "to throw off the yoke of Great Britain and pass again to the domination of Your Majesty." [53] If such feelings were indeed present in the Minorcan population, they undoubtedly existed as a result of secular rather than religious experiences. The high mortality incidence at New Smyrna was probably responsible for most of the dissatisfaction and despair. Only six hundred colonists eventually escaped to St. Augustine after New Smyrna disintegrated because of disease, deprivation, and revolt.

The crown eventually acquired additional security for the Catholic settlement at New Smyrna. In August, 1773, the king of Spain advised the bishop of Santiago de Cuba that his minister to Rome, Archbishop Don Lamas Acpuro of Valencia, had secured extended privileges for the clergymen in Florida. Father Camps and Vicar Casasnovas were granted twenty-year terms by the Roman court. When the indigo settlement collapsed in 1776–77, however, the clergy of New Smyrna had served only four years of the papal concession. The priests then accompanied their congregation in the flight to St. Augustine. Early in November, 1777, the San Pedro parish moved north to the former Spanish capital of Florida. In the old colonial city the refugees obtained new facilities for Roman Catholic worship. Other institutional arrangements were later implemented for the Minorcans when the Spaniards regained St. Augustine and the Florida provinces in 1783.[54]

Religious authority was smoothly transferred from the Roman Catholic Church to the Episcopal Church of England during the interchange of colonial rule in Florida. No international conflicts emerged from the exchange of religious institutions. British occupation of the French and Spanish colonies in Florida never really altered religious life or practice. The only significant problems of the transition period were related to the awkward processes of movement and settlement which each Church and clergy faced in 1763–64. The Spanish Church suffered a variety of socioeconomic losses as a result of resettlement. Settlement problems also perplexed the Church of England as it established centers of Anglicanism in the new colonies. Meanwhile at Mobile, French Catholicism continued to function without adequate clergymen. Throughout the British Period, the problem of clerical assignments continually concerned the Church and state officials in Florida. The shortage of clergy frustrated French Catholics and English Protestants alike. Because the Hispanic population emigrated en masse from Florida before the advent of Anglicanism, there were almost no contacts, and certainly no clashes between the Spanish and English churches. Similarly, the relationship between the new provincial governments and Catholicism remained quite cordial in both East and West Florida.

Great Britain did not interfere with either the departure of the Catholic Church or its continuing activities in Mobile and New Smyrna. England even permitted the Turnbull settlement to import Catholic colonists from Minorca and the surrounding Mediterranean area. Religious toleration for Catholicism, according to the Treaty of Paris, was evidently guaranteed under British rule. The case of Pedro Camps exemplified inevitable Catholic suspicion of English promises of toleration for Florida, but the exiled Church of St. Augustine could only complain of the seizure of its properties. The religious transfer of Florida from Franco-Spanish to British control was an almost uneventful international act. Anglicanism replaced Catholicism as the predominant Christian religion in Florida.

9

Indian Affairs
during the Transfer of Florida
from Franco-Spanish to British Rule

The Migration of the Catholic Indians
from Florida

The eighteenth century was a catastrophic time for Catholic institutions and clergy in Florida. In that era the Catholic Church probably experienced its only triumph when the proselytized Indians of the peninsula voluntarily joined the evacuation of 1763. After the collapse of the missionary system in the sixty years before 1763, the Church undoubtedly found some satisfaction in the decision of the Indians to accompany the Spaniards from British Florida. Indigenous people moved from the *presidios* of St. Augustine, Apalache, and Pensacola to Spanish havens in Cuba and New Spain.

Many of the Indians actually begged the Spaniards for permission to evacuate the old colony with Florida citizens and soldiers. Non-Christian Indians were reported to have displayed regret upon learning of the Spanish exodus. Even some of the hostile tribes of the hinterlands surprisingly requested the privilege of continuing under the protection of His Catholic Majesty. Amid such an appreciative feeling for Hispanic rule, the Spaniards abandoned East and West Florida with their remaining native allies.

Prior to 1763 the neighboring Indians frequently confounded the Spaniards throughout the eighteenth century. Vacillating between English and Spanish treaties, the aborigines of Florida frustrated Spain's endeavors to control central Florida, the Gulf Coast, and the ever changing Anglo-Spanish borders. Without the security of lasting alliances, Spain could not obstruct the southern advance of Great Britain, and the English colonies in southeastern America eventually expanded into Florida. Spanish officials continually discovered to their chagrin that unless the Indians were constantly deluged with feasts and gifts of rum, weapons, powder, and trinkets their loyalty to treaties soon languished. Even alliances based upon presents could be wrecked if France or Great Britain offered the natives better quantitative and qualitative arrangements. The annual cost of such uncertain unions often approximated 9,000 pesos. Spanish authority over Apalache, Gaule, and Timucua inevitably disintegrated as British and French colonies competed with the Spaniards for Indian friendship. By 1763, only Apalache remained under Spanish control, but the Creek tribes of the remote frontier were always undependable subjects of Spain.[1]

In the years following Moore's attack on Florida, Spain negotiated a number of Indian treaties. The Yamasees, Cavetas, and other Lower Creek peoples [2] became Spanish allies as the governors of St. Augustine attempted to reestablish control of the interior. By the spring of 1718, San Marcos de Apalache was established as a gift center and trading post to court new alliances and continue intimate contacts with previous Indian allies. The new outpost immediately needed a garrison. Anticipating the problem of recruiting colonists for the fort, Governor Antonio de Benavides hoped to settle immigrants from the Canary Islands at Apalache. Such a plan would have been particularly attractive to the residents of St. Augustine who resented the necessity of sharing their community with "foreigners" from the Canary Islands. The primary concern of the trading post, however, was not inhabitants, but insufficient supplies. Without adequate European goods to barter among their neighbors, the Spaniards at San Marcos de Apalache soon alienated the Tallapoosas and Uchizes.[3]

By the twenties, Indian relations at Apalache, and generally throughout Hispanic Florida, steadily deteriorated. Spanish alliances sundered especially as England increased its support of the Apalachicolas, Casistas, Cavetas, Tallapoosas, and Uchizes. In 1725 the distribution of British gifts finally culminated in a Creek raid upon Apalache. The attack was directed against the Yamasee allies of Spain. Three years later Colonel John Palmer and his Creek forces descended suddenly upon Florida, ruining the mission-village complex around St. Augustine. Palmer's attack probably delivered the *coup de grâce* to the Franciscan missionary system. Unable to compete financially with England in the contest for native friendship, the Spaniards eventually lost many of their Indian alliances in Florida. In the War of Jenkins' Ear (1739–43), Spanish Florida suffered the wrath of Anglo-Indian assaults organized by Governor James Oglethorpe of Georgia. After Queen Anne's War a majority of the non-Christian Indians agreed to military associations with the Spaniards of St. Augustine. Such alliances depended upon continual financial support. An era of peace followed until the late thirties and early forties when English gifts dislodged the Indians from previous commitments and enlisted their warriors in military activities against Spanish Florida.[4]

Only the cupidity of the indigenous population preserved Hispanic Florida from continuous attack and harassment. Realizing the economic advantages of alliances with the struggling European powers, and obviously enjoying the colonial wars in which there were opportunities to slay settlers and enemy Indians, the natives shrewdly shifted their allegiance back and forth from Great Britain to Spain. French Louisiana was also periodically involved in similar intrigue. Governor Manuel de Montiano of St. Augustine recognized the commanding position of the Indians and attempted to deprive them of their source of power. He tried to arrange a three-power agreement prohibiting the supply of arms to the tribes of Florida, Louisiana, and the southeastern English colonies. His negotiations were futile. Lacking British and French guarantees for a multilateral arms proposal, the Spanish governor was obliged to continue participating in the competition for Indian allies.[5]

Montiano then endeavored to win the allegiance of the Lower Creek tribes by transforming San Marcos de Apalache into a well-stocked trading commissary. These plans failed, too. Even though Philip V issued the royal *cédula* of February, 1744, sanctioning the governor's scheme, neither Manuel de Montiano nor his successors were able to improve the international status of St. Augustine or reduce the power of the Florida Indians. The age of Spanish authority in the interior had passed. Anglo-Indian alliances inevitably ended Spain's influence outside the *presidios* of St. Augustine, Apalache, and Pensacola. Because Apalache was supplied with a meager stock of provisions, and because of the "gift" policies of England and France, the Creeks continued to sell their services to the highest bidders. Unfortunately for Spanish Florida, His Catholic Majesty seldom offered the highest bid.[6]

During the ten years following the War of Jenkins' Ear, many tribes flocked to the Spaniards for financial support. The Indians sought Spanish assistance as their British allies adopted a thrifty policy after the war. The *presidios* of both St. Augustine and Pensacola allowed the Indians considerable amounts of goods after 1747 and consequently a time of peace prevailed in Florida. The period included less than a decade of tranquility, 1747–55. Those few years were probably quite peaceful because the English traders neglected their business contacts below the St. John's River. Bountiful supplies provided by the Havana Company also helped the Spaniards acquire Indian friendships, especially among the Lower Creeks. When the French and Indian War began in 1755, however, Great Britain once again "purchased" native allies. The Spaniards were similarly engrossed in buying friendship prior to their entrance into the Seven Years' War. English and Spanish officials therefore vied for Creek influence along the Florida frontier.[7]

Since Georgia and Carolina could apparently afford to provide the Indians with more presents than Spanish Florida, the competition did not remain long in doubt. The major tribes of the Lower Creeks and Uchizes were inveigled into English compacts. Yet, when Spain entered the Seven Years' War in 1761 the expected Indian attacks upon Florida never occurred. In the early sixties, Great Britain maintained a policy of containment in southeastern America, while launching a determined onslaught on French Canada. The Anglo-Spanish border actually remained relatively quiet in the two years before the Treaty of Paris.[8]

Although foreign offensives against Spanish Florida never materialized, native aggression was prominent in the late fifties. St. Augustine, Apalache, and Pensacola all felt the effect of tribal raids in that period. France and England were blamed for instigating the assaults. When Indians boldly attacked the fringes of the St. Augustine *presidio* in 1758 and 1759, the royal officials of Florida requested the crown to augment their military garrison. Spanish power no longer existed in the interior and now even the capital was insecure. According to the petitions from St. Augustine, the settlements of Canary Islanders were especially in need of soldiers which could not be spared from the defenses of the city or the Castillo de San Marcos. Upon arrival the governor situated these "foreigners" from Africa in peripheral stations north of St. Augustine. By 1760–61, however, the Indians were seemingly occupied elsewhere since Governor Lucas Fernando de Palacio reported to Julián de Arriaga, minister of the Council of the Indies, 1754 to 1776, that marauders had not crossed the St. John's River for more than a year. Unfortunately, the government of Fernando de Palacio prematurely mailed its report to Spain. Soon after Governor Palacio announced the absence of enemy braves, a party of warriors returned to St. Augustine in the spring of 1761 and alarmed the *presidio* throughout the following summer. Apparently these desperate Indians attacked Spanish Florida for pillage and food. The war party was finally routed by sixteen natives and four Negroes, who crossed the Río San Juan to engage the raiders in battle. In the same year the Spanish forces at Pensacola also withstood an assault. During October, 1761, Don Diego Ortiz Parrilla assumed the governorship of Pensacola as an insurrection destroyed the nearby Indian towns of Escambe and Punta Rosa. Spanish *haciendas* in proximity to Pensacola were also devastated before Ortiz Parrilla organized a counterattack.[9]

Indian affairs improved during the governorship of Melchor Feliú. With the advent of his administration in 1762, new endeavors were forthcoming to appease the Florida aborigines. Governor Feliú believed in the use of treaties to insure peaceful relations with the Lower Creek tribes. He concluded bilateral agreements with the frequently troublesome Tallapoosas and Uchizes as quickly as possible. The Yamasees, who remained faithful allies throughout the century, required no alterations in their relationship with Spanish Florida. Creek treaties would enable his government to settle Canary Island émigrés in Tolomato, an exposed area north of St. Augustine. Similarly, such arrangements could offer security to the unprotected inhabitants of La Chua and Santa Fe (two villages in proximity to today's Gainesville). Regardless of successful negotiations, Melchor Feliú recognized the necessity of strengthening the defenses of St. Augustine and its surrounding dependencies.[10]

The Spanish governor soon learned that his precautions were neither unnecessary nor inopportune. His ambivalent policy of military preparation and treaty negotiation worked effectively in the late eighteenth century. As the Floridians abandoned the old *presidio* in 1763–64, the natives reacted ferociously to news of the imperial exchange. Indian savagery ended Spain's contact with the interior of Florida and, afterwards, the British government would have to bargain its way into the backlands. Although Spanish officials notified the natives that their property rights would be guaranteed under Great Britain, skeptical tribes brutally assaulted outposts and plantations on the Anglo-Spanish frontier. In Georgia and South Carolina barbarities occurred even after the liberal distribution of food and presents. Merciless warriors were credited with murdering more than 4,000 persons and scattering approximately 1,000 families. According to rumors from the north, war parties boldly fought regular soldiers in formation achieving frequent victories. In certain battles the Indians even seized English forts.[11]

Despite such stories of savagery and aggression, the Spaniards continued to evacuate their colonists without significant interference. Christian Yamasees were not affected by the uprising since the St. Augustine authorities proceeded with plans to save their allies. From Florida the proselytized people voyaged to Cuba and New Spain. Yamasee Apalachinos from Pensacola were conveyed to Vera Cruz and a few Apalache Indians accompanied the Spanish soldiers to Havana. Catholic Indians from the Plaza de San Agustín were also transported to Havana for resettlement. More than two hundred Indians eventually left Florida during the evacuation of 1763–64.[12]

During the summer of 1763, nineteen Indian families were transported from St. Augustine to Havana. Previously, these Yamasees resided in the mission-villages of Nuestra Señora de la Leche and Nuestra Señora de Guadalupe de Tolomato. In proximity to St. Augustine, they planted maize and vegetables while serving the Spaniards as guides, scouts, and couriers. The exiles totaled eighty-nine persons. Twenty men,[13] thirty-two women, and thirty-seven children, including eighteen boys and nineteen girls ultimately moved to Cuba. When the Indians arrived in Havana they initially received one and one-half reales per diem from September, 1763, to April, 1764. Somewhat later the new arrivals were required to live on weekly stipends of only three and one-half reales. Lack of subsistence and yellow fever soon affected the Yamasees, and by 1766, the unsalutary conditions of Cuba seriously reduced the immigrant population from Florida. Of the total number of émigrés, only fifty-three remained alive in 1766 and that aggregate included less than one-half the original number of adult males voluntarily moved to Havana. Eleven Indian men perished during two years of exile.[14] The emigration from St. Augustine and subsequent settlement in Cuba unfortunately proved to be catastrophic for the Yamasees of Florida.

Other indigenous people eventually joined the Spanish exodus from East Florida. Several Apalache Indians sought refuge with the Spaniards in Cuba. Promising to convert to Catholicism, five local Indians from the towns of Sabacolo and Tamasca were permitted to travel with Captain Don Bentura Díaz and his detachment to Havana. The Apalache commander planned to leave Florida in the fall of 1763, but the misfortunes of Captain John Harries delayed his departure until February, 1764.[15] Presumably, the Indians of Sabacolo and Tamasca arrived in Havana to suffer the same fate as the Yamasees of St. Augustine.

Before the little outpost was abandoned in February, 1764, a large number of Indians ominously appeared in Apalache. The unwelcome visitors probably were Carolina Creeks, and their sudden appearance understandably concerned the Spaniards. Apprehensive of their intentions, Díaz hastily communicated with Conde de Ricla requesting Indian presents. The commander of San Marcos de Apalache implored the governor of Cuba for such desirable gifts as rum, syrup, tobacco, vermilion, mirrors, knives, glass beads, colored ribbons, colored silk and wool, muskets, shot, and gun powder. In his letter to the governor and captain general of Cuba, Díaz complained that he had been forced to give the menacing visitors seventy pesos worth of rum which his son purchased in Pensacola. West Indian rum was always an expensive but preferred bartering commodity in America. Several of the tribesmen who descended upon Apalache frequented the small fort to converse with three Florida Indians recently returned from Havana. The converts discoursed freely on their experiences in Cuba, profusely applauding Spanish generosity.[16]

Despite the lavish praise for the Spaniards of Cuba, Díaz suspiciously watched the movement of Creeks at Apalache while awaiting the advent of the British army. Captain Díaz continued to be quite wary of the Indians whom he claimed were unresponsive to kindness, compulsion, or obligations. This opinionated officer sarcastically asserted that Indian friendship was only negotiable with the distribution of gifts. In February, 1764, the Spanish garrison evacuated the "remote frontier" without encountering any native hostility. Following the exchange of command at Apalache, the English occupants of Fort St. Marks discovered many of the same indigenous problems reported by Captain Díaz.[17]

Spanish citizens, soldiers, and Catholic Indians abandoned West Florida on September 3, 1763. From Pensacola forty families of Yamasee Apalachinos sailed with Governor Don Diego Ortiz Parrilla and the *presidio* of San Miguel de Pensacola to Vera Cruz, New Spain. Only those Indians who claimed Catholic faith were voluntarily shipped to Vera Cruz. After more than a year of residence in Vera Cruz, the Yamasees journeyed north by land to Old Vera Cruz, the site of the Spanish landing in 1519. From Antigua Vera Cruz the Florida Indians moved to Tempoala (today called Tempoal), an area only 21 miles from the port-city of Vera Cruz. By February, 1765, the Yamasee Apalachinos were situated at Tempoala in a planned settlement known thereafter as San Carlos. Viceregal officials in New Spain founded the Indian village on uncultivated *realengas* in Tempoala. Upon arrival, farm lands and agricultural implements were distributed to the refugees with expectations that they could construct a self-sufficient community at San Carlos.[18]

According to royal instructions, Lieutenant Don Pedro de Amoscotigue y Bermudo became guardian and protector of the Catholic Indians of Pensacola after their exile. Lieutenant Amoscotigue was ordered to organize a Yamasee community in New Spain. The Spanish officer assumed his assignment in Vera Cruz under the command of Viceroy Marqués de Cruillas and the former governor of Pensacola, Don Diego Ortiz Parrilla. Joaquin de Monserrat, the Marqués de Cruillas, who was viceroy of New Spain from 1760 to 1766, instructed Lieutenant Amoscotigue to take charge of Yamasee affairs in the spring of 1764. During the first eight months of his employment, the lieutenant searched the Spanish Caribbean for "missing" Indian possessions. His mission was eventually successful. After a Pensacola merchant, Don Joseph de Rivera, apparently absconded with most of the Yamasee belongings, Amoscotigue sailed along the eastern coast of New Spain recovering the lost articles.[19]

Although most of the missing things were regained and eventually resold, the Yamasee Apalachinos suffered a serious loss of funds in the Rivera affair. The search for the embezzled goods cost 716 pesos. Similarly, the unexpected but extended stay of the Indians in Vera Cruz significantly decreased their assets, and after miscellaneous expenses, only 1,529 pesos remained in the treasury of the Florida immigrants. Their possessions prior to emigration were estimated to be worth approximately 3,000 pesos. With the forfeiture of half their reserves, the new settlers at San Carlos obviously required financial assistance.[20]

The population of the community consisted of only fifty-nine people. Few Florida Indians survived the sea and land exile from Pensacola. More than one hundred converts including forty families initially followed the Spaniards from Florida, but only forty-seven men, women, and children reached San Carlos in the winter of 1765. Twenty-two family units ultimately settled the crown territories of

Tempoala. Twelve of the fifty-nine refugees were Spanish soldiers whose marriages or engagements to Indian women motivated them to travel with the Yamasees to the new settlement.[21]

All residents of San Carlos were compelled to obey a code of eleven laws established by Lieutenant Don Pedro de Amoscotigue. Even the village officials—*gobernadores, mayores,* and *regidores*— entered the royal service under Amoscotigue's regulations. Initially, the townspeople of San Carlos were required to serve in the Spanish army at Antigua Vera Cruz. Military duty for every Indian man would be compulsory if foreigners invaded the Atlantic coastlands. The laws of the new community also ordered the arrest of all foreigners, deserters, or undesirable vagrants observed in the vicinity of the village. Protocol for elections, government administration, and financial management of San Carlos was carefully defined and systematized in the code of 1765. City maintenance likewise received meticulous attention under the new regulations. The guardian and protector of the Pensacola Indians even regulated social life and relations. The sanctity of marriage was assured. Anyone involved in illicit or extramarital relations faced severe punishment if apprehended by civil or ecclesiastical authorities. Although Lieutenant Amoscotigue provided a semiautonomous status for the new community, the code of 1765 obliged the Yamasee Apalachinos to live a Catholic, communal, and Hispanic life in San Carlos.[22]

Christian Indians continued to enjoy royal favor as Spain abandoned Florida in 1763–64. The crown even offered the converts special property and settlement opportunities in Cuba and New Spain after emigration from the peninsula. Spanish magnanimity, of course, depended upon proof of Catholicism or promises of future conversion. Immigration to Cuba and New Spain also involved additional discipline and supervision for native refugees. Unfortunately, the evacuation of Florida exacted a terrible toll of lives from the aboriginal population. Approximately half of the émigrés died during the two years following their departure from St. Augustine and Pensacola. Spain's chary policy of subsistence probably accounted for some of the deaths, although the royal officials of Charles III attempted to situate the Indians securely and comfortably in the Indies. The tragic fate of the Florida Indians was simply a circumstantial accident beyond the control of royal administration. These exiles actually suffered the same calamities as the Spanish *inmigrantes* in Cuba.

France and the West Florida Indians, 1700–1765

France and Spain experienced many of the same Indian problems in Florida. Throughout the eighteenth century both nations established inconclusive alliances with the natives of the Mississippi Valley. Without the security of lasting treaties, Indian wars were always an unpleasant possibility on the West Florida frontier. The competition for allies also created an international struggle in which the local tribes sold their allegiance for presents and provisions. All the involved European states obviously found such diplomacy to be expensive in money and anguish. Franco-Indian relations were inevitably predicated upon a policy emphasizing the continuous distribution of presents. French "eastern" Louisiana thus evolved and survived. From a few coastal settlements such as Biloxi and Mobile, Louisiana explorers eventually moved north and colonized the Illinois country. French control of the Mississippi Valley depended ultimately upon accord with the Alibamon, Chickasaw, Choctaw, and Natchez Indians. Peace could be purchased, but war was also often necessary as colonial policy. By the end of the period of French occupation, the tribes east of the Mississippi River apparently tolerated the development of trading communities in proximity to their towns and hunting grounds. After 1763 the Indian allies of France even seemed distressed to witness the departure of French administration from Louisiana.

In the early years of the eighteenth century, French Louisiana consisted of only five small forts. Possession of the colony in 1713–14 meant little more than the existence of outposts at Biloxi, Mobile, Dauphine Island, Ship Island, and an unnamed position near the mouth of the Mississippi River. The Mississippi station was called Fort De La Boulaye. By 1722 Louisiana included the settlements of Fort Rosalie at Natchez, Natchitoches, and New Orleans. Eventually during the era of the Mississippi Company (1718–31) there were nine territorial districts in French Louisiana: Alibamons, Arkansas, Biloxi, Illinois, Natchez, Natchitoches, New Orleans, Mobile, and Yazoo. An Indian massacre climaxed the last years of the Mississippi Company's control of the colony. In 1729 the Natchez tribes near Fort Rosalie murderously raided the settlement after the French commander threatened to expropriate their most prosperous lands. Nearby Yazoos later joined the insurrection. The massacre ultimately ruined the Mississippi settlement at Rosalie for the remainder of the French Period. It also resulted in the eradication of the Natchez Indians. Although the Natchez were annihilated as a nation, French Louisiana east of the Mississippi never evolved according to expectations. A severe drought in 1730 further distressed the state of the colony following the massacre. After these events and the financial crises that faced the Mississippi Company in France, the crown was requested to retrieve the charter to Louisiana.[23]

Indian problems continued to plague the colonists of Louisiana for the next thirty years. From 1731 to 1763 France waged an unending war against Indian adversaries. Throughout the eighteenth century the Chickasaws were inveterate enemies of French settlers east of the Mississippi River. Prompted by their English allies, the Chickasaws periodically raided French population centers in the northern country. French Louisiana like Spanish Florida continually suffered as Anglo-Indian alliances increased in size and significance in southeastern America. All attempts to crush the Chickasaws seemed unsuccessful. Several expeditions were planned to assault the Chickasaw strongholds, but only the attacks of 1736 and 1752 actually encountered the Indians in battle. In 1736 the French forces were repulsed in two engagements with these foes.[24]

Even such traditional allies as the Choctaws occasionally frightened the French settlements in the middle of the eighteenth century. The Choctaws customarily fought for France, especially against the Chickasaws, but a schism in 1747–48 separated these Indians into two European factions, one continuing its French allegiance and the other accepting English service. A short period of civil war and international strife followed. The French Choctaws eventually triumphed over the so-called "English Rebels" and the victors returned to their routine war with the Chickasaws. The fidelity of the Choctaws was related to the regularity of French supply shipments. As in Spanish Florida, Great Britain attempted to lure the Indians away from their Bourbon alliances by offering them more numerous and better provisions. The Choctaws, however, typically remained faithful to their French allies throughout the century of conflict.[25]

Prior to the cession of French Florida (Louisiana east of the Mississippi River) the colony also faced a variety of other internal crises. French settlements lacking provisions frequently seemed on the verge of famine. As a consequence, many Frenchmen abandoned their destitute circumstances and fled to Spanish Pensacola. The defectors, however, probably discovered similar conditions in Pensacola since numerous Spaniards had deserted Florida to find livelihoods in New Orleans. Natural calamities were especially cruel to the struggling French colony. Mobile was struck by a vicious storm in 1733 and two hurricanes in September, 1740. Six years later, in 1746, another hurricane devastated the French settlements destroying a significant portion of the crops and leaving lower Louisiana without sufficient food. Frenchmen also confronted several droughts and a flood in the period from 1731 to 1763. The suffering colonists even endured a smallpox epidemic in the early thirties. Despite all these catastrophic experiences, the royal province survived and continued its conflict with Anglo-Indian enemies.[26]

During the Seven Years' War the French position in Louisiana seemed especially precarious. Great Britain succeeded in blockading the Gulf Coast and almost severing communications between France and the Mississippi colonies. Lacking ammunition to face an Anglo-Indian attack, Governor Louis Kerlérec contracted a shipment of military supplies from Vera Cruz. Throughout the eighteenth century, French Louisiana and Spanish Florida maintained a continuing exchange of needed provisions.[27] On October 21, 1757, Kerlérec wrote to France describing his desperate situation,

> The English have taken very efficacious means to capture all ships bound to Louisiana. They have established a permanent cruise at Cape St. Antonio de Cuba, and their privateers, spreading desolation among our coasters, pounce upon them at the very mouth of the Mississippi. In a word, we are lacking in everything, and the discontent of our Indians is a subject of serious fears. So far, I have quieted them, but it has been at considerable expense. Had it not been for the distribution among them of some merchandise, procured from small vessels which had eluded the vigilance of our enemies, some revolution fatal to us would have sprung up among the Indians.[28]

Louisiana received an adequate quantity of supplies in August, 1758, to satisfy the demands of its Indian allies. The August shipment arrived opportunely. Without their customary presents, the Choctaws had begun to bother the Louisiana colonists and frighten the French governor. According to Kerlérec's calculations, the Alibamon and Choctaw Indians could together support a fighting force of seven thousand warriors. The governor notified his superiors that such nations required conciliation at any cost.[29]

Unfortunately for French Louisiana, the natives continued to complain of inadequate support because of the war. By July, 1761, the Alibamons and Choctaws were threatening to desert their allies for more profitable English terms. A year later the situation was worse. Although the French ambassador to Spain requested Spanish help in Louisiana, Charles III made no attempt to assist the "Family Compact" colony. Expecting Spanish supplies, however, Governor Kerlérec convinced the natives that presents and provisions would soon be forthcoming. Eventually, in the summer of 1762, several transports arrived at New Orleans from France, but their contents were insufficient to meet the needs of Louisiana. Near the end of June, 1762, Governor Kerlérec commented upon the consequences of the shortages of Indian commodities.

> They have brought none of the articles we wanted most, and hardly any of the things mentioned in the invoices. What they have brought is either not to the taste of the Indians, or is of so inferior or bad a quality, that it is without value. I am, therefore, under the shameful and humiliating necessity of not keeping my plighted faith to the savages. What shall I do with those Indian tribes I had convened, under the expectation of the supplies which I was led to believe would soon be at hand? What will be their feelings? How shall I keep them quiet? I am in a frightful position. Is the province of Louisiana destined to be the sport of cupidity and avarice? [30]

The Paris conferences and the conclusion of the Seven Years' War probably saved Louisiana from insurrection. After 1763 Great Britain inherited the indigenous problems of the French colony. The cession of Louisiana east of the Mississippi River freed the French government from all future responsibility for the Indians of West Florida. Many of the natives, however, initially refused to accept the Treaty of 1763. Some Indian spokesmen astutely argued that the king of France could not simply transfer them like livestock to English possession. Other people abandoned their property east of the Mississippi River and followed the French government to New Orleans. These loyal Indians were given lands in what remained of French Louisiana. Approximately four hundred Alibamon and Taensas tribesmen established villages at Bayou Lafourche. The Indians of Illinois apparently intended to contest the British occupation of their country.[31] A peaceful exchange of imperial rule in West Florida was ultimately possible because of French efforts in behalf of Great Britain.

Initially, the officials of Louisiana helped their English successors arrange meetings with the Mississippi Indians. As early as October 2, 1763, the government at New Orleans offered to organize a conference with England's new native subjects. Governor Kerlérec suggested "that it is of the utmost consequence for the reciprocal tranquility of the Subjects of the two Monarchs which are under our Subjection that the two Chiefs, English and French arrive at the same time, the Nations may perceive of themselves, all the union, and good understanding that for the present Unites us." [32] Governor d'Abbadie even attended some of the first conferences held by Major Farmar in Florida. Together, Jean d'Abbadie and Robert Farmar addressed the Alibamons and Choctaws respectively in November, 1763, and January, 1764, explaining the cession of eastern Louisiana and the exchange of imperial control. The attendance of Monsieur d'Abbadie was especially advantageous when Farmar conversed with such Francophiles as the Alibamons and Choctaws. In the presence of the Louisiana governor, and obviously with his prior agreement, Major Farmar made the following statements to the Choctaws.

The Lands of the French and English being intermixed, have occasioned hitherto continued Quarrels and Combats, which have caused Rivers of Blood to run among the English and French, and among the Red men who were Partizans of the One and of the other.

You weep, even this day for your Fathers, your Brothers and your Cousins who have lost their lives, some in supporting the side of the English, and others in fighting for the French.

The two Emperours of France and England, being desirous to clear the Roads, and make them smooth and white thrô' all the Countries, have laboured in good Affairs in their great Towns; and have said, that in order to fight no more, they must mark out distinct Boundaries to divide their Lands.

To this end they have promised, the one to the other, that their possessions shall be irrevocably fixed, by a Line drawn along the middle of this River Mississippi, from its source to the River Iberville, and from thence by a line along the middle of this River and the Lakes Maurepas & Ponchartrain, to the sea. And to this end the Most Christian King gives up in full property and guarantees to His Britanick Majesty the River and Port of Mobille and all which he possesses or ought to possess on the Left side of the River Mississippi, excepting the Town of New Orleans and the Island in which it is Situated which shall remain to France.

By this agreement to remain valid and True, your Nation, and the Nation of Alibamonts [Alibamons] find yourselves on the side of the English, who promise to provide for all your wants, and the wants of your Old men, your women & Children; but this only as long as your behavior shall be good, and as long as you shall be very attentive and mindfull of all the words they may speak to you.[33]

In addition to the assistance of Monsieur d'Abbadie at Mobile, French officials also served British interests in Illinois and later in the Mississippi Valley. Great Britain especially needed French intercession in Illinois. Nyon de Villiers, commander of the northern country, advised his superiors in New Orleans that the natives would not permit the English soldiers to possess Illinois. The commander nevertheless promised to seek an Indian conciliation for England. "I will, however, endeavor to dispose the Indians favorably towards the English, although their hostility to them is very great, and although they refuse to listen to words of peace on this subject." [34] Governor d'Abbadie later attempted in the spring of 1764 to guarantee safe passage for the Loftus expedition up the Mississippi River. Harangues in behalf of the British force had little effect upon the local natives. When the armada was routed by the Mississippi Valley Indians, French assistance was forgotten and Major Arthur Loftus accused Governor d'Abbadie of complicity in the ambuscade.[35] French efforts, however, appear to have been enacted in favor of Anglo-Indian accord.

Inevitable complaints and criticisms accompanied the exchange of Indian authority in West Florida. The new occupants of the province initially blamed their predecessors for the failure of the Loftus expedition. English commanders, like Major Farmar at Mobile, were similarly critical of the customary "gift" policies of France. In January, 1764, Farmar complained, "The French have established an Interest with the Indians that will not be removed without observing a very uniform steady Conduct with them, Sacrificing every thought of social Enjoyment, and conforming in a great degree with the vile custom the French have introduced. Your House constantly open to them, giving them Victuals when ever they ask it, and the Government making them Annually considerable Presents." [36] The French officials found British relations with the Indians to be equally deplorable. Nyon de Villiers charged England with atrocities against his country's former allies. According to the Illinois commander, Englishmen ignored their commitments with the native peoples after the Treaty of Paris and punished them with crucifixion and hanging. Nyon de Villiers also claimed that English spokesmen continually insulted the French name in their speeches to win the allegiance of the Indians. During the transition period, Governor d'Abbadie criticized Great Britain for demanding protection against Indian attacks. Among other complaints of British behavior the governor grumbled, "For instance . . . they maintain that we are bound to protect them against the incursions of the Indians!" [37] Despite Anglo-French discord the West Florida tribes soon accepted the international transfer.

Great Britain and the Florida Indians, 1763–65

In the post-war period, 1763–65, Great Britain and Spain were both busily occupied with the work of colonial settlement. The governments of Cuba and Nueva España eventually managed to complete the resettlement of Florida soldiers, citizens, and Catholic Indians. Meanwhile, British officials were quite concerned with the settlement of East and West Florida and the essential pacification of the rebellious southern tribes. The governors of the new provinces realized that pacification would have to be accomplished quickly if schemes to populate the Floridas could be executed without strife and bloodshed. A "general" Indian agreement thus became a colonial priority after the Spanish cession of Florida to Great Britain.

George III and the Board of Trade and Plantations subsequently made plans to arrange a meaningful accord with all the American Indians. Provisions to satisfy the indigenous population were included in the King's Proclamation of October 7, 1763. In the south, John Stuart, the Indian superintendent of the Southern Department from 1761 to 1779, endeavored to adapt English policy to native affairs in the Floridas. Recognizing the conciliatory value of local conferences, Stuart organized three populous assemblies in East and West Florida to win the friendship of the Gulf Coast tribes. Stuart held his first congresses in 1765 with the Chickasaws, Choctaws, and Creeks. The conferences at Mobile, Pensacola, and Picolata established Anglo-Indian relations and permitted the British occupancy of Florida. A precedent for peaceful coexistence now existed. Ultimately, the Stuart administration contributed significantly to the organization of the Southern Department and the maintenance of peace in the southern colonies from 1763 to 1775. [38]

John Stuart's congresses followed two cautious years of English residence in the new provinces. A policy of guarded contact was observed in East Florida, as well as in West Florida, where the aborigines seemed very aggressive. In West Florida, the first troops to arrive in the French and Spanish cities discovered that the Indians constantly demanded gifts as well as food and drink. Major Robert Farmar at Mobile complained on January 24, 1764, that "The most disagreeable Custom the French have Introduced amongst the Indians, is that of constantly giving them Victuals and drink, and which I have been under the Necessity of adopting." [39] Although annoyed and reluctant, the major followed French precedents in his treatment of natives.

> Not knowing the intention of the Government with respect to giving presents to the Indians, and at the same time the Fort being in so ruinous a Condition that it was not tenable with the fiew Men these two Regiments consisted of, against any considerable body with small Arms, the Covert way being entirely open, and also the Communication, one of the Principal Gates of the Fort unhinged, the Indians in the French Interest much displeased with the English for taking possession without previously treating with them, and condemning the Conduct of the French, I thought it most advisable to promise the Indians that the English in all respects would use them as the French had done, as will appear in the Counsel held with them herewith enclosed, and that those who for several years have been in the English Interests, and came in their way to Congratulate us, might go away with a good Impression, and endeavour to reconcile those of their Nation that have always been friends to the French, I gave them considerable presents of such things as I could purchase here, and I am sorry to say it at a verry advanced price. I have also given some small articles to those that were heretofore in the French Interest, not by way of presents (those I have assured them will be sent by His Majesty, with proper Medals for the Chiefs) but as a token of our good intentions towards them, . . . [40]

Two months before the Mobile commander mailed his report to the secretary of war, Lieutenant Ford wrote to Major Farmar from Tombecbe grumbling about the local inhabitants. Ford was irked at the "greatest necessity of giving Bread and Meat" and irritably remarked that "The French have accustomed the Chiefs of Grand Medals to Dine with them, which obliges me to keep up that Custom." [41] The commander of Pensacola also complained of insatiable Indians. Major William Forbes informed his superiors that "It is customary for the Indians to come frequently to this place in great numbers, insolently demanding provisions & other things neither of which I have in my power at present to give." [42] Forbes was concerned because his Creek neighbors supposedly possessed a force of 6,000 warriors in proximity to Pensacola. Fearing that presents might not satisfy the apparently voracious natives, Lieutenant Colonel Provost, Major Farmar, and Major Forbes all augmented their fortifications in West Florida. Major William Forbes even ordered a defensive trench, sixteen feet wide and five feet deep, to be dug around the Spanish fort at Pensacola. Until the congresses of 1765, the commanders and civilian officials of Mobile and Pensacola placated the Indians with a variety of gifts and foodstuffs. Meanwhile, the British garrisons gradually bolstered their defenses against the possibility of sudden attack and war. [43]

Although the colonial governments anticipated eventual conflict with the Florida Indians, relations remained surprisingly peaceful in the months after the Franco-Spanish cessions of 1763 and before the conferences of 1765. A mood of impending strife seemed to pervade that brief period. The existing tranquility was only apprehensively enjoyed by the new colonists, however, since the Creeks threatened war over the settlement of hunting grounds. At Pensacola Commander William Forbes was warned by a Creek chief "that as soon as the English should begin to settle the land they would declare War & begin to Scalp the Settlers." [44] Several incidents such as Indian sniping at Mobile in March of 1764 also aggravated the fears of the English settlers in Florida. But the uneasy peace continued. By the summer of 1764, Mobile officers reported that peace and quiet prevailed on the frontier, and similar reports were also forthcoming from Pensacola in the fall of 1764. Much of the credit for the preservation of peace in West Florida probably belonged to the British military commanders who countered Indian suspicion with presents, promises of fair treatment, and patient explanations of the change of colonial administration. [45] These tactics had considerable success.

The English officers attempted to establish rapport with the Indians by means of integrated councils, negotiation, orations, and the influence of traders and interpreters. Relationships of faith and trust, however, required time. Hoping to convince the Indians of England's fidelity to previous French commitments, Major Farmar delivered several harangues to the Creek and Choctaw nations in the neighborhood of Mobile. The major met with the Indians in the winter of 1763–64. Governor d'Abbadie assisted his English successor at the meetings attended by the Alibamons and Choctaws. Farmar promised his audiences food and other supplies and pledged "Presents to those who shall deserve them." [46] The officer implied that gifts would only be provided if peace was observed and the murder of Europeans outlawed. Major Farmar sought agreements with the indigenous people which would guarantee punishment for any murderers of either English or Indian nationality. Such a policy proposed "Blood for Blood." He also instructed his subordinates to insure that traders bartered fairly with the Indians. Imprisonment or banishment was authorized by Farmar as suitable penalties for unlicensed and dishonest dealings. [47]

Realizing the relationship of Indian satisfaction to the welfare of his settlements, Robert Farmar issued appropriate orders to the commanders of all West Florida outposts. His commands concerned soldiers and civilians. The major obviously intended to organize military supervision of all native affairs in an attempt to secure peace in West Florida.

> You are on no pretence what ever, to suffer the men under your Command to abuse, ill treat, or take any thing from the present Inhabitants, or the Native Indians, but oblige them to pay a reasonable price for what they want, keeping up a Strict Discipline, and not to suffer less then a Corporal and four men, to go any distance from the Fort, that his Majesty's Troops may not be exposed, or Insulted.
>
> You are to use your utmost endeavours to Cultivate, and preserve a good understanding with the Indians, obliging all that Trade with them, to deal Justly, taking care that they give full, and just weight, and measure, such as shall attempt in any respect to defraud them, Seize their persons, and Effects, and after satisfying the Indians (which I take for granted will be the Injured party) oblige the aggressors to leave the Country, that by these acts of Strict Justice, the Indians may receive a good impression of the English Nation, which their late Masters have endeavoured by every artifice to figure to them in the worst Light. [48]

In his persuasive speeches, Rober Farmar stressed the importance of mutual efforts to keep peace for all peoples of West Florida. The English officer hoped to achieve accord with the neighboring tribes by suggesting that "white and red men" could together, under "the great Emperor of England" share the burdensome affairs of Florida. [49] One of Farmar's appeals therefore stated:

> I hope you our good Friends and Brothers, will endeavour to maintain and keep up that Friendship, and harmony that ought to subsist between white and red men, for the mutual Happiness of both.

If you continue to act as good Brothers, I shall not fail to make the great Emperor of England my Master acquainted therewith, who will not fail to make manifest to you the tender regard he has for you as his Children, and who earnestly wishes the red men will use their endeavours to procure peace amongst themselves as they are now become Children of the great English Emperor.[50]

After the interval of military government in West Florida, Governor George Johnstone and John Stuart cooperated to stabilize Indian affairs in the province. The employment of Superintendent Stuart to manage such matters in the Floridas complied with royal instructions to all governments in America. Colonial governors were urged "to appoint a proper person or persons to assemble and treat with the said INDIANS, promising and assuring them of protection and friendship on our part and delivering them such presents as shall be sent to you for that purpose." [51] The crown also advised the governors of British America "UPON NO account to molest or disturb them in the possession of said parts of the said province as they at present occupy or possess, BUT to use the best means you can for the conciliating their affections and uniting them to our government." [52] The two officials faithfully observed the instructions from overseas. Realizing the necessity of coordinating all colonial services toward the solution of Indian problems, Johnstone and Stuart jointly issued regulations for West Florida. According to mutual agreement, the governor and superintendent ordered the enforcement of the laws by both civil and military authorities. Superintendent Stuart expected officers of his department to work in conjunction with provincial commanders and governors. Stuart departed from West Florida in June, 1765, after completing his arrangements with Johnstone and concluding the Indian congresses. Later in the same year he returned to Florida to assist Governor James Grant at the Picolata Congress.[53]

While residing in West Florida, John Stuart prepared a set of nineteen regulations with the approval of Governor George Johnstone. The new code was written to eliminate trading irregularities among the Chickasaws, Choctaws, and Creeks, and to organize government control of all barter with the West Florida Indians. Imperial authority over Indian life in America appeared as an implicit principle in the Proclamation of 1763, but control of native relations was explicitly proposed by the Plan for the Future Management of Indian Affairs. The latter plan evidently contained many of Stuart's ideas concerning the centralization of the Southern Department. He recommended that the superintendents possess sufficient power to institute and enforce regulations for Indian commerce in America.[54]

Resolving to employ "the Plan" in West Florida, Stuart obtained Johnstone's promise to make the traders obey the restrictions under threat of license and bond forfeiture. With the cooperation of George Johnstone, the superintendent then procured Indian endorsement for the establishment of trade regulations. The West Florida tribes as well as their agents approved the program, but Stuart and his commissaries were unable to police their system or enforce its provisions. Unfortunately, the plan failed because of outside interference. Colonists in other provinces could not be convinced to accept trade limitations. Less than six months after the Pensacola Congress, Governor Johnstone discontinued his efforts in behalf of the commercial scheme. When unlicensed traders from other southern colonies entered Florida and continually ignored the laws in their transactions with the Chickasaws, Choctaws, and Creeks, the governor lost interest in Stuart's plans and regulations.[55]

Superintendent Stuart's regulations generally protected the socioeconomic interests of the Indian people of West Florida. The laws demanded fair trade with all Florida aborigines. In every transaction traders were ordered to use the same weights and measures as "shall conform exactly to the standard weight and measure lodged with the commissary." [56] For purposes of supervision, John Stuart confined Indian commerce to the towns where negotiations would be open to observation. He also placed tariffs upon all goods passing from colonial traders to Indians. Physical abuse of the natives was strictly forbidden. The superintendent also prohibited the use of Indians, half-breeds, or Negroes as hired employees. Without the permission of the commissaries, traders were not allowed to hold assemblies or secret and private negotiations with the indigenous people. Other prohibitions included the sale of "spirituous liquor," rifled guns, and shot, and the unlimited purchase of undressed hides and pelts. Stuart's regulations even limited the amount of credit that could be extended to West Florida natives; a local Indian could not obtain credit beyond thirty pounds of deerskins. Finally, the prices of all items of barter were fixed and attached to a comprehensive list of trade provisions.[57]

The culmination of John Stuart's official visit to West Florida occurred during the spring of 1765. From March to June, the superintendent and his staff labored to negotiate Indian treaties which would establish friendly relations and definite channels of colonial trade. Stuart also hoped to arrange "permanent" boundaries in the new province. The existence of West Florida required extensive land cessions from the Chickasaws, Choctaws, and Creeks. Talks with those tribes were begun on March twenty-sixth and concluded two and one-half months later. Superintendent Stuart generally attained his ambitious objectives in West Florida. At Mobile the Indian superintendent arranged a compact with the Chickasaws and Choctaws, and at Pensacola the Upper and Lower Creeks reluctantly agreed to a similar treaty.[58]

The successful negotiations in West Florida were really the work of English officials in conjunction with Chevalier Montault de Monberaut. Although the correspondence of Superintendent Stuart and Governor Johnstone neglected to mention Monberaut, the Frenchman actually deserved their praise for his crucial service in the organization of the Indian congresses and the conclusion of treaties with Chickasaw, Choctaw, and Creek tribes in 1765. Montault de Monberaut became a British civil servant in December, 1764, after twenty-five years of colonial life in French Louisiana. Since this resident of Mobile found difficulty in the disposition of his property, he decided to accept employment in British West Florida. Montault de Monberaut approached the military occupants of Mobile seeking an appointment in Indian affairs. Lieutenant Colonel James Robertson and General Thomas Gage enthusiastically agreed to enlist the services of Monberaut whose influence with the Creeks and reputation among the Frenchmen in Florida were even well known to the British army. Governor Johnstone and Superintendent Stuart subsequently appointed the French officer as deputy superintendent of Indian affairs. In this position, Chevalier Montault de Monberaut contributed his experience, *savoir-faire,* and influence with the Indians to the congresses of 1765. The Frenchman creditably served his English employers at Mobile and Pensacola. His personal appeals, conversations, and harangues provided climactic assistance to the Anglo-Indian conferences in both cities. After only six months of service as deputy superintendent, Montault de Monberaut had helped Great Britain settle some of the burdensome problems in the province of West Florida.[59]

The Mobile Congress lasted from March 26 to April 4, 1765. Stuart's congress was actually the second Indian assembly in Mobile. Major Farmar organized the first meetings in June, 1764, less than a year before Stuart arrived in West Florida. The British commander met with the Chickasaws and Choctaws to obtain guarantees of free passage for Major Loftus and his Mississippi expedition; security from Chickasaw and Choctaw interference, however, could not protect the Loftus command from other Indian attacks. The conference established by John Stuart considered several other significant topics besides peaceful relations. Because of the importance of the Mobile Congress, Governor Johnstone and several members of the council of West Florida joined the English deputation that conferred with the chiefs of the Chickasaws and Choctaws.[60]

During the proceedings the Indians were treated to daily feasts and the persuasive speeches of Stuart and Johnstone. In their talks, the English delegates stressed the necessity of friendship and land cessions. Seeking to secure additional property from the natives, the Englishmen advised the congress that "the Great King George" could not properly entertain his "Red Children" in the following year if his new province was not awarded a grant of productive land. Both Chickasaws and Choctaws, eagerly awaiting the distribution of presents, agreed with the request for territory and promised to continue peaceful relations with Great Britain. On April 4, 1765, the Mobile Congress was concluded with an Anglo-Indian treaty. After surrendering their French medals and signing the seven-article agreement, six Indian chiefs received great medals and five lesser chiefs were given small medals in a special military ceremony. The festivities included the discharge of cannon and the drums and fifes of the Twenty-second and Thirty-fourth Regiments. Six Choctaw villages shunned the conferences because of their continuing allegiance to France. Somewhat later, on April twenty-second, their representatives journeyed to Mobile and offered their assent to the treaty.[61]

Great Britain gained a number of concessions in the Mobile treaty. The Indian chiefs agreed to "a perfect & perpetual Peace & Sincere friendship" with His Majesty King George the Third. Chickasaw and Choctaw representatives also promised to restrain their tribesmen from inciting disturbances and molesting or stealing the property of English settlers. The Indians vowed "to give the Utmost attention to preserve & maintain Peace & friendship between their people & the King of Great Brittain and his Subjects and Shall not Commit or Permit any kind of Hostility, injuries or damage whatsoever Against them henceforward." [62] Without any persuasion, the native delegates readily agreed to "blood for blood" punishment for English and Indian murderers. Stuart and Johnstone were even able to convince the Chickasaws and Choctaws to assist the West Florida government in the apprehension of colonial fugitives. In regard to regulation of trade, the indigenous assembly willingly accepted "specified" prices and rates. Finally, the chiefs granted Great Britain a relatively generous land cession north and west of Mobile. The Indian boundary extended approximately fifty miles north of Mobile, west to the Mississippi Valley at a distance of about fifty to seventy-five miles from the Gulf Coast, and north again to the meeting of the Mississippi and Yazoo Rivers. Natchez and the east bank of the Mississippi River to the northern junction of the Yazoo River were included within the ceded territories.[63]

The British administrators certainly appreciated their unexpected success in the conferences. Great Britain actually yielded the Indians little of importance. The governor and superintendent only promised to "encourage Persons to furnish & Supply the Said Nations of Indians aforesaid with all sorts of Goods usually carried amongst them in the manner which they now are, and which will be Sufficient to answer all their wants." [64] Governor Johnstone was especially proud of the treaty. After remarking to their superiors that the "Creeks and Chactaws have been educated in an inveterate Hatred to the English," [65] the governor of West Florida and the superintendent boasted of their results in a detailed report to Whitehall.

> The Effect of the whole has been, First by the Congress at Mobile to gain the principal men of the Chactaw Nation; To induce the whole to give up their French Medals and Commissions, and accept of others from His Majesty; to grant to the Province a Tract of Rich, Convenient, and extensive Territory; to agree to render Blood for Blood; to restore Negroes and Deserters, and to refrain from plundering the Inhabitants; to submit to the Regulations of Trade prescribed; and really, to their Honor be it said, tho' they were near two Months at Mobile, from first to last, and often two thousand men together; Yet no Damage worthy of notice, was committed.[66]

The Creek Congress at Pensacola commenced on May 27, 1765, and was concluded a week later on June 4, 1765. Once again Johnstone and Stuart presided at the Indian meetings. The Upper Creeks were officially represented by The Mortar, Emistsiguo, Gun Merchant, and Devols Land Lord. Lower Creeks followed the leadership of Topalga, The White Lieutenant, and The Beaver Tooth King. At the treaty ceremonies, the Upper Creek chiefs acquired titles of

Great Medal Chiefs, while the Lower Creek chiefs were given the authority of Small Medal Chiefs. Since a multitude of Indians attended the Pensacola Congress, their English hosts reluctantly spent 1,700 pounds for gifts and entertainment. General Thomas Gage wanted Creek friendship at any cost.[67]

Although expensive, the conference at Pensacola created a cordial atmosphere for negotiations. In demonstration of his affection, The Mortar visited the West Florida council chambers to present Governor Johnstone and John Stuart with the symbolic white wings signifying peace and friendship. The Mortar's visit apparently pleased the entire assembly. Amid other peaceful gestures, the English officials were fanned with eagle tails, although The Mortar later complained that the presence of the "red-crossed" flag of Great Britain indicated hostility.[68] The Creeks were not as easily conciliated as the Chickasaws and Choctaws. But the Indian superintendent eventually convinced The Mortar of England's good will and arranged a treaty satisfying all the Creek tribes. On May 28, 1765, the assembled chiefs signed the British agreement.

The terms of the second treaty were quite similar to the arrangements made in Mobile. "Blood for Blood" again appeared as an essential provision. The Indians obviously appreciated Article IV which stated "And if any white Man shall kill or Murder an Indian such white Man, shall be tried for the offence, in the same manner as if he had Murdered a White man & if found Guilty shall be executed accordingly in the presence of some of the Relations of the Indian who may be Murdered if they chuse to be present." [69] Naturally, the pact included other boundary provisions. After a session of haggling, the Creeks ceded Great Britain a section of territory—approximately 15 miles wide—around Pensacola. The Creek boundary limited the capital of West Florida to a coastal location where infertile soils and sands would dissatisfy later settlers. There were also different prices for trade goods in the two treaties. British commodities cost the Creeks more money because John Stuart could not lower the existing rates employed by the colonial traders of Georgia and South Carolina. Stuart's agreement with the Creeks also omitted the section of the Chickasaw and Choctaw treaty concerning the establishment of commissaries in native territory.[70]

On June 12, 1765, Governor Johnstone and Superintendent Stuart informed Whitehall of their accomplishments at Pensacola. The two officials recognized that the second congress was probably not as popular with the Indians as the first meetings at Mobile. But they felt confident "with proper Attention, in future, that they [the Creeks] may be perfectly conciliated to our Interest." [71] Johnstone and Stuart also admitted that the government would have to continue the gift-giving customs of the previous rulers of West Florida. Despite the disturbing knowledge that Indian presents were necessary for peace, the West Florida report indicated England's improved position after the meetings at Mobile and Pensacola.

> The Effect with the Creeks has been, To induce the Mortar, and five hundred of his Warriors, together with most of the Principal men of the Nation, especially those who had been opposed to our Interest, and who had never set foot upon English Land before, to come down to Pensacola. They have given us a tolerable large Boundary, tho not all which we could have wished, being only about fifteen miles back, which does not reach the rich Soil, and so around the Sea Coast, up along the East side of the Bay of Mobile, as high as the Confluence of the River Alibamont. They have likewise solemnly promised to give Blood for Blood for the future; to refrain from any Outrages, to admit a free Trade, and to deliver up Deserters. Tho' they did not depart in so perfect a good Humor as the Chactaws, yet we have Reason to believe, with proper Attention, in future, that they may be perfectly conciliated to our Interest. The Mortar has really all the Talents which Fame reports of him, and his Friendship ought to be cultivated, if we wish to preserve Peace with his Nation. But, we think it our Duty to say, that, unless Presents are given, or a superior Force maintained in the Province, it will be impossible to insure that Blessing for any Duration.
> The French have accustomed both the Upper Creeks and Chactaws to such large Presents, that it will be difficult to break that Custom, until they are convinced of Our Superiority and their Dependence, which can only be done by Time, and a well regulated Trade restraining the general Licences; Or, by an immediate War.[72]

An Indian settlement for East Florida followed in November, 1765. The Creek Congress was convened at Picolata approximately five and one-half months after John Stuart completed his conference at Pensacola. Prior to the negotiations at Picolata, the government of East Florida established very cautious contacts with the neighboring Indians. Governor James Grant intended to avoid meeting the Creeks en masse until the arrival of Superintendent Stuart and the organization of local native assemblies.[73]

In a letter to the Lords of Trade, the governor announced that he would "avoid having any Intercourse with them 'till that time (Stuart's arrival)." [74] Grant also said he would feel relieved if more troops were available at St. Augustine. "We have not 200 men to do Duty, which are by no means sufficient to protect this Country against a numerous Nation of Indians consisting of near four thousand Men." [75] The new governor almost immediately realized the importance of presents for peaceful relations. Following the policy of his Spanish predecessors in East Florida, James Grant recommended that "it will no doubt be expedient, to give them a favorable Impression . . . by making presents to them, which will keep them in good Humor, and will induce them to relinquish any Claim, which they may pretend to have to the new Country." [76] The British governments of East and West Florida would reluctantly appease the Indians with the same expensive policy previously employed by France and Spain. When local tribes visited both St. Augustine and Apalache before the arrival of Superintendent Stuart, they were welcomed with gifts and provisions. The Creek Assembly finally convened in November, 1765, but a "gift" policy remained in all future Indian relations. Even after Stuart's congresses were completed in 1765, the distribution of presents continued throughout the British Period. [77]

Yearly subsidies later supported Florida expenses for the purchase of Indian provisions. The treasury forwarded special funds to the governments of East and West Florida. East Florida was initially assigned 1,500 pounds in 1764, but thereafter received 1,000 pounds regularly each year. Financial assistance for West Florida included an annual payment of 2,000 pounds to cover the cost of native goods. British money provided such assorted provisions as combs, knives, razors, scissors, hoes, hatchets, pots, blankets, calico, shirts, corn, rice, and rum. [78] Indian supplies were very expensive. But trading goods cost Great Britain considerably less than the price of savage wars which seemed frequently to be related to native feelings of dissatisfaction.

Until the arrival of John Stuart, the settlers of East Florida attempted to satisfy those tribesmen who visited St. Augustine and Apalache and demanded supplies. St. Augustine authorities waited more than two years for an Indian settlement. From the summer of 1763 to the late fall of 1765, the colonists continued to be apprehensive of Indian aggression. Stuart initially visited Apalache in September, 1764, to assure the nearby Creeks that their boundaries would be strictly respected. His meeting at Apalache temporarily mollified the Creek chiefs. The Indian frontier thereafter remained peaceful but ominous prior to the Picolata Congress. [79]

John Stuart finally arrived in St. Augustine in the autumn of 1765. To the obvious satisfaction of Governor Grant, the superintendent almost immediately planned an Indian conference. James Grant was especially eager to arrange a Creek convention in order to fix the boundaries of his province and proceed with property settlement. The Picolata Congress officially opened on November fifteenth, and after three days of talks a treaty was concluded on November 18, 1765. This session only incurred expenses of 500 pounds, 1,200 pounds less than the cost of the Pensacola Congress.[80]

On November 15, 1765, Governor James Grant, Superintendent John Stuart, and his deputy superintendent convened their assembly with the Upper and Lower Creek chiefs. Because the Indians refused to cross the St. John's River with their horses, Picolata, rather than St. Augustine, became the site of the East Florida Congress. The Creeks were represented by Tallechea, Estimé, Captain Aleck, Sempoyaffé, Latchigé, Wioffké, Chayhagé, Tellegeia, and several other prominent headmen and warriors. Cow-keeper, chief of Latchaway (Alachua) declined to attend the gathering because of "the Sickness of his Family" and the Alachua chief did not visit St. Augustine until somewhat later, on December 23, 1765. When Cow-keeper learned of the generous reception given the other Creek chiefs, he traveled to St. Augustine for an eight day sojourn. An entourage of sixty persons accompanied the chief. After receiving a great medal, Cow-keeper and his family departed for home with many presents and provisions.[81]

At Picolata the British commissioners quickly discerned that the Indians were "disposed to be Refractory" concerning territorial cessions. A postponement of the talks was even considered. But the younger Creek chiefs, anxious to acquire rum and presents, convinced their elders to cede England "a little Land, of which they had such Plenty." [82]

> The Leading Men appeared Averse to Our Measures, expressed the greatest Indignation at the Interpreters, for daring to make such proposals, And upon One of the young Ones saying that he did not see why they came to the Meeting, if they intended to differ with the white People about a little Land, of which they had such Plenty, that he could see no good Reason for their Conduct, & therefore thought that the Land should be given up—Our other Friends immediately altered their Sentiments, and agreed in Opinion with him, the rest of their Council did not oppose the Measure, and when they were in this Disposition We sent for them to agree about

the Terms for Limits, And the Treaty was signed the 18th of November, by which they have Ceded a very extensive Territory to His Majesty, which in all probability will be sufficient for the Settlement of this Province for many Years.[83]

All negotiations were concluded on Sunday, November 17, 1765, and ceremonies honoring the various chiefs followed on Monday. According to precedents established in West Florida, the festivities included the presentation of English medallions to attending Indian chieftains. Tallechea, Estimé, and Captain Aleck accepted large medals, while small medals were awarded to Sempoyaffé, Latchigé, Wioffké, and Chayhagé. "The Superintendent presented the Chiefs to the Govʳ who hung the Medals about their Necks the Superintendᵗ afterwards gave them a Charge Explaining to them the dutys of their Office which ceremony was performed under the discharge of the Fort Guns repeated by those on board the East Florida Schooner." [84]

A treaty of five articles was prepared at Picolata. This agreement basically contained the same terms as the other treaties. Indian arrangements in East Florida, however, excluded trade or commissary stipulations since Stuart's system was only applicable to West Florida trade. The first article bound all parties to "a Perfect Sincere & Perpetual Peace and Lasting friendship." According to Article I, the Creeks were obliged to follow a peaceful policy which would never permit them to perpetrate any act of hostility, injury, or damage against the subjects of the Great King George III. In the second article, Great Britain vaguely promised to support the Creek nations with adequate provisions to "Answer all their wants." The third and fourth articles established a "Blood for Blood" punishment for individuals guilty of international murder. Article V settled the Anglo-Indian boundaries of East Florida. Great Britain was ceded all territory east of the St. John's River as well as a large section of land on the west bank of that waterway. After the Creek treaty, East Florida actually included substantial territories north and west of the St. John's River. England acquired all the lands bounded on the north by the St. Mary's River, on the south by Lake George (seventy miles southwest of St. Augustine), and on the west by an inland line extending from the St. Mary's River to Lake George, approximately thirty-five miles from the Atlantic coast. Below Lake George, the boundary followed the course of the St. John's River and a coastal line running along the entire edge of the peninsula to the Apalachicola River. The belt of British territory included about ten to fifteen miles of area along the Atlantic and Gulf Coasts. James Grant and John Stuart signed the agreement for England and thirty-one chiefs of thirteen nations placed their seals on the November treaty.[85]

Other assemblies were convened during the British era in both East and West Florida. Since the first conferences could not settle all indigenous disputes, further negotiations were later required, especially in West Florida where war erupted between the Creeks and the new English colony. In East Florida, Governor James Grant urged the Board of Trade to organize new Indian congresses. "A Measure of that kind, when we have nothing to ask, would be very pleasing to them. It would remove the Suspicion they have of our Intention to get possession of their whole Country, & would gain their Affections at no great Expence. The Superintendant is of the same way of thinking." [86]

The Province of East Florida enjoyed very peaceful relations with the Creek tribes following the Picolata Congress. Stuart's arrangements apparently satisfied the Creeks, although later reports from Apalache and Don Juan Elixio de la Puente suggested that many natives preferred Spanish administration of Florida. Such reports obviously related Spanish prejudice and opinion. Puente, who relished every rumor supporting his feeling that English possession of the old colony was in jeopardy, claimed that the Indians wanted the Spaniards to return as rulers of Florida. Puente's assertions were probably wishful rather than real. Regardless of their complaints and criticisms of British dominion, the East Florida Indians generally cooperated with the new residents of St. Augustine and Apalache, despite Puente hopes to the contrary.[87]

In November, 1767, Lord Shelburne, president of the Board of Trade, wrote to St. Augustine congratulating Governor James Grant for the tranquil state of affairs in his colony: "Your Manner of treating the Indians has been very judicious, and the perfect Tranquility in which the Colony under your Command has remained while they have been exposed to several Insults in the neighbouring Province, bears ample Testimony in your Favour." [88] The governments of both Floridas continued to offer the aborigines gifts and supplies in conjunction with occasional conferences. But the Indians of West Florida appeared to be much less receptive to the profitable and peaceful overtures of the British officials than the Creeks of East Florida.[89]

Indian affairs in the Floridas were not significantly affected by the Spanish exodus. Spain abandoned Florida and the Florida Indians. The Spaniards carried away their few Christianized allies and willed the remaining Indians and the unpleasant indigenous problems to the future occupants of the peninsula. Spanish Cubans, however, continued to trade with the East Florida natives during the British Period. To the chagrin of English colonial officials, Lower Creeks and Cubans continued to barter in Havana, and Spanish fishing vessels surreptitiously transported goods and Creek chiefs to and from Cuba.[90] Except for such limited contacts, Spain left Florida without further interest in Indian activities.

Soon after the acquisition of Florida, Great Britain sought to pacify the suspicious and somewhat hostile inhabitants. The spreading Pontiac rebellion in the north required immediate attention and the British colonial office wished to secure the south from the contagion of native insurrection. Initially, the King's Proclamation of 1763 provided the legal authority to stabilize Anglo-Indian relations and establish peace in the Floridas. But the new provinces and the Indian superintendency inherited the actual obligation of employing the proclamation to satisfy native complaints and demands. In West Florida, British officials were fortunate to secure the services of the French government and Montault de Monberaut in their efforts to conciliate the Chickasaws, Choctaws, and Creeks. Ultimately, the distribution of gifts and the organization of occasional congresses became British devices to obtain accord with the Indians. In the first few years of English rule, such colonial measures seemed to be successful. Later Indian affairs, however, were altered by mutual antagonism and treaty violations.

10

The Triple-Nation Transfer
of Florida

Spanish Florida was smoothly transferred to British control following the ratification of the Treaty of Paris. The official exchange of authority occurred in the summer and early autumn of 1763. Despite the illegal property activities of England and Spain, the two European states typically obeyed the treaty as international law. The transfer of Florida therefore followed without significant complications and with surprisingly few incidents of controversy. Real estate transactions produced the only serious sources of discord between the governments of Great Britain and Spain. But such problems of colonial proprietorship seemed considerably less important across the seas from America. Property irregularities really affected the subjects of the two states rather than the relationship between George III and Charles III.

The process of imperial transfer was obviously accommodated by Spain's decision to evacuate and resettle the total population of Florida. Instructions for the abandonment of the old colony arrived in St. Augustine early in April, 1763. Spanish Floridians and their possessions were removed to New Spain and Cuba before the beginning of any significant British movement to Florida. The hasty evacuation was calculated and not coincidental. Because the subjects of Great Britain and Spain experienced limited contact with each other, there were correspondingly limited opportunities for international strife during the exchange. Most of the administrative and political problems of the period were actually related to the awkward operations of migration and settlement which each nation faced from 1763 to 1765. The need for urgency intensified all activities of transfer. Spain wished to liberate its citizenry from English influence as soon as possible, while Great Britain sought with alacrity to establish Florida as an area for future colonization. Spanish anxiety seemed to be related to the arduous tasks of resettling and reemploying several thousand Florida people. Simultaneously, British energies were fully extended to the work of organizing and populating the new provinces.

The French surrender of Louisiana created a number of international conflicts. Anglo-French relations actually deteriorated with the arrival of the first British soldiers at Mobile Bay. French delays and procrastination in the cession of Mobile initially damaged the intercolonial transfer and provided an unfriendly atmosphere for the development of later disputes. The contested evacuation of Fort Condé further complicated the affairs of England and France. Continued French occupation of West Florida probably exacerbated all international activities and contributed daily friction to the period of transition. The exchange was finally troubled by English property regulations and loyalty requirements. French Louisiana passed under British control far more controversially than Spanish Florida.

England and Spain worked well together to achieve harmony during the official and demographic transfer of the old colony. Consequently, the cession was quietly and quickly concluded. St. Augustine and Pensacola passed easily from Spanish to English rule, but the odyssey of Captain John Harries unfortunately detained the delivery of Apalache to British dominion. The delay of imperial exchange at the "remote frontier," however, had no serious repercussions. Although the Harries affair incited certain international tensions, the responsible officials of Great Britain and Spain (General Thomas Gage and Governor Conde de Ricla) resolved the situation and calmly directed the exchange of control at Apalache. Outside of San Marcos de Apalache, the other unpleasant incidents and personality conflicts that occurred in the period of transition were likewise pacified under the orders of the Spanish and English commanders. Local issues never became important. Both countries simply shunned any altercations in the transfer of Florida which could have affected their post-war conciliation.

Many more incidents of controversy appeared in the cession of Louisiana. Although only one city and several outposts were transferred to English control, a number of conflicts emerged from the colonial exchange. Mobile became the center of the struggle. The French governors, d'Abbadie and Kerlérec, and the British soldiers, Farmar and Loftus, were all intimately involved in the difficult transfer of Louisiana. All of these officials contributed to the bad relations between France and Great Britain. The issues of discord, however, were international. They included the delayed surrender of Mobile, the military state of Fort Condé after the French departure, and the disastrous fate of the Loftus expedition. The transfer of Louisiana was apparently an awkward and tense intercolonial event.

The emigration of Spanish Catholicism from Florida and the entrance of Anglicanism into the new provinces were accomplished without complications. Actually, the two systems had few opportunities for intercolonial contacts. With the movement of the Spanish clergy to New Spain and Cuba in 1763–64, all religious authority over Florida devolved upon the Episcopal Church of England. Anglicanism simply replaced Spanish Catholicism and coexisted with French Catholicism. Anglican ministers thereafter managed the religious life of East and West Florida for the next nineteen years. Yet, Catholicism was permitted to exist in Mobile and New Smyrna. Frenchmen at Mobile and Minorcans at New Smyrna enjoyed Catholic services without interference. Great Britain guaranteed toleration according to the provisions of the Treaty of Paris. The religious transfer of French Louisiana and Spanish Florida was uneventful, although the Catholic clergy understandably complained about the seizure of Church properties at St. Augustine.

Indian affairs in Florida were abandoned by the Spaniards as they transported their people and possessions to other areas in the Spanish Indies. Except for those converts who sailed with the Floridians from St. Augustine, Pensacola, and Apalache, the remaining natives of the colony were ignored during the transfer and evacuation of Florida. Frenchmen also abandoned their indigenous allies in eastern Louisiana. But before leaving, French officials helped establish peaceful relations between the English soldiers and their former native enemies. In the future all the Indians east of the Mississippi River would be under British rule.

Great Britain inherited an ominous situation with many indigenous problems. The new provinces needed a colonial policy which would improve Indian relations and maintain peace in southeastern America. Land for settlement was also in urgent demand. Somehow the tribes of French Louisiana and Spanish Florida would have to be convinced to cede generous grants of territory to the new colonies. The King's Proclamation of 1763 almost immediately provided an imperial solution to colonial problems in East and West Florida. Effectively employing the proclamation, a powerful Indian superintendency, native congresses, and a program of gift-distribution, England managed to stabilize the frontier in the early years after the departure of France and Spain.

The transfer of sovereignty in Florida was complicated by Anglo-Spanish property problems. Since both England and Spain adopted "national" interpretations of the provisions of the Treaty of Paris, international law was readily compromised during the transition period. In 1763–64 France apparently avoided involvement in illegal property activities. Meanwhile, the other two imperial states simply ignored or evaded those articles of the Treaty of 1763 which conflicted with their political and / or economic objectives in Florida. Through the employment of English agents, Spain conspired to sell real estate beyond the stipulated limits of the treaty. Spanish realtors attempted to preserve the value of property by negotiating fictitious sales with unscrupulous speculators in St. Augustine and Pensacola. Great Britain also acted unilaterally and arbitrarily. British officials recognized only those transactions that conformed with Whitehall's plans for East and West Florida.

The subjects of both countries subsequently forfeited their investments and territory because of such policy. Despite loyalty demands, French proprietorship in West Florida was not similarly affected by British occupation. Great Britain accepted the principle of property exchange between Franco-Spanish and British inhabitants of Florida, but denied those transactions which threatened the colonial system presented in the October Proclamation of 1763. National objectives were more important than international law. Although later settlers enjoyed the land grant opportunities of the King's October Proclamation, the Spanish Church, many of the St. Augustine and Pensacola proprietors, and several English realtors suffered severe financial losses after the period of 1763–64. Certain opportunists like Fish and Gordon ultimately profited from the "time" provisions of the Treaty of Paris. They exacted exorbitant commissions as a price for representing Spain's interests in the new English provinces. Property became "the" economic problem of the period as Franco-Spanish Florida passed into English control.

The Proclamation of 1763 provided the colonial organization for Canada and the Floridas. From its provisions there emerged a monarchial plan for Florida populations and property. The October Proclamation also settled a number of long-standing problems in British America. Initially, the proclamation was prepared to meet the demands of the American Indians, many of whom were involved in Pontiac's insurrection. The general security of British America required Indian satisfaction and peace. Hoping that the opportunities of the king's declaration would divert frontiersmen away from the hunting grounds of the Alleghenies and toward the sparsely populated Florida provinces, British officials anticipated peaceful relations with the Indians. After 1762–63 the specter of Pontiac apparently haunted the personnel who formulated colonial policy. Because of the movement of population to the Floridas, the Board of Trade envisaged the economic development of the former French and Spanish colonies. Peace and prosperity were the expected possibilities of Florida settlement. The colonial office also intended to establish imperial control over all contacts with the indigenous population of America. Indian superintendencies, empowered by the crown, were expected to support monarchial power in the colonies and maintain peace with the native peoples.

Finally, the acquisition of Florida enabled England to settle the vexing controversy between Georgia and South Carolina regarding the control of the country south of the Altamaha River. Georgia's petition was ultimately approved. Employing the St. Mary's River as the northern boundary of East Florida, the Board of Trade disallowed South Carolina's claims, permitted Georgia to expand southward to the Florida border, and granted the new province the potentially rich lands between the St. John's and St. Mary's Rivers. The petition of Governor James Grant saved the St. Mary's River Valley for Florida. Great Britain's first few years in the Floridas were therefore devoted to the organization of the ceded territories, a project which appeared to be initially successful.

During the early months of the English occupation of Florida, the Spaniards effected a "total" evacuation of their colonial population. From April, 1763, to February, 1764, the Spanish and proselytized-Indian peoples of Florida emigrated en masse to Cuba and New Spain with all their portable possessions. Only a few Spaniards remained behind to manage the king's unfinished business in Florida. The emigration was complete, orderly, and swiftly executed. Spain relinquished little of value to the new residents of Florida except immovable property and real estate. After the exodus of 1763–64, England's legacy included the residential, municipal, and military buildings, the unfriendly Indians, and the territory of Florida.

For the Spanish crown, the evacuation provided an international victory over Great Britain. England obviously preferred to see the French and Spanish citizenry remain in the new provinces for their commercial potential. The Treaty of Paris deprived Spain of Florida and its strategic coastline, but the Spaniards salvaged their colonial population and possessions as they abandoned the peninsula. For the émigrés the exodus was a tragic experience. They suffered physically, psychologically, and financially in the process of resettlement in Cuba and New Spain. Disease and death and a subsistence life in Ceiba Mocha, Havana, or San Carlos were the unfortunate results of their migration from Florida. Almost all the immigrants suffered—civilians, clergymen, soldiers, and Indians. The memorial from San Agustín de la Nueva Florida clearly revealed the misery encountered by the exiles in their new environment. Spain emptied Florida of people, but resettlement seriously reduced the refugee population.

The transfer of Franco-Spanish Florida to British control was really accomplished with very few complications. In comparison to other colonial interchanges of the eighteenth century, it seemed especially uneventful. The Franco-Spanish exchange of Louisiana (1763–68) and the Anglo-Spanish exchange of Florida (1783–85) certainly included many more incidents of conflict and discord. Confusion, lawlessness, and even revolution accompanied those intercolonial adjustments. In 1763–64 the triple-nation transfer significantly altered the imperial structure of the New World. After the Treaty of Paris, the French empire was almost excluded from eastern America and the Spanish empire ceased to exist above the Gulf of Mexico. The Spanish Indies in Middle America were thereafter menaced by their proximity to the English colonies east of the Mississippi River. Without Florida the Spanish empire in America no longer controlled the Bahama Channel, the Gulf of Mexico, or the Caribbean Sea.

Appendices
Notes
Bibliography
Index

Appendix A

Articles IV, VII, XIX, and XX
of the February 10, 1763, Treaty of Paris*

IV. His most Christian majesty renounces all the pretensions which he has heretofore formed, or might form, to Nova Scotia, or Acadia, in all its parts, and guaranties the whole of it, and with all its dependencies, to the king of Great Britain: moreover his most Christian majesty cedes, and guaranties to his said Britannic majesty, in full right, Canada, with all its dependencies, as well as the island of Cape Breton, and all the other islands, and coasts, in the gulph and river St. Laurence, and, in general, every thing that depends on the said countries, lands, islands, and coasts, with the sovereignty, property, possession, and all rights acquired by treaty or otherwise, which the most Christian king, and the crown of France, have had, till now, over the said countries, islands, lands, places, coasts, and their inhabitants, so that the most Christian king cedes and makes over the whole to the said king, and to the crown of Great Britain, and that in the most ample manner and form, without restriction, and without any liberty to depart from the said cession and guaranty, under any pretence, or to disturb Great Britain in the possessions above mentioned. His Britannic majesty, on his side, agrees to grant the liberty of the Catholic religion to the inhabitants of Canada, he will, consequently, give the most precise and most effectual orders, that his new Roman Catholic subjects may profess the worship of their religion, according to the rites of the Romish Church, as far as the laws of Great Britain permit. His Britannic majesty further agrees, that the French inhabitants, or others who had been subjects of the most Christian king in Canada, may retire, with all safety and freedom, wherever they shall think proper, and may sell their estates, provided it be to subjects of his Britannic majesty,

* T. C. Hansard (ed.), *The Parliamentary History of England from the Earliest Period to the Year 1803* (London: T. C. Hansard, 1813), XV, 1291–1301; *The London Magazine*, March, 1763, 152–53.

and bring away their effects, as well as their persons, without being restrained in their emigration, under any pretence whatsoever, except that of debts, or of criminal prosecutions: the term limited for this emigration shall be fixed to the space of 18 months, to be computed from the day of the exchange of the ratifications of the present Treaty.

VII. In order to re-establish peace on solid and durable foundations, and to remove for ever all subject of dispute with regard to the limits of the British and French territories on the continent of America; it is agreed, that, for the future, the confines between the dominions of his Britannic majesty, and those of his most Christian majesty, in that part of the world, shall be fixed irrevocably by a line drawn along the middle of the river Mississippi, from its source to the river Iberville, and from thence, by a line drawn along the middle of this river, and the lakes Maurepas and Pontchartrain, to the sea; and for this purpose, the most Christian king cedes in full right, and guaranties to his Britannic majesty, the river and port of the Mobile, and every thing which he possesses, or ought to possess, on the left side of the river Mississippi, except the town of New Orleans, and the island in which it is situated, which shall remain to France; provided that the navigation of the river Mississippi shall be equally free, as well to the subjects of Great Britain, as to those of France, in its whole breadth and length, from its source to the sea, and expressly that part which is between the said island of New Orleans, and the right bank of that river, as well as the passage both in and out of its mouth: it is further stipulated, that the vessels belonging to the subjects of either nation, shall not be stopped, visited, or subjected to the payment of any duty whatsoever. The stipulations, inserted in the 4th Article, in favour of the inhabitants of Canada, shall also take place, with regard to the inhabitants of the countries ceded by this Article.

XIX. The king of Great Britain shall restore to Spain all the territory which he has conquered in the Island of Cuba, with the fortress of the Havanna, and this fortress, as well as all the other fortresses of the said island, shall be restored in the same condition they were in when conquered by his Britannic majesty's arms; provided, that his Britannic majesty's subjects, who shall have settled in the said island, restored to Spain by the present treaty, or those who shall have any commercial affairs to settle there, shall have liberty to sell their lands, and their estates, to settle their affairs, to recover their debts, and to bring away their effects, as well as their persons, on board vessels which they shall be permitted to send to the said island restored as above, and which shall serve for that use only, without being restrained on account of their religion, or under any other pretence whatsoever, except that of debts, or of criminal prosecutions: and for this purpose, the term of eighteen months is allowed to his Britannic majesty's subjects, to be computed from the day of the exchange of the ratifications of the present treaty: but as the liberty, granted to his Britannic majesty's subjects, to bring away their persons, and their effects, in the vessels of their nation, may be liable to abuses, if precautions were not taken to prevent them; it has been expressly agreed, between his Britannic majesty and his Catholic majesty, that the number of English vessels, which shall have leave to go to the said island restored to Spain, shall be limited, as well as the number of tons of each one; that they shall go in ballast; shall set sail at a fixed time; and shall make one voyage only; all the effects belonging to the English being embarked at the same time: it has been further agreed, that his Catholic majesty shall cause the necessary passports to be given to the said vessels; that, for the greater security, it shall be allowed to place two Spanish clerks, or guards, in each of the said vessels, which shall be visited in the landing-places, and ports of the said island restored to Spain, and that the merchandizes, which shall be found therein, shall be confiscated.

XX. In consequence of the restitution stipulated in the preceeding article, his Catholic majesty cedes and guaranties, in full right, to His Britannick majesty, Florida, with fort St. Augustin, and the bay of Pensacola, as well as all that Spain possesses on the continent of North America, to the east, or to the south east, of the river Mississippi. And, in general, every thing that depends on the said countries, and lands, with the sovereignty, property, possession, and all rights, acquired by treaties or otherwise, which the Catholic king, and the crown of Spain, have had, till now, over the said countries, lands, places, and their inhabitants; so that the Catholic king cedes and makes over the whole to the said king, and to the crown of Great Britain, and that in the most ample manner and form. His Britannick majesty agrees, on his side, to grant to the inhabitants of the countries, above ceded, the liberty of the Catholic religion: he will consequently give the most express and the most effectual orders, that his new Roman Catholic subjects may profess the worship of their religion, according to the rites of the Romish church, as far as the laws of Great Britain permit: his Britannick majesty further agrees, that the Spanish inhabitants, or others who had been subjects of the Catholic king in the said countries, may retire, with all safety and freedom, wherever they think proper; and may sell their estates, provided it be to his Britannick majesty's subjects, and bring away their effects, as well as their persons, without being restrained in their emigration, under any pretence whatsoever, except that of debts or of criminal prosecutions: the term, limited for this emigration, being fixed to the space of eighteen months, to be computed from the day of the exchange of the ratifications of the present treaty. It is moreover stipulated, that his Catholic majesty shall have the power to cause all the effects, that may belong to him, to be brought away, whether it be artillery, or other things.

Appendix B

The Puente-Fish Property Transaction
of July 28, 1764*

I further certify that another document, whose caption is as follows, sayeth:

"Account of the houses and lots, which, up to the present, have not been sold for want of purchasers, for which reason they have been sold or passed over in confidence to Jesse Fish, a vassal of his Britannic majesty, giving him only for the precise formality of the case a deed of sale upon the margin, of which is cited the value of each property and the name of the proprietor. They are as follows: to the south of the front entrance of the governor's house there appears to be included one hundred and eighty-five possessions, amongst which are the lot of ground and the walls of the new church, valued at one hundred dollars. At the foot of that statement is found the declaration of the aforementioned Jesse Fish in the following terms: I, Jesse Fish, a vassal of his Britannic majesty, do hereby acknowledge to have received from John Joseph Elijah Puente, general commissioner for the sale of property, both moveable and immoveable, belonging to Spanish subjects who left this garrison, two deeds, dated one on the twenty-fourth and the other on the twenty-seventh of this present month and year, in which a real sale is executed to me of all the houses and lots belonging to the aforesaid subjects as expressed in the preceding account or note, and at the low prices stated in the margin, giving the names of the proprietors of each house and lot of ground, upon which I do hereby declare that I have not paid to him anything on account of the said houses and lots, and that the aforesaid deeds or contracts of sale were made in confidence, and for the purpose of securing to the legitimate owners their right therein, which they were about to lose under the provi-

* U.S., Congress, Senate, *Claims of the Catholic Church Pertaining to Certain Properties Held by the United States,* 30th Congress, Second Session, January 30, 1849, Senate Executive Document 21, 29–31.

sions of twentieth article of the preliminaries for peace. I further add, that both now and hereafter I oblige myself to give to the aforesaid Puente, or to his order, a most punctual account, and payment of the proceeds of the said houses and lots—the sale of which I promise to verify as soon as purchasers may offer, and to the best possible advantage. In order that it may so appear, I sign these presents in St. Augustine, Florida, on this twenty-eighth day of July, one thousand seven hundred and sixty-four years.

"Jesse Fish."

Notes

List of archival abbreviations herein included:

AGI   Archivo General de las Indias
AGI, SD Archivo General de las Indias, Santo Domingo
AGNM   Archivo General de la Nación, México
BNM   Biblioteca Nacional de Madrid
EFP   East Florida Papers
NCCSR   North Carolina Collection of Spanish Records
PPC   Papeles Procedentes de Cuba
PRO:CO   Public Record Office: Colonial Office

1   Spanish Colonial Florida, 1513–1763

1.   *Tratado definitivo de paz concluido entre el rey nuestro señor y s. m. christianísima por una parte, y s. m. británica por otra, en Paris á 10. de Febrero de 1763, con sus artículos preliminares y la accesión de s. m. fidelísima á ellos, y al mismo tratado* (Madrid: En la Imprenta Real de la Gaceta, 1763), 3–97; T. C. Hansard (ed.), *The Parliamentary History of England from the Earliest Period to the Year 1803* (London: T. C. Hansard, 1813), XV, 1291–1305; Frances Gardner Davenport and Charles Oscar Paullin (eds.), *European Treaties Bearing on the History of the United States and Its Dependencies* (Washington, D.C.: Carnegie Institution of Washington, 1937), IV, 92–98.

2.   Manuel Giménez Fernández, *Las bulas alejandrinas de 1493 referentes á las Indias* (Sevilla: Escuela de Estudios Hispano-Americanos, 1944), 182–85; Anthony Kerrigan (trans.), *Barcia's Chronological History of the Continent of Florida . . . from the Year 1512, in which Juan Ponce de León Discovered Florida, until the Year 1722* (Gainesville: University of Florida Press, 1951), 191; John W. Monette, *Extent of Florida: History of the Discovery and Settlement of the Valley of the Mississippi by Three Great Powers, Spain, France, and Great Britain and the Subsequent Occupation, Settlement and Extension of*

Civil Government by the United States up to the Year 1846 (New York: Harper & Brothers, 1846) , 46.

3.   Florida's discovery, exploration, and colonization are thoroughly studied in the following histories and document collections: Herbert E. Bolton, *The Spanish Borderlands, A Chronicle of Old Florida and the Southwest* (New Haven: Yale University Press, 1921) , 1–79, and 120–65; Eugenio Ruidiaz y Caravia, *La Florida: su conquista y colonización por Pedro Menéndez de Avilés* (Madrid: Hijos de J. A. Garcia, 1893) , I, and II; Woodbury Lowery, *The Spanish Settlements within the Present Limits of the United States, 1513–1574* (New York: G. P. Putnam's Sons, 1905) , I, 3–338, and II, 123–53; Francis Parkman, *Pioneers of New France* (New York: Charles Scribner's Sons, 1915) , I, 9–158; Jeannette Thurber Conner (trans.) , *Pedro Menéndez de Avilés, Adelantado, Governor and Captain General of Florida: Memorial by Gonzalo Solís de Merás* (De Land, Florida: Florida State Historical Society, 1913) .

4.   Verne E. Chatelain, *The Defenses of Spanish Florida, 1565–1763* (Washington, D.C.: Carnegie Institution of Washington Publications, 1941) , 35–58.

5.   An intimate portrait of the last difficult years of the sixteenth century may be obtained in the following works: Jeannette Thurber Conner (trans. and ed.) , *The Colonial Records of Spanish Florida, 1570–1580* (De Land, Florida: Florida State Historical Society, 1925 and 1930) , I, and II; Charles W. Arnade, "The Failure of Spanish Florida," *The Americas*, XVI (January, 1960) , 271–84; Chatelain, *Defenses of Spanish Florida*, 35–58.

6.   Charles W. Arnade, *Florida on Trial* (Coral Gables, Florida: The University of Miami Press, 1959) , 1–90.

7.   Herbert E. Bolton, *The Mission as a Frontier Institution in the Spanish American Colonies* (El Paso: Texas Western College Press, 1960) , 1–23; Maynard Geiger, O.F.M., *The Franciscan Conquest of Florida, 1573–1618* (Washington, D.C.: Catholic University of America Press, 1931) , 52–70, and 116–265; John Tate Lanning, *The Spanish Missions of Georgia* (Chapel Hill: University of North Carolina Press, 1935) , *passim;* Rubén Varges Ugarte, S.J., *Los mártires de Florida, 1566–1572* (Lima: A. Castañeda, 1940) , 5–99; Felix Zubillaga, S.I., *La Florida; la misión jesuítica, 1566–1572 y la colonización española* (Roma: Institutum Historicum S.I., 1941) , 161–391.

8.   The term "uncivilized" refers here to a culture without the essential political and socio-economic organization that characterized certain other early Indian cultures in Mexico and Peru, e.g., the Aztecs, Incas, and Mayas.

9.   Arnade, "Failure of Spanish Florida," 277.

10.   Charles W. Arnade estimates that Spanish Florida in 1689 possessed about 14,500 people including Indians, Negroes, and 500 Spanish families. Charles W. Arnade, *The Siege of St. Augustine in 1702* (Gainesville: University of Florida Press, 1959) , 9–11. Before 1650 there were no more than 600 persons included within the St. Augustine *presidio*. Without the Indian population the colony therefore indicated little demographic importance. John R. Dunkle, "St. Augustine, Florida: A Study in Historical Geography," Ph.D. dissertation, Clark University, 1957) , 30–31.

11.   Mark F. Boyd, Hale G. Smith, and John W. Griffen, *Here They Once Stood: The Tragic End of the Apalache Missions* (Gainesville: University of Florida Press, 1951) , 1–106; Mark F. Boyd, "Further Considerations of the

Apalache Missions," *The Americas*, IX (April, 1953), 459–79; Chatelain, *Defenses of Spanish Florida*, 59–76; Arnade, "Failure of Spanish Florida," 271–81; Charles W. Arnade, "Cattle Raising in Spanish Florida, 1513–1763," *Agricultural History*, XXXV (July, 1961), 116–24.

12. Jeannette Thurber Conner, "The Nine Old Wooden Forts of St. Augustine," *Florida Historical Quarterly*, IV (January and April, 1926), 103–11; L. A. Vigneras, "Fortificaciónes de la Florida," *Anuario de Estudios Americanos*, XVI (1955), 533–52; Chatelain, *Defenses of Spanish Florida*, 59–76.

13. Queen Anne's War was the American colonial phase of the European War of the Spanish Succession, 1701–13. Herbert E. Bolton, *Arredondo's Historical Proof of Spains' Title to Georgia* (Berkeley: University of California Press, 1925), 1–111; Arnade, *Siege of St. Augustine*, 8–9 and 61.

14. Charles W. Arnade, "The English Invasion of Spanish Florida, 1700–1706," *Florida Historical Quarterly*, XLI (July, 1962), 29–37; Arnade, *Siege of St. Augustine*, 14–62; Mark F. Boyd, "Diego Peña's Expedition to Apalache and Apalachicola in 1716," *Florida Historical Quarterly*, XXVII (July, 1949), 1–27; Mark F. Boyd (trans.), "The Siege of St. Augustine by Governor Moore of South Carolina in 1702 as Reported to the King by Don Joseph de Zúñiga y Zerda, Governor of Florida," *Florida Historical Quarterly*, XXVI (April, 1948), 345–52; Boyd, et al., *Here They Once Stood*, 6–19; Chatelain, *Defenses of Spanish Florida*, 41–46.

15. Mark F. Boyd, unpublished history of eighteenth-century Florida and Don Juan Elixio de la Puente (Mark F. Boyd Library of Florida History, Tallahassee, Florida); John Jay TePaske, *The Governorship of Spanish Florida, 1700–1763* (Durham: Duke University Press, 1964), 77–107. This latter study offers a superb portrait of Spanish administration in the eighteenth century.

16. William E. Dunn, *Spanish and French Rivalry in the Gulf Region of the United States, 1678–1702* (Austin: University of Texas Bulletin No. 1705, 1917), 8–81 and 110–40; Lawrence C. Ford, *The Triangular Struggle for Spanish Pensacola, 1689–1739* (Washington, D.C.: Catholic University of America Press, 1939), 1–63; Irving A. Leonard, *The Spanish Approach to Pensacola, 1689–1693* (Albuquerque: Quivira Society, 1939), 1–76. The best sources of information on the New World expeditions of Tristan de Luna are found in the following works: Herbert I. Priestley, *Tristan de Luna, Conquistador of the Old South* (Glendale, California: Arthur H. Clark Company, 1936), 95–135; Herbert I. Priestley (trans. and ed.), *The Luna Papers: Documents Relating to the Expedition of Don Tristan de Luna y Arellano for the Conquest of Florida, 1557–1561* (De Land, Florida: Florida State Historical Society, 1928), I and II, *passim;* Lowery, *Spanish Settlements*, I, 351–81.

17. Dunn, *Spanish and French Rivalry in the Gulf Region*, 185–217; Ford, *Triangular Struggle for Spanish Pensacola*, 33–156.

18. Chatelain, *Defenses of Spanish Florida*, 88–91.

19. John Tate Lanning, *The Diplomatic History of Georgia* (Chapel Hill: University of North Carolina Press, 1936), 174–230; *A Geographical and Historical Description of the Principal Objects of the Present War in the West Indies, viz. Cartagena, Puerto Bello, La Vera Cruz, The Havana and St. Augustine Shewing Their Situation, Strength, Trade, etc.* (London: Printed for T. Gardner, 1741), 186–92.

20.   Fort Mosa was occupied by Negro fugitives from the English colonies. Governor Manuel de Montiano, according to the instructions of the Royal *cédula* of October 29, 1733, liberated the Negro slaves in 1738 and settled the new freedmen at Pueblo de Gracia Real de Santa Teresa de Mosa. Wilbur H. Siebert, "Slavery and White Servitude in East Florida," *Florida Historical Quarterly*, X (July, 1931), 3–23.

21.   *The St. Augustine Expedition of 1740: A Report to the South Carolina General Assembly, Reprinted from the Colonial Records of South Carolina* (Columbia: South Carolina Archives Department, 1954), xi–xxviii; Chatelain, *Defenses of Spanish Florida*, 88–92; TePaske, *Governorship of Spanish Florida*, 139–54.

22.   Chatelain, *Defenses of Spanish Florida*, 90–92; TePaske, *Governorship of Spanish Florida*, 154–57.

23.   U.S., *American State Papers: Public Lands* (Washington, D.C.: Gales and Seaton, 1834), I, 51–52; Lawrence Shaw Mayo, *The St. Mary's River, A Boundary* (Privately printed, 1914), 10–11; Lanning, *Diplomatic History of Georgia*, 230–34.

2   *The 1763 Treaty of Paris*

1.   Lawrence Henry Gipson, *The Great War for the Empire: The Culmination, 1760–1763*, VIII, *The British Empire before the American Revolution* (New York: Alfred A. Knopf, 1954), 228–52; Henry Folmer, *Franco-Spanish Rivalry in North America, 1524–1763* (Glendale, California: Arthur H. Clark Company, 1953), 307.

2.   Frances Gardner Davenport and Charles Oscar Paullin (eds.), *European Treaties Bearing on the History of the United States and Its Dependencies* (Washington, D.C.: Carnegie Institution of Washington, 1937), IV, 83–84; Zenab Esmat Rashed, *The Peace of Paris, 1763* (Liverpool: The University Press, 1951), viii, 38, 43–45, 115–91, 235–43; Gipson, *The Great War for the Empire: The Culmination*, VIII, 245–52; Folmer, *Franco-Spanish Rivalry in North America*, 307–10; Rafael Altamira, *A History of Spain*, trans. M. Lee (New York: D. Van Nostrand Company, Inc., 1951), 440–41; Francis Parkman, *Montcalm and Wolf*, III (New York: Charles Scribner's Sons, 1915), 241–44. For further information concerning the colonial politics of the family compact see, A. S. Aiton, "Spanish Colonial Reorganization under the Family Compact," *Hispanic American Historical Review*, XII (August, 1932), 269–80.

3.   Francis Russell Hart, *The Siege of Havana, 1762* (New York: Houghton Mifflin Company, 1931), 23–52; Gipson, *The Great War for the Empire: The Culmination*, VIII, 260–68, and 275–82; Antonio Ballesteros y Beretta, *Historia de España y su influencia en la historia universal* (Barcelonia: Salvat Editores, S.A., 1929), I, 163–65; Rashed, *Peace of Paris*, viii, 23, 201–11.

4.   Lawrence Henry Gipson, *The Great War for the Empire: The Victorious Years, 1758–1760*, VII, *The British Empire before the American Revolution* (New York: Alfred A. Knopf, 1949), 167–467; Gipson, *The Great War for the Empire: The Culmination*, VIII, *passim*.

5.   Rashed, *Peace of Paris*, 115–91; Parkman, *Montcalm and Wolfe*, III,

219–21; W. T. Selley, *England in the Eighteenth Century* (London: Adam and Charles Black, 1934), 90–92; William E. H. Lecky, *A History of England in the Eighteenth Century* (New York: D. Appleton and Company, 1891), II, 538–40.

6.   Rashed, *Peace of Paris*, 159–211; Folmer, *Franco-Spanish Rivalry in North America*, 308–9; Clarence W. Alvord, *The Mississippi Valley in British Politics* (Cleveland: Arthur H. Clark Company, 1917), I, 71–72; Charles L. Mowat, *East Florida as a British Province, 1763–1784* (Berkeley: University of California Press, 1943), 15.

7.   Alvord, *Mississippi Valley in British Politics*, I, 71–72; Folmer, *Franco-Spanish Rivalry in North America*, 308–10; Parkman, *Montcalm and Wolfe*, III, 248–50; Ballesteros, *Historia de España*, 165–66.

8.   Horace Walpole, *Memoirs of the Reign of King George the Third* (London: Lawrence and Bullen, 1894), I, 16.

9.   George L. Beer, *British Colonial Policy, 1754–1765* (New York: Peter Smith, 1933), 143; Lecky, *History of England in the Eighteenth Century*, III, 292–93; Lewis Namier, *England in the Age of the American Revolution* (New York: St. Martin's Press, Inc., 1961), 273–82; Rashed, *Peace of Paris*, 201–5.

10.   Beer, *British Colonial Policy*, 143.

11.   *Ibid.*, 140–54; Alvord, *Mississippi Valley in British Politics*, I, 49–74; Parkman, *Montcalm and Wolfe*, III, 250.

12.   Walpole, *Memoirs of the Reign of King George the Third*, I, 174; Mowat, *East Florida as a British Province*, 16.

13.   Alvord, *Mississippi Valley in British Politics*, I, 66–103; *Scots Magazine*, XXV (November, 1763), 627; *Scots Magazine*, XXIX (January, 1767), 50.

14.   Alfred J. Hanna, "The Beginnings of Florida," *American Heritage*, IV (December, 1952), 64.

15.   William Stork, *A Description of East Florida with a Journal Kept by John Bartram of Philadelphia, Botanist to His Majesty for the Floridas: Upon a Journey from St. Augustine to the River St. Johns as Far as the Lakes* (London: W. Nicoll, 1769), ii–vii and 10–49, and *passim;* William Roberts, *An Account of the First Discovery and Natural History of Florida with a Particular Detail of the Several Expeditions and Descents Made upon that Coast* (London: Printed for T. Jefferys, 1768), vii and 3, and *passim;* Charles L. Mowat, "The First Campaign of Publicity for Florida," *Mississippi Valley Historical Review*, XXX (December, 1943), 359–76.

16.   Folmer, *Franco-Spanish Rivalry in North America*, 309–10; Rashed, *Peace of Paris*, viii, 115–200.

17.   *Ibid.*

18.   Davenport and Paullin, *European Treaties Bearing on the History of the United States*, IV, 91.

19.   *Ibid.*, 86–90; T. C. Hansard (ed.), *The Parliamentary History of England from the Earliest Period to the Year 1803* (London: T. C. Hansard, 1813), XV, 1291–1305; *London Magazine* (March, 1763), 149–58; The English, Spanish, and French respectively ratified the Preliminary Articles of Peace on November 12, 13, and 14, 1763. *Tratado definitivo de paz concluido entre el rey nuestro señor y s. m. christianisima por una parte, y s. m. británica por otra, en Paris á 10. de Febrero de 1763, con sus articulos preliminares y la accesión de s.*

m. fidelísima á ellos, y al mismo tratado (Madrid: En la Imprenta Real de la Gaceta, 1763) , 3–97.

20. *Ibid.,* 300–314; Rashed, *Peace of Paris,* 212–29.

21. *Tratado definitivo de paz,* 155–73; Davenport and Paullin, *European Treaties Bearing on the History of the United States,* IV, 93–95; Hansard, *Parliamentary History of England,* XV, 1300–1301; Rashed, *Peace of Paris,* 204–9.

22. *Ibid.;* See Appendix A for translated versions of Articles IV and VII of the Paris Treaty of 1763.

23. *Ibid.*

24. *Ibid.*

25. *Tratado definitivo de paz,* 187–91; Davenport and Paullin, *European Treaties Bearing on the History of the United States,* IV, 95–96; Hansard, *Parliamentary History of England,* XV, 1300–1301.

26. *Ibid.;* Hart, *Siege of Havana,* 54.

27. *Tratado definitivo de paz,* 191–94, and 199–305; Davenport and Paullin, *European Treaties Bearing on the History of the United States,* IV, 96; *London Magazine* (March, 1763) , 153.

28. *Ibid.;* See Appendix A for translated versions of Articles XIX and XX.

29. *Tratado definitivo de paz,* 191–94; Davenport and Paullin, *European Treaties Bearing on the History of the United States,* IV, 96; Hansard, *Parliamentary History of England,* XV, 1305.

30. George Nobbe, *The North Briton: A Study in Political Propaganda* (New York: Columbia University Press, 1939) , 119.

31. Beer, *British Colonial Policy,* 132.

32. *Ibid.*

33. Alvord, *Mississippi Valley in British Politics,* I, 73.

34. *Ibid.,* 56; Rashed, *Peace of Paris,* 208–9.

35. Beer, *British Colonial Policy,* 154–58; Parkman, *Montcalm and Wolfe,* III, 253–54; Rashed, *Peace of Paris,* 202–3.

36. Alvord, *Mississippi Valley in British Politics,* I, 73.

37. Parkman, *Montcalm and Wolfe,* III, 250–51.

38. *A Geographical and Historical Description of the Principal Objects of the Present War in the West Indies, viz. Cartagena, Puerto Bello, La Vera Cruz, The Havana, and St. Augustine Shewing Their Situation, Strength, Trade, etc.* (London: Printed for T. Gardner, 1741) , 191–92; Lecky, *History of England in the Eighteenth Century,* III, 293–95; Rashed, *Peace of Paris,* 203–5.

39. Parkman, *Montcalm and Wolfe,* III, 255.

40. Rashed, *Peace of Paris,* 204.

41. *Ibid.*

42. Colonel Melchor Feliú replaced Acting Governor Alonso de Cárdenas on March 4, 1762. When Governor Lucas de Palacio y Valenzuela died on December 6, 1761, Sergeant Major Alonso de Cárdenas became acting governor of Florida according to accepted legal and traditional procedure. When Cárdenas was removed as acting governor because of his extreme age, Feliú assumed the provisional governorship of Florida. Esteban de Peña to Minister Julián de Arriaga. St. Augustine, December 15, 1761. MS, AGI (Archivo General de las

Indias) 87–2–23/1; Governor Juan de Prado to Minister Julián de Arriaga. Havana, March 12, 1762, MS, AGI 86–6–6/34; Conde de Ricla to Minister Julián de Arriaga. Havana, August 3, 1763, MS, AGI 86–7–11/8; Conde de Ricla to Minister Julián de Arriaga. Havana, April 12, 1763, MS, AGI 86–7–11/23; *South Carolina Gazette*, July 16–23, 1763.

43. Governor Feliú to Conde de Ricla. St. Augustine, August 3, 1763, MS, AGI 86–7–11/8; General William Keppel to Major Francis Ogilvie. On board the *Conquistador*, July 19, 1763; Captain Hedges to the Secretary of War. Portsmouth, September 4, 1763, Dunbar Rowland (ed.), *Mississippi Provincial Archives, 1763–1766: English Dominion* (Nashville: Brandon Printing Company, 1921), I, 128–32; Sir Jeffrey Amherst to General Thomas Gage. New York, November 17, 1763, Clarence E. Carter (ed.), *The Correspondence of General Thomas Gage with the Secretaries of State and with the War Office and the Treasury, 1763–1775* (New Haven: Yale University Press, 1933), II, 213–14.

44. According to his biographer, Mark F. Boyd, Juan Elixio de la Puente was the most prominent Floridian of the eighteenth century. His distinguished career included thirty years of military and civil service under the Spanish crown. Puente was therefore appropriately chosen by the royal officials of Cuba to be the realtor of St. Augustine's remaining possessions. Mark F. Boyd, unpublished history of eighteenth-century Florida and Don Juan Elixio de la Puente (Mark F. Boyd Library of Florida History, Tallahassee, Florida).

45. Puente to the governor of Cuba. Havana, February 26, 1766, MS, AGI 87–1–5/2–3, SD (Santo Domingo) 2595; Charles W. Arnade, "The Florida Keys: English or Spanish in 1763?" *Tequesta*, XV (1955), 41–53.

46. *Ibid.*

47. In order to emphasize Ogilvie's rage to his superiors, Puente underlined the statements attributed to the English soldier.

48. Puente to the governor of Cuba. Havana, February 26, 1766, MS, AGI 87–1–5/2–3, SD 2595; Arnade, "Florida Keys: English or Spanish in 1763?" 51–53.

49. *Ibid.*; Royal officials to Minister Julián de Arriaga. Havana, February 12, 1765, MS, AGI 86–6–7/1; The international cession of Florida, witnessed by Puente, only included the local ceremonies attended by Governor Melchor Feliú and Ogilvie's subordinate, Captain John Hedges.

50. *Ibid.*

51. Puente to the governor of Cuba. Havana, February 26, 1766, MS, AGI 87–1–5/2–3, SD 2595; Arnade, "Florida Keys: English or Spanish?" 46–50.

52. *Ibid.*

53. Governor James Grant to the Board of Trade. St. Augustine, April 26, 1766, PRO:CO 5/541; Governor Grant to the Board of Trade. St. Augustine, April 26, 1766, PRO:CO 5/548; *South Carolina Gazette*, November 3–10, 1766; James W. Covington, "Trade Relations between Southwestern Florida and Cuba, 1600–1840," *Florida Historical Quarterly*, XXXVIII (October, 1959), 116–19.

54. Lord Shelburne to Governor James Grant. Whitehall, December 11, 1766, PRO:CO 5/548; *Tratado definitivo de paz*, 191–94; Davenport and Paullin, *European Treaties Bearing on the History of the United States*, IV, 96; also, see Appendix A.

55.   *Ibid.*

56.   The famous Florida traveler, Bernard Romans, commented "that the crown would not allow the transfer of Spanish landed interest to be good, although mentioned in articles of peace." Bernard Romans, *A Concise Natural History of East and West Florida.* Facsimile reproduction of 1775 edition. (Gainesville: University of Florida Press, 1962), 223; Great Britain, *By the King: A Proclamation, October 7, 1763* (Mark Baskett, 1763); a copy is located in the P. K. Yonge Memorial Library of Florida History, Gainesville, Florida; *Tratado definitivo de paz,* 191–94; Davenport and Paullin, *European Treaties Bearing on the History of the United States,* IV, 96; also, see Appendix A.

57.   For a fine study of the Pontiac rebellion see Howard H. Peckham, *Pontiac and the Indian Uprising* (Chicago: The University of Chicago Press, 1947).

58.   Charles L. Mowat, "The Land Policy in British East Florida," *Agricultural History,* XIV (April, 1940), 75.

59.   The king to Governor Grant. Whitehall, April 3, 1764, PRO:CO 5/548; Fowler Walker, *The Case of Mr. John Gordon with Respect to Certain Lands in East Florida, Purchased of His Catholic Majesty's Subjects by Him and Mr. Jesse Fish for Themselves and Others, His Britannick Majesty's Subjects: In Conformity to the Twentieth Article of the Last Definitive Treaty of Peace* (London: printed in 1772), 19; Leonard Woods Labaree (ed.), *Royal Instructions to British Colonial Governors, 1670–1776* (New York: D. Appleton-Century, 1935), I, 515–16.

60.   The Jesse Fish Account Book. St. Augustine, 1763–70, EFP, 319.

61.   John Gordon even obtained affidavits from Governor Melchor Feliú and Major Francis Ogilvie bearing testimony to his proprietorship of certain territories along the St. John's River. Major Ogilvie's testimony of Gordon's ownership of the disputed lands. St. Augustine, December 1, 1763, PRO:CO 5/550; Testimony of Governor Feliú and Esteban de Peña to Gordon's ownership of the disputed lands. St. Augustine, December 2, 1763, PRO:CO 5/550; Letter from John Greg to commissioners of Trade and Plantations. London, February 22, 1764; PRO:CO 5/540; Walker, *The Case of Mr. John Gordon,* 19–21.

62.   Walker, *The Case of Mr. John Gordon,* 19–21.

63.   *Ibid.,* 30–31; Account of Mr. Gordon's purchases in East Florida for himself and other British subjects. East Florida, February 16, 1775, PRO:CO 5/546; Mowat, "Land Policy in British East Florida," 75–76; Lawrence Henry Gipson, *The Triumphant Empire: New Responsibilities within the Enlarged Empire, 1763–1766,* IX, *The British Empire before the American Revolution* (New York: Alfred A. Knopf, 1956), 183–89.

3   *Property Transactions during the Transfer of Empires: East Florida*

1.   Governor of Cuba to Minister Julián de Arriaga. Havana, May 18, 1772, MS, AGI 86–7–11/150, SD 2574; Residents of St. Augustine to Don Juan Elixio de la Puente—delivery of powers of attorney to Puente for property sales. Havana, February 10, 1772, MS, PPC, Legajo 372.

2.   *Tratado definitivo de paz concluido entre el rey nuestro señor y s. m. christianisma por una parte, y s. m. británica por otra, en París á 10. de Febrero de 1763. Con sus artículos preliminares y la accesión de s. m. fidelísima á ellos, y al mismo tratado* (Madrid: En la Imprenta Real de la Gaceta, 1763), 191–94; Frances Gardner Davenport and Charles Oscar Paullin (eds.), *European Treaties Bearing on the History of the United States and Its Dependencies* (Washington, D.C.: Carnegie Institution of Washington, 1937), IV, 96; Residents of St. Augustine to Don Juan Elixio de la Puente—delivery of powers of attorney to Puente for property sales. Havana, February 10, 1772, MS, PPC, Legajo 372.

3.   Clarence H. Haring, *The Spanish Empire in America* (New York: Oxford University Press, 1941), 257.

4.   *Ibid.*

5.   *Ibid.;* Charles Gibson, *The Aztecs under Spanish Rule: A History of the Indians of the Valley of Mexico, 1519–1810* (Stanford: Stanford University Press, 1964), 257–99.

6.   Haring, *Spanish Empire in America,* 257–58.

7.   Verne E. Chatelain, *The Defenses of Spanish Florida, 1565–1763* (Washington, D.C.: Carnegie Institution of Washington Publications, 1941), 16; John Jay TePaske, *The Governorship of Spanish Florida, 1700–1763* (Durham: Duke University Press, 1964), 77–107.

8.   Royal officials to the crown. St. Augustine, October 6, 1685, MS, NCCSR (North Carolina Collection of Spanish Records) 6–16; TePaske, *Governorship of Spanish Florida,* 4–10; Chatelain, *Defenses of Spanish Florida,* 16; Woodbury Lowery, *The Spanish Settlements within the Present Limits of the United States, 1513–1574* (New York: G. P. Putnam's Sons, 1905), II, 142–44; Eugenio Ruidiaz y Caravia, *La Florida: su conquista y colonización por Pedro Menéndez de Avilés* (Madrid: Hijos de J. A. Garcia, 1893), II, 401–27; Hernando de Miranda was Menéndez' son-in-law. Anthony Kerrigan (trans.), *Barcia's Chronological History of the Continent of Florida . . . from the Year 1512, in which Juan Ponce de León Discovered Florida, until the Year 1722* (Gainesville: University of Florida Press, 1951), 163–64.

9.   Royal officials to the crown. St. Augustine, October 6, 1658, MS, NCCSR 6–16; TePaske, *Governorship of Spanish Florida,* 4–11; Chatelain, *Defenses of Spanish Florida,* 16.

10.   Royal *cédula* to the governor of Florida. San Carlos de Real, October 15, 1680, MS, NCCSR 4–65, AGI 58–1–21/210 or 270; Royal officials to the crown. St. Augustine, October 6, 1685, MS, NCCSR 6–116, AGI 54–5–12/30.

11.   *Ibid.;* Royal officials to the crown. St. Augustine, March 20, 1685, MS, NCCSR 6–13, AGI 54–5–12/13; Royal officials to the crown. St. Augustine, July 10, 1685, MS, NCCSR 6–20, AGI 54–5–12/25.

12.   Royal officials to the crown. St. Augustine, March 2, 1680, MS, NCCSR 4–70, AGI 54–5–14/152; Crown to the governor of Florida. Buen Retiro, November 16, 1683, MS, NCCSR 5–33, AGI 58–1–21/376; Crown to the governor of Florida. San Lorenzo, March 6, 1685, MS, NCCSR 6–14, AGI 54–5–12/12; T. Frederick Davis, "Pioneer Florida: An Interpretation of Spanish Law and Land Titles," *Florida Historical Quarterly,* XXIV (October, 1945), 119–20.

13.   A *vara* in New Spain was equivalent to 32.99 inches. J. Villasana

Haggard, *Handbook for Translators of Spanish Historical Documents* (Oklahoma City: Semco Color Press, 1941), 84–86.

14.   A *fanega* was approximately equal to 2.6 bushels. *Ibid.*, 76–77.

15.   The amount of land that one ox could plow during a day's effort or approximately one-half acre was designated as a *huebra. Ibid.*, 78.

16.   Florida. *Spanish Land Grants in Florida, Unconfirmed Claims,* I, U.S., WPA (Works Progress Administration) Division of Professional and Service Projects (Tallahassee: State Library Board, 1940), xix–xx; Haring, *Spanish Empire in America,* 257.

17.   Royal officials to the crown. St. Augustine, October 6, 1685, MS, NCCSR 6–116, AGI 54–5–12/30; Crown to the governor of Florida. Buen Retiro, November 16, 1683, MS, NCCSR 5–33, AGI 58–1–21/376; Royal *cédula* to the governor of Florida. San Carlos de Real, October 15, 1680, MS, NCCSR 4–65, AGI 58–1–21/210 or 270; Fowler Walker, *The Case of Mr. John Gordon with Respect to Certain Lands in East Florida, Purchased of His Catholic Majesty's Subjects by Him and Mr. Jesse Fish for Themselves and Others, His Britannick Majesty's Subjects: In Conformity to the Twentieth Article of the Last Definitive Treaty of Peace* (London: Printed in 1772), 32–37.

18.   The actual percentage of titled land in 1763–64 is not known. Such knowledge would require a detailed study of each piece of property in the old Spanish colony.

19.   Residents of St. Augustine to Don Juan Elixio de la Puente—delivery of powers of attorney to Puente for property sales. Havana, February 10, 1772, MS, PPC, Legajo 372; Walker, *The Case of Mr. John Gordon,* 32–37, and *passim;* The Jesse Fish Account Book. 1763–70, MS, EFP 319, and *passim.*

20.   Acts establishing the Pensacola Indians near Vera Cruz. 1764–66, MS, AGNM 911, Ramo de Tierras, Legajo 466; Audiencia of Guadalajara. Guadalajara, October 21, 1767, MS, AGI 104–6–17/21; Governor Parrilla to Conde de Ricla. Pensacola, September 2, 1763, MS, AGI 86–7–11/228, SD 2574; Governor Feliú to Minister Julián de Arriaga. Havana, April 16, 1764, MS, AGI 86–6–6/43, SD 2543; Wilbur H. Siebert, "The Departure of the Spaniards and Other Groups from East Florida, 1763," *Florida Historical Quarterly,* XIX (October, 1940), 149–50; Wilbur H. Siebert, "How the Spaniards Evacuated Pensacola in 1763," *Florida Historical Quarterly,* XI (October, 1932), 53–57.

21.   Governor Parrilla to Conde de Ricla. Pensacola, August 16–20, September 2, 1763, MS, AGI 86–7–11/228, SD 2574; Governor Feliú to Minister Julián de Arriaga. Havana, February 5, 1764, MS, AGI 86–7–11/21; Governor Feliú to Minister Julián de Arriaga. Havana, April 16, 1764, MS, AGI 86–6–6/43, SD 2543; Captain Díaz to Conde de Ricla. Apalache, January 19 and 21, 1764, MS, AGI 86–7–11/20; Juan Elixio de la Puente to the Governor of Cuba. Havana, January 22, 1764, and January 27, 1770, MSS, AGI 87–1–5/4.

22.   Conde de Ricla to Governor Feliú. Havana, July 8, 1763, MS, AGI 86–7–11/3; Governor Feliú to Minister Julián de Arriaga. Havana, April 16, 1764, MS, AGI 86–6–6/43, SD 2543; Inventory of the Church property in 1764. Havana, February 10, 1765, MS, PPC, Legajo 372; A complete inventory of the *presidio's* material possessions at the time of the evacuation is available in the following documents: Esteban de Peña's inventory of the possessions of the Plaza of St. Augustine, Florida. Havana, May 14, 1764, MS, AGI 87–1–14/4; The warehouse account of Don Joachin Blanco. Havana, December 6, 1765, MS, AGI 87–3–27.

23.   Governor Feliú to Conde de Ricla. St. Augustine, August 29, 1763, MS, AGI 86–7–11/11; Governor Feliú to Conde de Ricla. St. Augustine, November 12, 1763, MS, AGI 86–7–11/19; Joachin Blanco's inventory of artillery, munitions, and other war materials. St. Augustine, December 28, 1763, MS, AGI 86–6–6/43, SD 2543.

24.   Governor Feliú to Conde de Ricla. St. Augustine, August 29, 1763, MS, AGI 86–7–11/11.

25.   *Ibid.;* Cotilla was another former Floridian. He has been credited with designing Fort San Marcos de Apalache in the period, 1756–59. Charles W. Arnade, "The Architecture of Spanish St. Augustine," *The Americas,* XVIII (October, 1961), 161–63.

26.   Conde de Ricla to Governor Feliú. Havana, July 20, 1763, MS, AGI 86–7–11/3; Instructions concerning the 1763 evacuation. July 6 and November 24, 1763, MS, AGNM 425, Documents: 14–24, and 60–64; Minister Julián de Arriaga to Governor Parrilla. Havana, April 19, 1763, MS, AGI 86–7–11/228, SD 2574; Lieutenant Colonel James Robertson to General Thomas Gage. New York, March 8, 1764, PRO:CO 5/83; Charles L. Mowat, *East Florida as a British Province, 1763–1784* (Berkeley: University of California Press, 1943), 8.

27.   Conde de Ricla to Governor Feliú. Havana, November 2, 1766, MS, AGI 86–7–11/15; Instructions concerning the 1763 evacuation. July 6 and November 24, 1763, MS, AGNM 425, Documents: 14–24, and 60–64; James Robertson to General Gage. New York, March 8, 1764, PRO:CO 5/83.

28.   Governor Feliú to Conde de Ricla. St. Augustine, November 15, 1763, MS, AGI 86–7–11/18; Arnade, "Architecture of St. Augustine," 165.

29.   Both Mark F. Boyd and Charles W. Arnade suspect that the famous Don Juan Elixio de la Puente map of 1764 is an improvised copy of a similar, but missing, chart that was drawn by Pablo Castelló about a year before Puente's map became operational. The index of the Puente map provides the best description of St. Augustine in 1760–70 presently extant. Governor Feliú to Minister Julián de Arriaga. St. Augustine, April 16 and 18, and May 30, 1763, MSS, AGI 86–6–6/41/44/45; Governor Feliú to Minister Julián de Arriaga. St. Augustine, May 28, 1763, MS, AGI 87–3–13/31, SD 2659; Governor Feliú to Conde de Ricla. St. Augustine, August 29, 1763, MS, AGI 86–7–11/11; Governor Feliú to Conde de Ricla. St. Augustine, December 28, 1763, MS, AGI 86–7–11/19; Governor Feliú to Conde de Ricla. Havana, April 12, 1764, MS, AGI 86–7–11/23, SD 2660; Arnade, "Architecture of St. Augustine," 167–69 and 181–86.

30.   Governor Feliú to Minister Julián de Arriaga. Havana, April 16, 1764, MS, AGI 86–6–6/43, SD 2543.

31.   Don Juan Elixio de la Puente to the governor of Cuba. Havana, February 26, 1766, MS, AGI 87–1–5/2/3, SD 2595; Charles W. Arnade, "The Avero Story: An Early St. Augustine Family with Many Daughters and Many Houses," *Florida Historical Quarterly,* XXXX (July, 1961), 6–7.

32.   Puente to the governor of Cuba. Havana, February 26, 1766, MS, AGI 87–1–5/2, SD 2595.

33.   Governor Feliú to Minister Julián de Arriaga. Havana, April 16, 1764, MS, AGI 86–6–6/43, SD 2543.

34.   *Ibid.;* James Robertson to General Gage. New York, March 8, 1764, PRO:CO 5/83. For a descriptive account of British St. Augustine, see Wilbur H. Siebert, "The Port of St. Augustine during the British Regime," *Florida Historical Quarterly,* XXIV (April, 1946), 247–65, and XXV (July, 1946), 76–93.

35.   James Robertson to General Gage. New York, March 8, 1764, PRO:CO 5/83; Mowat, *East Florida as a British Province,* 8; George Nobbe, *The North Briton: A Study in Political Propaganda* (New York: Columbia University Press, 1939), 160–67.

36.   *Ibid.*

37.   The Jesse Fish Contract with St. Augustine. St. Augustine, February 1, 1754, MS, AGI 87–3–13/20A; James Robertson to General Gage. New York, March 8, 1764, PRO:CO 5/83; Arnade, "Avero Story," 6–8; James G. Wilson, *Memorial History of the City of New York* (New York: 1892–93), 305.

38.   U.S. Congress, Senate, *Claims of the Catholic Church Pertaining to Certain Properties Held by the United States,* 30th Congress, Second Session, January 30, 1849, Senate Executive Document 21, 29–31.

39.   *Ibid.*

40.   A number of properties that Fish held during the twenty years of British control were returned to the Spanish owners or their descendants when Spain regained Florida in 1783–84. U.S. Congress, Senate, *Claims of the Catholic Church,* 29–31; Puente to the Governor of Cuba. Havana, February 10, 1772, MS, PPC, Legajo 372; Florida, *Florida Deeds: Town Lots and Lands,* Vol. 357, Document: 20, Field Note Division, Department of Agriculture, Tallahassee, Florida. The text of the Puente-Fish property transaction can be found in Appendix B.

41.   *Ibid.*

42.   U.S. Congress, Senate, *Claims of the Catholic Church,* 27–28; Puente to the governor of Cuba. Havana, March 4, 1772, MS, AGI 86–7–11/24.

43.   *Ibid.*

44.   General Gage to Secretary of State Henry Conway. New York, March 28, 1766, Clarence E. Carter (ed.), *The Correspondence of General Thomas Gage with the Secretaries of State and the War Office and the Treasury, 1763–1775* (New Haven: Yale University Press, 1933), I, 87; General Gage to Brigadier Taylor. New York, March 9, 1766, and December 9, 1767, Gage Papers, Microfilm, Reel II, P. K. Yonge Memorial Library of Florida History, Gainesville, Florida. Governor James Grant to the Board of Trade. East Florida, November 22, 1764, PRO:CO 5/540; Charles L. Mowat, "St. Francis Barracks, St. Augustine: A Link with the British Regime," *Florida Historical Quarterly,* XXI (January, 1943), 269–70; Rev. Michael J. Curley, C.S.S.R., *Church and State in the Spanish Floridas, 1783–1822* (Washington, D.C.: Catholic University of America Press, 1940), 21–22.

45.   Governor Feliú to Minister Julián de Arriaga. Havana, March 14, 1764, MS, AGI 86–7–11/22; Puente to the governor of Cuba. Havana, February 10, 1772, MS, PPC, Legajo 372; Puente to the governor of Cuba. Havana, March 4, 1772, MS, AGI 86–7–11/24.

46.   *Ibid.*

47. James Robertson to General Gage. New York, March 8, 1764, PRO:CO 5/83.

48. *Ibid.;* Esteban de Peña to the viceroy of New Spain. March 2, 1763, MS, AGNM 529, Documents: 1–11; Royal officials to the crown. Havana, May 14, 1764, MS, AGI 87-1-14/4; Memorial of William Walton of the City of New York to Sir Charles Hardy, Governor and Captain General of the Province of New York. New York, January 29, 1757, New York Colonial Manuscripts, Volume 84, Document 51, New York State Library, Albany, New York, and Mark F. Boyd Library of Florida History, Tallahassee, Florida.

49. James Robertson to General Gage. New York, March 8, 1764, PRO:CO 5/83.

50. Major Ogilive to Lord Amherst. St. Augustine, November 11, 1763, Gage Papers, Microfilm, Reel I, in the P. K. Yonge Memorial Library of Florida History, Gainesville, Florida; Mowat, *East Florida as a British Province,* 8–9.

51. Governor Grant to the Board of Trade. East Florida, November 22, 1764, PRO:CO 5/540.

52. Puente to the governor of Cuba. Havana, February 10, 1772, MS, PPC, Legajo 372; Puente to the governor of Cuba. Havana, March 4, 1772, MS, AGI 86-7-11/24; Governor of Cuba to Minister Julián de Arriaga. Havana, May 18, 1772, MS, AGI 86-7-11/150, SD 2574.

53. Herrera later was recruited as a spy when Spain attempted to regain Florida during the Revolutionary War. Katherine S. Lawson, "Luciano de Herrera: Spanish Spy in British St. Augustine," *Florida Historical Quarterly,* XXIII (January, 1945), 170–76.

54. Puente to the governor of Cuba. Havana, February 10, 1772, MS, PPC, Legajo 372; Puente to the governor of Cuba. Havana, March 4, 1772, MS, AGI 86-7-11/24; Governor of Cuba to Minister Julián de Arriaga. Havana, May 18, 1772, MS, AGI 86-7-11/150, SD 2574.

55. *Ibid.*

56. The precise property stipulations of Article XX are available in Appendix A.

57. Puente to the governor of Cuba. Havana, February 10, 1772, MS, PPC, Legajo 372; Puente to the governor of Cuba. Havana, March 4, 1772, MS, AGI 86-7-11/24; Governor of Cuba to Minister Julián de Arriaga. Havana, May 18, 1772, MS, AGI 86-7-11/150, SD 2574.

58. *Ibid.*

59. Thomas Jefferys' Plan of St. Augustine and Surrounding Area in 1765. PRO:CO Florida 8, Library of Congress photostat; The Jesse Fish Account Book. 1763–70, MS, EFP 319; Wilbur H. Siebert, *Loyalists in East Florida, 1774 to 1785* (De Land, Florida: Florida State Historical Society, 1929), II, 191.

60. *Ibid.;* T. Frederick Davis (ed.), *Florida Events of History* (Jacksonville: The Jacksonville Times Union Publication, 1942), 35. Santa Anastasia Island appears on Thomas Jefferys' map of the Town and Harbor of St. Augustin, 1763.

61. Siebert, *Loyalists in East Florida,* I and II, *passim;* Maxfield Parrish (ed.), Mrs. Lydia Austin Parrish Papers, uncataloged, microfilm collection, P. K. Yonge Memorial Library of Florida History, Gainesville, Florida, *passim.* The socio-economic status of Turnbull's agricultural colony from settlement to collapse is thoroughly narrated in the following history: Kenneth H. Beeson, Jr.,

"Fromjadas and Indigo: The Minorcan Colony in Florida" (Master's thesis, University of Florida, 1960).

62. Governor James Grant to the secretary of state. St. Augustine, April 26, 1766, PRO:CO 5/548; The Jesse Fish Account Book. 1763–70, MS, EFP 319.

63. *Ibid.;* Florida, Jesse Fish Property Sales, Volume 357, Document: 28, Field Note Division, Department of Agriculture, Tallahassee, Florida; Testamentary Proceedings. 1756–1821, EFP 301–18, Reels, I, II, III, V, and VI, uncataloged, microfilm collection, P. K. Yonge Memorial Library of Florida History, Gainesville, Florida; Governor Grant to the secretary of state. St. Augustine, April 26, 1766, PRO:CO 5/548; U.S., *American State Papers: Documents of the Congress of the United States* (Washington, D.C.: Gales and Seaton, 1859), IV, 568, 588, and 646.

64. Governor of Florida to Ministro de Gracia y Justicia. St. Augustine, October 6, 1789, uncataloged, Edward Lawson Papers, P. K. Yonge Memorial Library of Florida History, Gainesville, Florida; *Spanish Land Grants in Florida, Confirmed Claims,* V, U.S., WPA Division of Professional and Service Projects (Tallahassee: State Library Board, 1940), 120.

65. In New Spain a league was equivalent to 2.6 miles according to Haggard, *Handbook for Translators of Spanish Historical Documents,* 79–80; General Gage to Lord Halifax. New York, March 10, 1764, Clarence E. Carter (ed.), *The Correspondence of General Thomas Gage with the Secretaries of State and with the War Office and the Treasury, 1763–1775* (New Haven: Yale University Press, 1933), I, 19; Governor of Cuba to Minister Julián de Arriaga. Havana, May 18, 1772, AGI 86–7–11/150, SD 2574; Walker, *The Case of Mr. John Gordon,* 1–36.

66. Memorial of William Thomson, William Greenwood, and William Higginson, Merchants of London, in behalf of John Gordon. London, September 6, 1765, PRO:CO 5/540; Testimony of Governor Melchor Feliú and Esteban de Peña to Gordon's ownership of the disputed lands. St. Augustine, December 2, 1763, PRO:CO 5/550; Major Ogilvie's testimony of Gordon's ownership of the disputed lands. St. Augustine, December 1, 1763, PRO:CO 5/550.

67. James Robertson to General Gage. New York, March 8, 1764, PRO:CO 5/83.

68. General Gage to Lord Halifax. New York, March 10, 1764, Carter, *The Correspondence of General Thomas Gage,* I, 19.

69. *Ibid.*

70. Governor Grant to the Board of Trade. East Florida, November 22, 1764, PRO:CO 5/540.

71. Memorial of John Gordon. St. Augustine, September 3, 1768, PRO:CO 5/550; Attorney General of East Florida commenting on the Gordon case. St. Augustine, September 6, 1768, PRO:CO 5/550; His Majesty's order in Council relating to claim of John Gordon. St. James, December 3, 1766, PRO:CO 5/541; Governor Grant to the Board of Trade. St. Augustine, September 9, 1768, PRO:CO 5/550.

72. Governor Grant to the Board of Trade. St. Augustine, September 9, 1768, PRO:CO 5/550.

73. *Ibid.*

74. *Ibid.;* Council chambers meeting. Whitehall, April 5, 1773, PRO:CO 5/545; Lawrence Henry Gipson, *The Triumphant Empire: New Responsibilities within the Enlarged Empire, 1763-1766*, IX, *The British Empire before the American Revolution* (New York: Alfred A. Knopf, 1956), 183-89; Robert Walpole to the Lords of the Committee of Council for Plantation Affairs. London, October 8, 1765, PRO:CO 5/540; Memorial of William Thomson, William Greenwood, and William Higginson, Merchants of London, in behalf of John Gordon. London, September 6, 1765, PRO:CO 5/540; Walker, *The Case of Mr. John Gordon*, 1-36.

4 Property Transactions during the Transfer of Empires: West Florida

1.   Instructions concerning the 1763 evacuation .July 6 and November 24, 1763, MS, AGNM 425, Documents: 14-24, and 60-64; Acts establishing the Pensacola Indians in Vera Cruz. 1764-66, MS, AGNM 911, Ramo de Tierras, Legajo 466; Audiencia of Guadalajara. Guadalajara, October 21, 1767, MS, AGI 104-6-17/21; Minister Julián de Arriaga to Conde de Ricla and Conde de Ricla to Minister Julián de Arriaga. Havana, April 19, July 6 and 15, and September 24, 1763, MSS, AGI 86-7-11/228, SD 2574; Wilbur H. Siebert, "How the Spaniards Evacuated Pensacola in 1763," *Florida Historical Quarterly*, XI (October, 1932), 48-57.

2.   *Ibid.*

3.   Lieutenant Colonel Provost to the secretary of war. Fort Pensacola, September 7, 1763; Lord Halifax to Governor Johnstone. St. James, April 14, 1764, Dunbar Rowlands (ed.), *Mississippi Provincial Archives, 1763-1766: English Dominion* (Nashville: Brandon Printing Company, 1921), I, 136 and 145; Governor Parrilla to Conde de Ricla. Pensacola, September 2, 1763, MS, AGI 86-7-11/228, SD 2574; Captain Philip Pittman, *The Present State of the European Settlements on the Mississippi*, reprint of original edition, London, 1770 (Cleveland: Arthur H. Clark, 1906), 24-26; Lieutenant Colonel James Robertson to General Thomas Gage. New York, March 8, 1764, PRO:CO 5/83; Clinton N. Howard, "Some Economic Aspects of British West Florida, 1763-1768," *Journal of Southern History*, VI (May, 1940), 201.

4.   James Robertson to General Gage. New York, March 8, 1764, PRO:CO 5/83; Lieutenant Colonel Provost to the secretary of war. Fort Pensacola, September 7, 1763, Rowland, *Mississippi Provincial Archives*, I, 136-37; Clinton N. Howard, "Colonial Pensacola: The British Period," *Florida Historical Quarterly*, XIX (October, 1940), 111; Howard, "Economic Aspects of British West Florida," 209-11; Lord Halifax to Governor Johnstone. St. James, May 12, 1764, Rowland, *Mississippi Provincial Archives*, I, 147-49.

5.   Clarence W. Alvord, "The Genesis of the Proclamation of 1763," *Michigan Pioneer and Historical Society*, XXXVI (1908), 20-52; Clinton N. Howard, "Alleged Spanish Grants in British West Florida," *Florida Historical Quarterly*, XXII (October, 1943), 83-84.

6.   For an excellent study of land grants in British West Florida, see Clinton N. Howard, *The British Development of West Florida, 1763-1769* (Berkeley: University of California Press, 1947); Dunbar Rowland, *History of Mississippi Heart of the South* (Chicago: S. J. Clarke Publishing Company, 1925), I, 275-84 offers land grant statistics for Natchez and the Eastern Mississippi Valley from 1768–78.

7.   Major William Forbes to the secretary of state. Pensacola, January 29, 1764; The governor's complaint of the chief justice. Pensacola, April 1, 1766, Rowland, *Mississippi Provincial Archives*, I, 143–44, and 466–67; Howard, "Alleged Spanish Grants in British West Florida," 77–85; Howard, "Economic Aspects of British West Florida," 210–11; Cecil Johnson, "Expansion in West Florida, 1770–1779," *Mississippi Valley Historical Review*, XX (March, 1934), 481.

8.   Ibid.

9.   Francis Parkman, *A Half-Century of Conflict, Part VI, France and England in North America* (Boston: Little, Brown and Company, 1933), I, 298–325; Charles Gayarré, *History of Louisiana: The French Domination* (New York: William J. Widdleton, Publisher, 1866), I, 9–114, 191–232, 353–89, 390–441, and *passim;* Dunbar Rowland and Albert G. Sanders (eds.), *Mississippi Provincial Archives: French Dominion, 1701–1729* (Jackson, Mississippi: Press of the Mississippi Department of Archives and History, 1927), I, 54–71, 117–26, 167, and *passim;* Dunbar Rowland and Albert G. Sanders (eds.), *Mississippi Provincial Archives: French Dominion, 1704–1743* (Jackson, Mississippi: Press of the Mississippi Department of Archives and History, 1932), III, 173–78, 489–539, 557–76, 586–607, and *passim.*

10.   Ibid.

11.   Ibid.

12.   The king to Jean Baptiste, Sieur de Bienville and Edmé Gatlen Salmon. Marly, February 2, 1732, Rowland and Sanders, *Mississippi Provincial Archives: French Dominion,* III, 568.

13.   Parkman, *A Half Century of Conflict, Part VI,* 298–325; Gayarré, *History of Louisiana,* 9–114, 191–232, 353–89, 390–441, and *passim;* Rowland and Sanders, *Mississippi Provincial Archives: French Dominion,* I, 54–71, 117–26, 167, and *passim;* Rowland and Sanders, *Mississippi Provincial Archives: French Dominion,* III, 173–78, 489–539, 557–76, 586–607, and *passim.*

14.   Reply of Bienville and Salmon to the king's memorial. New Orleans, May 12, 1733, Rowland and Sanders, *Mississippi Provincial Archives: French Dominion,* III, 597–98.

15.   Parkman, *A Half Century of Conflict, Part VI,* 298–325; Gayarré, *History of Louisiana,* 9–114, 191–232, 353–89, 390–441, and *passim;* Rowland and Sanders, *Mississippi Provincial Archives: French Dominion,* I, 54–71, 117–26, 167, and *passim;* Rowland and Sanders, *Mississippi Provincial Archives: French Dominion,* III, 173–78, 489–539, 557–76, 586–607, and *passim.*

16.   *Ibid.;* Rowland, *History of Mississippi Heart of the South,* I, 269.

17.   Major Farmer to the secretary of war. Mobile, January 24, 1764, Rowland, *Mississippi Provincial Archives,* I, 10–11; Great Britain, *Par Monsieur Robert Farmar Majeur du 34me Regiment & Commandant des Troupes de Sa Majesté Britannique, dans la Lousiane . . .* (Chicago: Students of Chicago School of Printing, 1939); Pittman, *European Settlements on the Mississippi,* 26; James Robertson to General Gage. New York, March 8, 1764, PRO:CO 5/83; Howard, *British Development of West Florida, 1763–1769,* 8–15; Howard, "Economic Aspects of British West Florida," 205–12.

18. Howard, "Economic Aspects of British West Florida," 109–13; Clinton N. Howard, "The Interval of Military Government in West Florida," *Louisiana Historical Quarterly,* XXII (January, 1939), 4–5; Clinton N. Howard, "The Military Occupation of British West Florida," *Florida Historical Quarterly,* XVII (January, 1939), 196–97; Lord Halifax to Governor Johnstone. St. James, May 12, 1764, Rowland, *Mississippi Provincial Archives,* I, 147–49.

19. Report of Governor d'Abbadie. New Orleans, January 10, 1764, Gayarré, *History of Louisiana: The French Domination,* II, 101–2.

20. Ibid.

21. Ibid.; Lord Halifax to Governor Johnstone. St. James, May 12, 1764, Rowland, *Mississippi Provincial Archives,* I, 147–49.

22. Milo B. Howard, Jr., and Robert R. Rea (ed. and trans.), *The Mémoire Justificatif of the Chevalier Montault de Monberaut: Indian Diplomacy in British West Florida* (University, Alabama: University of Alabama Press, 1965), 21–25, 47–50, and 68–69.

23. Major Farmar to Chevalier Sieur de Ville. On board the *Stag,* September 21, 1763, Rowland, *Mississippi Provincial Archives,* I, 33.

24. Major Farmer to the secretary of war. Mobile, January 24, 1764, Rowland, *Mississippi Provincial Archives,* I, 15.

25. Ibid., 33. *26.* Ibid., 15.

5 *The Official and Demographic Transfer of Spanish East Florida to British Control*

1. A number of the Spanish documents present different figures for the evacuation totals. Typically, population assessments vary in number and category according to the particular date of preparation. Don Juan Elixio de la Puente to Minister Julián de Arriaga. Havana, April 16, 1764, MS, AGI 86–6–6/43, SD 2543; Puente to the governor of Cuba. Havana, January 22, 1764, September 26, 1766, and January 27, 1770, MSS, AGI 87–1–5/3/4, SD 2595; Puente to the governor of Cuba. Havana, February 10, 1772, MS, PPC, Legajo 372; Puente to the governor of Cuba. Havana, March 4, 1772, MS, AGI 86–7–11/24; Mark F. Boyd, unpublished history of eighteenth-century Florida and Don Juan Elixio de la Puente (Mark F. Boyd Library of Florida History, Tallahassee, Florida).

2. Instructions concerning the 1763 evacuation. July 6 and November 24, 1763, MSS, AGNM 425, Documents: 14–24, and 60–64; Conde de Ricla to Governor Feliú. Havana, July 2, and 13, 1763, MSS, AGI 86–7–11/3; Puente to Minister Julián de Arriaga. Havana, April 16, 1764, MS, AGI 86–6–6/43, SD 2543; Puente to the governor of Cuba. Havana, January 22, 1764, September 26, 1766, and January 27, 1770, MSS, AGI 87–1–5/3/4, SD 2595; Wilbur H. Siebert, "The Departure of the Spaniards and Other Groups from East Florida," *Florida Historical Quarterly,* XIX (October, 1940), 145–49.

3. Instructions concerning the 1763 evacuation. July 6, and November 24, 1763, MSS, AGNM 425, Documents: 14–24, and 60–64; Conde de Ricla to Governor Feliú. Havana, July 2 and 13, 1763, MS, AGI 86–7–11/3.

4. Governor Alonzo Fernández de Heredia to Minister Julián de Arriaga. St. Augustine, October 14, 1757, MS, AGI 87–3–13/23, SD 2659; Governor of

Cuba to Minister Julián de Arriaga. Havana, October 26, 1757, MS, AGI 87–3–13/25, SD 2659; Governor Lucas Fernando de Palacio to Minister Julián de Arriaga. St. Augustine, January 20, 1761, MS, AGI 86–7–22/10; Governor Alonzo de Cárdenas to the crown. St. Augustine, December 22, 1761, MS, AGI 86–7–22/13/23; Governor of Cuba to Minister Julián de Arriaga. Havana, December 22, 1761, and Governor Feliú to Minister Julián de Arriaga. St. Augustine, March 24, 1762, MSS, AGI 86–6–6/34, SD 2660; Puente to Minister Julián de Arriaga. Havana, April 16, 1764, MS, AGI 86–6–6/43, SD 2543; Puente to the governor of Cuba. Havana, January 22, 1764, September 22 and 26, 1766, and January 27, 1770, MSS, AGI 87–1–5/3/4, SD 2595.

5. Puente to Minister Julián de Arriaga. Havana, April 16, 1764, MS, AGI 86–6–6/43, SD 2543.

6. Governor Feliú to Conde de Ricla. St. Augustine, September 12, 1763, MS, AGI 86–7–11/12; Puente to Minister Julián de Arriaga. Havana, April 16, 1764, MS, AGI 86–6–6/43, SD 2543; Puente to the governor of Cuba. Havana, January 22, 1764, and January 27, 1770, MSS, AGI 87–1–5/4, SD 2595.

7. Juan de Cotilla to Conde de Ricla. St. Augustine, July 31, 1763, MS, AGI 87–7–11/4.

8. Governor Feliú and Don Juan Elixio de la Puente to Minister Julián de Arriaga. Havana, April 16, 1764, MSS, AGI 86–6–6/43, SD 2543; Puente to the governor of Cuba. Havana, January 22, 1764, and January 27, 1770, MSS, AGI 87–1–5/4, SD 2595.

9. Ibid.

10. Lieutenant Colonel James Robertson to General Thomas Gage. New York, March 8, 1764, PRO:CO 5/83; Lieutenant Colonel Provost to the secretary of war. Fort Pensacola, September 7, 1763, Dunbar Rowland (ed.), *Mississippi Provincial Archives, 1763–1766: English Dominion* (Nashville: Brandon Printing Company, 1921), I, 136–37; Joseph A. Scoville, *The Old Merchants of New York City* (New York: Carleton Company, 1863), 103–4; *South Carolina Gazette,* June 20, 1757; Memorial of William Walton of the City of New York to Sir Charles Hardy, Governor and Captain General of the Province of New York, New York, January 29, 1757, New York Colonial Manuscripts, Volume 84, Document 51, New York State Library, Albany, New York, and the Mark F. Boyd Library of Florida History, Tallahassee, Florida.

11. Governor Feliú to Conde de Ricla. St. Augustine, August 25, 1763, MS, AGI 86–7–11/11; James Robertson to General Gage. New York, March 8, 1764, PRO:CO 5/83; Puente to Minister Julián de Arriaga. Havana, April 16, 1764, MS, AGI 86–6–6/43, SD 2543; Puente to the governor of Cuba. Havana, January 22, 1764, and January 27, 1770, MSS, AGI 87–1–5/4, SD 2595; Governor Feliú and Juan Elixio de la Puente to Minister Julián de Arriaga. Havana, March 14, 1764, MS, AGI 86–7–11/22; *South Carolina Gazette,* November 12–19, 1763; Siebert, "The Departure of the Spaniards and Other Groups from East Florida," 145–49.

12. Ibid.

13. Ibid.

14. Governor Feliú to Conde de Ricla. St. Augustine, August 25, 1763, MS, AGI 86–7–11/11; James Robertson to General Gage. New York, March 8, 1764, PRO:CO 5/83; Puente to Minister Julián de Arriaga. Havana, April 16, 1764,

MS, AGI 86–6–6/43, SD 2543; Puente to the governor of Cuba. Havana, January 22, 1764, and January 27, 1770, MSS, AGI 87–1–5/4, SD 2595; Governor Feliú and Juan Elixio de la Puente to Minister Julián de Arriaga. Havana, March 14, 1764, MS, AGI 86–7–11/22; *South Carolina Gazette,* November 12–19, 1763.

15. Conde de Ricla to Minister Julián de Arriaga. Havana, November 1, 1763, MS, AGI 86–7–11/24; Conde de Ricla to Minister Julián de Arriaga. Havana, November, 1763, MS, AGI 86–7–11/14; Puente to the governor of Cuba. Havana, September 22, and 26, 1766, MSS, AGI 87–1–5/3, SD 2595; James Robertson to General Gage. New York, March 8, 1764, PRO:CO 5/83; Duvon C. Corbitt, "Spanish Relief Policy and the East Florida Refugees of 1763," *Florida Historical Quarterly,* XXVII (July, 1948), 67–70.

16. Conde de Ricla to the royal officials of Matanzas. Havana, March 17, 1764, MS, AGI 87–1–5/1, SD 2595; Memorial of former inhabitants of Florida. Havana, August 26, 1766, MS, AGI 87–1–5/1, SD 2595; Puente to the governor of Cuba. Havana, September 22, and 26, 1766, MS, AGI 97–1–5/3, SD 2595; Corbitt, "Spanish Relief Policy and the East Florida Refugees of 1763," 67–70.

17. Memorial of former inhabitants of Florida. Havana, August 26, 1766, MS, AGI 87–1–5/1, SD 2595; Puente to the governor of Cuba. Havana, September 22, and 26, 1766, MSS, AGI 87–1–5/3, SD 2595.

18. Conde de Ricla to the royal officials of Matanzas. Havana, March 17, 1764, MS, AGI 87–1–5/1, SD 2595.

19. *Ibid.*

20. *Ibid.*

21. *Ibid.*

22. *Ibid.*

23. Puente to the governor of Cuba. Havana, September 22 and 26, 1766, MSS, AGI 87–1–5/3, SD 2595; Memorial of former inhabitants of Florida. Havana, August 26, 1766, MS, AGI 87–1–5/1, SD 2595.

24. Puente to the governor of Cuba. Havana, September 22, and 26, 1766, MSS, AGI 87–1–5/3, SD 2595; Memorial of former inhabitants of Florida. Havana, August 26, 1766, MS, AGI 87–1–5/1, SD 2595.

25. *Ibid.*

26. Puente to the governor of Cuba. Havana, September 22 and 26, 1766, MSS, AGI 87–1–5/3, SD 2595; Puente to the governor of Cuba. Havana, January 22, 1764, and May 8, 1770, MSS, AGI 87–1–5/4, SD 2595; Murat Halstead, *The Story of Cuba* (Akron: The Werner Company, 1896), 233, and 240–51; Francis Russell Hart, *The Siege of Havana, 1762* (New York: Houghton Mifflin Company, 1931), 32.

27. Puente to the governor of Cuba. Havana, September 22, and 26, 1766, MSS, AGI 87–1–5/3, SD 2595; Memorial of former inhabitants of Florida. Havana, August 26, 1766, MS, AGI 87–1–5/1, SD 2595.

28. *Ibid.;* Various obligations of the Plaza of St. Augustine. Havana, March 17, 1764, MS, AGI 87–1–5/1, SD 2595.

29. *Ibid.*

30. Memorial of former inhabitants of Florida. Havana, August 26, 1766, MS, AGI 87–1–5/1, SD 2595; Puente to the governor of Cuba. Havana, September 22, and 26, 1766, MSS, AGI 87–1–5/3, SD 2595.

31. *Ibid.*

32.   *Ibid.*

33.   *Ibid.;* Memorial of former inhabitants of Florida. Havana, August 26, 1766, MS, AGI 87–1–5/1, SD 2595.

34.   *Ibid.*

35.   Memorial of former inhabitants of Florida. Havana, August 26, 1766, MS, AGI 87–1–5/1, SD 2595.

36.   *Ibid.*

37.   Royal *cédula* to the governor of Florida. Sevilla, January 1, 1731, MS, AGI 86–5–20/97; James Robertson to General Gage. New York, March 8, 1764, PRO:CO 5/83; Corbitt, "Spanish Relief Policy and the East Florida Refugees of 1763," 67–75.

38.   *Ibid.*

39.   Spanish cession orders to General Keppel. Havana, April 18, 1763, PRO:CO 5/549; Conde de Ricla to Minister Julián de Arriaga. Havana, July 2, and August 3, 1763, MSS, AGI 86–7–11, and AGI 86–7–11/3; Conde de Ricla to Minister Julián de Arriaga. Havana, August 3, 1763, MS, AGI 86–7–11/8; Conde de Ricla to Minister Julián de Arriaga. Havana, April 12, 1764, MS, AGI 86–7–11/23; Governor Feliú to Conde de Ricla. Havana, November 2, 1763, MS, AGI 86–7–11/13.

40.   *South Carolina Gazette,* February 5–12, 1763; *Georgia Gazette,* April 14, 1763; Charles L. Mowat, *East Florida as a British Province, 1763–1784* (Berkeley: University of California Press, 1943) , 7.

41.   General William Keppel played a significant part in the siege of Morro Castle during the conquest of Cuba in 1762. His brother, the Earl of Albemarle, commanded the land campaign against Spanish Cuba. Conde de Ricla to Minister Julián de Arriaga. Havana, July 2, 1763, MS, AGI 86–7–11/3; Clinton N. Howard, "The Military Occupation of British West Florida," *Florida Historical Quarterly,* XVII (January, 1939) , 182–88; *South Carolina Gazette,* July 10–23, 1763; General William Keppel to Major Francis Ogilvie. On board the *Conquistador,* July 19, 1763; General Keppel to Colonel Provost. Havana, July 3, 1763, Rowland, *Mississippi Provincial Archives,* I, 127–28.

42.   Captain Hedges to the secretary of war. St. Augustine, September 4, 1763, Rowland, *Mississippi Provincial Archives,* I, 132.

43.   Governor Feliú to Minister Julián de Arriaga. St. Augustine, August, 1763, MS, AGI 86–7–11/7; Governor Feliú to Minister Julián de Arriaga. Havana, April 16, 1764, MS, AGI 86–6–6/43, SD 2543; Conde de Ricla to Minister Julián de Arriaga. Havana, November, 1763, MS, AGI 86–7–11/14; Conde de Ricla to Minister Julián de Arriaga. Havana, August 3, 1763, MS, AGI 86–7–11/8; Conde de Ricla to Minister Julián de Arriaga. Havana, April 12, 1764, MS, AGI 86–7–11/23; General Keppel to Major Ogilvie. On board the *Conquistador,* July 19, 1763; Captain Hedges to the secretary of war. Portsmouth, September 4, 1763, Rowland, *Mississippi Provincial Archives,* I, 127–32; Sir Jeffrey Amherst to General Gage. New York, November 17, 1763, Clarence E. Carter (ed.) , *The Correspondence of General Thomas Gage with the Secretaries of State and the War Office and the Treasury, 1763–1775* (New Haven: Yale University Press, 1933) , II, 213–14; Frances Gardner Davenport and Charles Oscar Paullin (eds.) , *European Treaties Bearing on the History of the United States and Its Dependencies* (Washington, D.C.: Carnegie Institution of Washington, 1937), IV, 96; Zenab Esmat Rashed, *The Peace of Paris, 1763* (Liverpool: The University Press, 1951), *passim*.

44. Royal *cédula* to Governor Melchor Feliú. San Lorenzo, November 12, 1762, MS, AGI 86-7-18/22; John Jay TePaske, *The Governorship of Spanish Florida, 1700-1763* (Durham: Duke University Press, 1964), 7-57; Verne E. Chatelain, *The Defenses of Spanish Florida, 1565-1763* (Washington, D.C.: Carnegie Institution of Washington Publications, 1941), 27-29.

45. *Ibid.*

46. Governor Feliú to Conde de Ricla. St. Augustine, August 29, 1763, MS, AGI 86-7-11/11; Conde de Ricla to Minister Julián de Arriaga. Havana, February 5, 1764, MS, AGI 86-7-11/21; Governor Feliú to Minister Julián de Arriaga. Havana, March 14, 1764, MS, AGI 86-7-11/22; Governor Feliú to Minister Julián de Arriaga. Havana, April 16, 1764, MS, AGI 86-6-6/43, SD 2543.

47. Conde de Ricla to Governor Feliú. Havana, November 2, 1763, MS, AGI 86-7-11/15; Governor Feliú to Conde de Ricla. St. Augustine, November 15, 1763, MS, AGI 86-7-11/18.

48. Puente to the governor of Cuba. Havana, February 10, 1772, MS, PPC, Legajo 372; Puente to the governor of Cuba. Havana, March 4, 1772, MS, AGI 86-7-11/29; Thomas Sothvel to Conde de Ricla. St. Augustine, August 3, 1763, MS, AGI 86-7-11; Instructions concerning the 1763 evacuation. July 6 and November 24, 1763, MSS, AGNM 425, Documents: 14-24, and 60-64; The provisions report of Juan Thomas de la Barrera Sotomayor. St. Augustine, November 22, 1763, MS, AGI 86-7-11/19; Governor Feliú to Minister Julián de Arriaga. Havana, April 16, 1764, MS, AGI 86-6-6/43, SD 2543. The latter two manuscripts offer inventories of the military equipment and supplies which were hauled from Florida to Cuba.

49. Bernard Romans, *A Concise Natural History of East and West Florida.* Facsimile reproduction of 1775 edition. (Gainesville: University of Florida Press, 1962), 223; William W. Dewhurst, *The History of St. Augustine, Florida* (New York: G. P. Putnam's Sons, 1881), 108; Mowat, *East Florida as a British Province,* 9.

50. Major Ogilvie to the Board of Trade. St. Augustine, January 26, 1764, PRO:CO 5/540.

51. Major Ogilvie to Lord Amherst. St. Augustine, November 11, 1763, Gage Papers, Microfilm, Reel I, P. K. Yonge Memorial Library of Florida History, Gainesville, Florida; General Gage to the secretary of war. New York, April 26, 1765, Carter, *Correspondence of General Gage,* II, 282, and 314.

52. James Robertson to General Gage. New York, March 8, 1764, PRO:CO 5/83.

53. Governor Feliú to Minister Julián de Arriaga. Havana, April 16, 1764, MS, AGI 86-6-6/43, SD 2543.

54. Captain Díaz to the British garrison of Pensacola. Apalache, November 12, 1763, MS, AGI 86-7-11/20; Mark F. Boyd, "From a Remote Frontier: Letters and Documents Pertaining to San Marcos de Apalache, 1763-1769, during the British Occupation of Florida," *Florida Historical Quarterly,* XIX (January, 1941), 180-81, 184, and 190-92; James Robertson to General Gage. New York, March 8, 1764, PRO:CO 5/83.

55. Captain Díaz to Conde de Ricla. Apalache, November 6, 1763, MS, AGI 86–7–11/16: Captain Díaz to Conde de Ricla. Apalache, January 19, 1764, MS, AGI 86–7–11/20; Boyd, "From a Remote Frontier," 192–200.

56. Captain Díaz to Conde de Ricla. Apalache, January 19, 1764, MS, AGI 86–7–11/20; James Robertson to General Gage. New York, March 8, 1764, PRO:CO 5/83.

57. Captain Díaz to Colonel Provost. Apalache, January 21, 1764, MS, AGI 86–7–11/20; Boyd, "From a Remote Frontier," 200–209.

58. Captain Díaz to Conde de Ricla. Apalache, January 21, 1764, MS, AGI 86–7–11/20; Boyd, "From a Remote Frontier," 206–9.

59. Captain Díaz to Colonel Provost. Apalache, January 21, 1764, MS, AGI 86–7–11/20; Conde de Ricla to Colonel Robertson. Havana, February 5, 1764, MS, AGI 86–7–11/20; Boyd, "From a Remote Frontier," 209–12.

60. Captain Harries to Lord Amherst. Pensacola, December 11 and 14, 1763, Mark F. Boyd, "From a Remote Frontier: Letters Passing between Captain Harries in Command at Apalache (St. Marks), 1763–1764, and the Commanders-in-Chief, Amherst and Gage," *Florida Historical Quarterly*, XIX (April, 1941), 402–6.

61. *Ibid.*

62. *Ibid.*

63. *Ibid.*

64. Captain Harries to General Gage. Pensacola, February 7, 1764, Boyd, "From a Remote Frontier: Harries in Command at Apalache," 406–9.

65. *Ibid.*

66. General Gage to Captain Harries. New York, March 31, 1764, Boyd, "From a Remote Frontier: Harries in Command at Apalache," 409; James Robertson to General Gage. New York, March 8, 1764, PRO:CO 5/83.

67. General Gage to Captain Harries. New York, March 31, 1764, Boyd, "From a Remote Frontier: Harries in Command at Apalache," 409–12.

68. Great Britain occupied San Marcos de Apalache only until the autumn of 1769. Captain Harries to General Gage. Apalache, February 25, 1764; General Gage to Captain Harries. New York, May 7, 1764, Mark F. Boyd, "From a Remote Frontier: Letters Passing between Captain Harries in Command at Apalache (St. Marks) in 1764 and His Commander-in-Chief, General Gage, in New York," *Florida Historical Quarterly*, XX (July, 1941), 82–92.

6 *The Official Transfer of Franco-Spanish West Florida to British Control*

1. Conde de Ricla to Governor Parrilla. July 6, and November 24, 1763, MSS, AGNM 425, Documents: 14–24, and 60–64; Minister Julián de Arriaga to Conde de Ricla, Conde de Ricla to Governor Parrilla, and Governor Parrilla to Minister Julián de Arriaga. Havana, and Pensacola, July 6, and November 21 and 24, 1763, MSS, AGI 86–7–11/228, SD 2574; Wilbur H. Siebert, "How the Spaniards Evacuated Pensacola in 1763," *Florida Historical Quarterly*, XI (October, 1932), 48–54.

2. *Ibid.*

3.   *Ibid.*

4.   *Ibid.;* Siebert's transportation figures indicate a total of 722 emigrants, although the listed Pensacolans leaving Florida actually numbered 622 persons. The author and/or the periodical unintentionally included a typographical error in the evacuation statistics.

5.   Acts establishing the Pensacola Indians near Vera Cruz. 1764–66, MS, AGNM 911, Ramo de Tierras, Legajo 466; Conde de Ricla to Governor Parrilla. July 6, and November 21, and 24, 1763, MSS, AGNM 425, Documents: 14–24, and 60–64; Minister Julián de Arriaga to Conde de Ricla, Conde de Ricla to Governor Parrilla, and Governor Parrilla to Minister Julián de Arriaga. Havana, and Pensacola, July 6 and November 21, and 24, 1763, MSS, AGI 86–7–11/228; Siebert, "How the Spaniards Evacuated Pensacola in 1763," 53–54.

6.   Antigua Vera Cruz, known currently as José Cardel, is located approximately fifteen miles north of the present port-city of Vera Cruz. Old Vera Cruz apparently occupies the site of Hernando Cortés' famous landing in April, 1519.

7.   Today, Tempoala is simply called Tempoal. Lieutenant Pedro de Amoscotigue y Bermudo to Viceroy Marqués de Cruillas. Vera Cruz and San Carlos, December 12 and 19, 1764, January 26, March 6, and November 22, 1765, MSS, AGNM, 911, Ramo de Tierras, Legajo 466; The San Carlos reports of Viceroy Marqués de Croix. Mexico City, August 27, and 29, 1766, MSS, AGNM 911, Ramo de Tierras, Legajo 466.

8.   *Ibid.;* The Don Pedro de Amoscotigue y Bermudo Map and Plan of the Pueblo of San Carlos and the surrounding area. Vera Cruz, February 26, 1766, MS, AGNM 911, Ramo de Tierras, Legajo 466.

9.   The list of the Pensacola Indians moving to Tempoala. Vera Cruz, January 16, 1765, MSS, AGNM 911, Ramo de Tierras, Legajo 466; Lieutenant Pedro de Amoscotigue y Bermudo to Viceroy Marqués de Cruillas. Tempoala, January 26, 1765, MSS, AGNM 911, Ramo de Tierras, Legajo 466; The San Carlos reports of Viceroy Marqués de Croix. Mexico City, August 27, and 29, 1766, MSS, AGNM 911, Ramo de Tierras, Legajo 466.

10.   After concluding the evacuation of San Miguel de Pensacola, Don Diego Ortiz Parrilla became interim governor of San Francisco de Coaguila (Coahuila), New Spain. Parrilla held that post from 1764 until October, 1765. Audiencia of Guadalajara. Guadalajara, October 21, 1767, MS, AGI 104–6–17/21.

11.   Acts establishing the Pensacola Indians near Vera Cruz. 1764–66, MSS, AGNM 911, Ramo de Tierras, Legajo 466; Conde de Ricla to Governor Parrilla. July 6, and November 21, and 24, 1763, MSS, AGNM 425, Documents: 14–24, and 60–64; Minister Julián de Arriaga to Conde de Ricla, Conde de Ricla to Governor Parrilla, and Governor Parrilla to Minister Julián de Arriaga. Havana, and Pensacola, July 6, and November 21, and 24, 1763, MS, AGI 86–7–11/228.

12.   General Keppel to Lieutenant Colonel Provost. Havana, July 3, 1763, Dunbar Rowland (ed.), *Mississippi Provincial Archives, 1763–1766: English Dominion* (Nashville: Brandon Printing Company, 1921), I, 130–31.

13.   Lieutenant Colonel Provost to the secretary of war. Fort Pensacola, September 7, 1763, Rowland, *Mississippi Provincial Archives,* I, 136–37; *South Carolina Gazette,* November 12–19, 1763; Clinton N. Howard, "The Military Occupation of British West Florida," *Florida Historical Quarterly,* XVII (January, 1939), 183–85.

14.   Conde de Ricla to Minister Julián de Arriaga. Havana, November, 1763, MS, AGI 86–7–11/14; Howard, "Military Occupation of British West Florida," 181–86; Siebert, "How the Spaniards Evacuated Pensacola in 1763," 49–50.

15.   Report of Major William Forbes on Pensacola. Pensacola, January 30, 1764, Rowland, *Mississippi Provincial Archives*, I, 113.

16.   Captain Machinen to the secretary of war. Pensacola, October 30, 1764, Rowland, *Mississippi Provincial Archives*, I, 123; Cecil Johnson, *British West Florida, 1763–1783* (New Haven: Yale University Press, 1943), 13; General Gage to Secretary of State Henry Conway. New York, November 9 and December 21, 1765, and General Gage to Lord Halifax. New York, November 9, 1764, Clarence E. Carter (ed.), *The Correspondence of General Thomas Gage with the Secretaries of State and with the War Office and the Treasury, 1763–1775* (New Haven: Yale University Press, 1933), I, 43, 73–74, and 76; General Gage to Secretary of War Barrington. New York, December 21, 1765, Carter, *Correspondence of General Thomas Gage*, II, 329–30.

17.   Webster Merritt, "West Florida, Three Centuries under Four Flags, Conquest and Disease," *Journal of the Florida Medical Association*, XXXIX (April, 1953), 758; Captain Philip Pittman, *The Present State of the European Settlements on the Mississippi,* reprint of original edition, London, 1770 (Cleveland: Arthur H. Clark Company, 1906), 24–25; Major Farmar to the secretary of war. Mobile, September 15, 1764, Rowland, *Mississippi Provincal Archives*, I, 120.

18.   Lieutenant Colonel James Robertson to General Thomas Gage. New York, March 8, 1764, PRO:CO 5/83; Major Farmar to the secretary of war. Mobile, January 24, 1764; General Keppel to Major Farmar. On board the *Conquistador*, July 19, 1763; Duc de Choiseul to Governor Kerlérec of New Orleans. Versailles, April 13, 1763, Rowland, *Mississippi Provincial Archives*, I, 9–10, 128–29, and 135; Howard, "Military Occupation of British West Florida," 187–92.

19.   Major Farmar to the secretary of war. Mobile, January 24, 1764; Major Farmar to Captain de Ville. On board the H.M.S. *Stag* in Pensacola harbor, October 2, 1763; General Keppel to Major Farmar. On board the *Conquistador*, July 19, 1763, Rowland, *Mississippi Provincial Archives*, I, 9–10, 58–59, and 128–29.

20.   Major Farmar to Captain de Ville. Aboard the H.M.S. *Stag*, September 21, 1763; Captain de Ville to Major Farmar. Mobile, October 14, 1763; Governor Kerlérec to Major Farmar. New Orleans, October 2, 1763; Governor d'Abbadie to Major Farmar. New Orleans, October 4, 1763, Rowland, *Mississippi Provincial Archives*, I, 33–35; 54–58.

21.   *Ibid.*

22.   Governor Kerlérec to Major Farmar. New Orleans, October 2, 1763, Rowland, *Mississippi Provincial Archives*, I, 56–57.

23.   *Ibid.,* 58.

24.   *Ibid.,* 54–58; James Robertson to General Gage. New York, March 8, 1764, PRO:CO 5/83.

25.   Major Farmar to Governor d'Abbadie. Mobile, November 9, 1763, Rowland, *Mississippi Provincial Archives*, I, 36.

26.   *Ibid.*

27.   *Ibid.*

28.   *Ibid.;* Major Farmar to the secretary of war. Mobile, January 24, 1764, Rowland, *Mississippi Provincial Archives,* I, 9-12.

29.   See Appendix A for the terms of Article VII of the Treaty of 1763.

30.   Governor d'Abbadie to Colonel James Robertson. New Orleans, December 7, 1763, Charles Gayarré, *History of Louisiana: The French Domination* (New York: William J. Widdleton, Publisher, 1866), II, 98.

31.   *Ibid.,* 10; Howard, "Military Occupation of British West Florida," 192-95.

32.   Major Farmar to the secretary of war. Mobile, January 24, 1764, Rowland, *Mississippi Provincial Archives,* I, 10-11; Clinton N. Howard, *The British Development of West Florida, 1763-1769* (Berkeley: University of California Press, 1947), 11.

33.   *Ibid.;* Governor d'Abbadie to Major Farmar. New Orleans, October 4, 1763; Captain de Ville to Major Farmar. Mobile, October 14, 1763, Rowland, *Mississippi Provincial Archives,* I, 34-35.

34.   *Ibid.;* James Robertson to General Gage. New York, March 8, 1764, PRO:CO 5/83.

35.   The French always considered the territory on the east bank of the Mississippi as being an integral part of the Louisiana Territory. Under the English colonial system, eastern Louisiana was incorporated into the West Florida province which also included Spanish Florida west of the Apalachicola River.

36.   The Mobile cession. Mobile, October 20, 1763, Rowland, *Mississippi Provincial Archives,* I, 77-79. A translation of the cession of Mobile is included in the above work.

37.   Reports of Major Farmar concerning the state of the revenue and produce of Louisiana, with appointments civil and military whilst under the French government. Mobile, January 24, 1764; Major Farmar to the secretary of war. Mobile, August 1, 1764, Rowland, *Mississippi Provincial Archives,* I, 30-31, and 119.

38.   *Ibid.;* James Robertson to General Gage. New York, March 8, 1764, PRO:CO 5/83; Peter J. Hamilton, *Colonial Mobile* (New York: Houghton Mifflin Company, 1898), 191; Howard, "Military Occupation of British West Florida," 195-97.

39.   Great Britain, *Par Monsieur Robert Farmar Majeur du 34ᵐᵉ Regiment & Commandant des Troupes de Sa Majesté Britannique, dans la Louisiane . . .* (Chicago: Students of Chicago School of Printing, 1939); Major Farmar's Mobile Manifesto. Mobile, October 20, 1763, Rowland, *Mississippi Provincial Archives,* I, 60-63.

40.   *Ibid.;* The list of inhabitants taking the Oaths of Allegiance. Mobile, October 2, 1764, Rowland, *Mississippi Provincial Archives,* I, 121-22.

41.   Report of Lieutenant Ford at Tombecbe. Tombecbe Fort, November 24, 1763; Text of the cession of Tombecbe post. Tombecbe Fort, November 22, 1763, Rowland, *Mississippi Provincial Archives,* I, 23-25, and 97-100.

42.   *Ibid.;* General Gage to Lord Halifax. New York, February 11, 1764, Carter, *Correspondence of General Gage,* I, 14-15; Major Farmar to the secretary of war. Mobile, January 24, 1764, Rowland, *Mississippi Provincial Archives,*

I, 12; James Robertson to General Gage. New York, March 8, 1764, PRO:CO 5/83.

43.   Major Farmar to the secretary of war. Mobile, January 24, 1764; Major Farmar to Lord Egremont. Mobile, January 24, 1764, Rowland, *Mississippi Provincial Archives*, I, 12–13, and 137–38.

44.   Major Loftus to General Gage. Pensacola, April 9, 1764; Extracts of Governor d'Abbadie's letter of June 20, 1764. New Orleans, June 20, 1764, Clarence Walworth Alvord and Clarence Edwin Carter (eds.), *The Critical Period, 1763–1765*, British Series (Springfield, Illinois: State Historical Library, 1915), I, xl–lvii, 225–32, and 237–39; Howard, "Military Occupation of British West Florida," 198–99; Clinton N. Howard, "The Interval of Military Government in West Florida," *Louisiana Historical Quarterly*, XXII (January, 1939), 7–12; Pittman, *European Settlements on the Mississippi*, 10–11; Hamilton, *Colonial Mobile*, 188–90.

45.   Report of Monsieur Aubry, Commandant of New Orleans. New Orleans, April 7, 1764, Gayarré, *History of Louisiana*, II, 102–104.

46.   Captain Campbell to Governor George Johnstone. Mobile, December 12, 1764, Rowland, *Mississippi Provincial Archives*, I, 267.

47.   Governor George Johnstone to John Pownall, Secretary to Lords Commissioners for Trade and Plantations. Pensacola, February 19, 1765, Rowland, *Mississippi Provincial Archives*, I, 271–72.

48.   The Mobile cession. Mobile, October 20, 1763; Major Farmar to the secretary of war. Mobile, September 15, and October 20, 1764, Rowland, *Mississippi Provincial Archives*, I, 77–79, and 120–21; Clinton N. Howard, "Some Economic Aspects of British West Florida, 1763–1768," *Journal of Southern History*, VI (May, 1940), 204–5; Merritt, "West Florida, Conquest and Disease," 758; Howard, "The Interval of Military Government in West Florida," 3–15; Pittman, *European Settlements on the Mississippi*, 24–25.

7   *The King's Proclamation of October 7, 1763*

1.   Great Britain, *By the King: A Proclamation, October 7, 1763* (Printed by Mark Baskett, 1763). A copy is located in the P. K. Yonge Memorial Library of Florida History, Gainesville, Florida; *South Carolina Gazette*, December 21, 1763.

2.   *Ibid.*

3.   By "including all Islands within Six Leagues of the Sea Coast" within the jurisdiction of East Florida, the authors of the king's proclamation were obviously ignoring Spanish claims to the Florida Keys. Great Britain, *By the King: A Proclamation, October 7, 1763* (Mark Baskett, 1763).

4.   Pensacola was designated as the seat of government for West Florida, while St. Augustine continued to be the capital city of East Florida. Leonard Woods Labaree (ed.), *Royal Instructions to British Colonial Governors, 1670–1776* (New York: D. Appleton-Century Company, 1935), I, 5, 14, and 18; Great Britain, *By the King: A Proclamation, October 7, 1763* (Mark Baskett, 1763).

5.   Great Britain, *By the King: A Proclamation, October 7, 1763* (Mark Baskett, 1763).

6.   *Ibid.*

7.   *Ibid.*

8.   Clinton N. Howard, *The British Development of West Florida, 1763–1769* (Berkeley: University of California Press, 1947), 32–33; J. E. Dovell, *Florida—Historic, Dramatic, Contemporary* (New York: Lewis Historical Publishing Company, Inc., 1952), I, 85–86, and 105; Charles L. Mowat, "The Land Policy in British East Florida," *Agricultural History*, XIV (April, 1940), 75–77; Charles L. Mowat, "The First Campaign of Publicity for Florida," *Mississippi Valley Historical Review*, XXX (December, 1943), 363–64.

9.   Lawrence Henry Gipson, *The Triumphant Empire: New Responsibilities within the Enlarged Empire, 1763–1766, IX, The British Empire before the American Revolution* (New York: Alfred A. Knopf, 1957), 196–97.

10.   Beverley W. Bond, *The Quit-Rent System in the American Colonies* (New Haven: Yale University Press, 1919), 367, 374, and 382; Labaree, *Royal Instructions to British Colonial Governors*, I, 548–49; Great Britain, *By the King: A Proclamation*, October 7, 1763 (Mark Baskett, 1763); Additional instructions for the reservation of quit-rents. Whitehall, May 14, 1766. PRO:CO 5/540.

11.   Great Britain, *By the King: A Proclamation, October 7, 1763* (Mark Baskett 1763).

12.   *Ibid.*

13.   *Ibid.*

14.   Clarence W. Alvord, *The Mississippi Valley in British Politics* (Cleveland: Arthur H. Clark Company, 1917), I, 182–84; Clarence W. Alvord, "The Genesis of the Proclamation of 1763," *Michigan Pioneer and Historical Society*, XXXVI (1908), 20–52; Helen L. Shaw, *British Administration of the Southern Indians, 1756–1783* (Lancaster, Pennsylvania: Lancaster Press, 1931), 26–31; Wilbur R. Jacobs (ed.), *Indians of the Southern Colonial Frontier: The Edmond Atkin Report and Plan of 1755* (Columbia, South Carolina: University of South Carolina Press, 1954), *passim;* Clarence E. Carter, "Some Aspects of British Administration in West Florida," *Mississippi Valley Historical Review*, I (December, 1914), 365; Albert T. Volwiler, *George Croghan and the Westward Movement, 1741–1782* (Cleveland: Arthur H. Clark Company, 1926), 171; Oliver M. Dickerson, *American Colonial Government, 1696–1765* (New York: Russell and Russell, Inc., 1962), 253; John Richard Alden, "The Albany Congress and the Creation of the Indian Superintendencies," *Mississippi Valley Historical Review*, XXVII (September, 1940), 193–210.

15.   Alvord, "Genesis of the Proclamation of 1763," 22–31.

16.   *Ibid.;* Jack M. Sosin, *Whitehall and the Wilderness: The Middle West in British Colonial Policy, 1760–1775* (Lincoln, Nebraska: University of Nebraska Press, 1961), 51–64.

17.   *Ibid.;* Volwiler, *George Croghan and the Westward Movement*, 171; Clinton N. Howard, "Early Settlers in British West Florida," *Florida Historical Quarterly*, XXIV (July, 1945), 45–46.

18.   *Ibid.*

19.   Great Britain, *By the King: A Proclamation, October 7, 1763* (Mark

Baskett, 1763) ; John Richard Alden, *John Stuart and the Southern Colonial Frontier, 1754–1775* (Ann Arbor: University of Michigan Press, 1944) , 240–42, 265, 290–93, and 302; Clarence E. Carter, "The Beginnings of British West Florida," *Mississippi Valley Historical Review,* IV (December, 1917) , 314–41; Charles Metzger, "An Appraisal of Shelburne's Western Policy," *Mid-America,* XVIII (July, 1937) , 169–81; Sosin, *Whitehall and the Wilderness,* 56–64; Alvord, "Genesis of the Proclamation of 1763," 31–33.

20.   Great Britain, *By the King: A Proclamation, October 7, 1763* (Mark Baskett, 1763) ; Alden, *John Stuart and the Southern Colonial Frontier,* 207–14; Ray Allen Billington, *Western Expansion: A History of the American Frontier* (New York: Macmillan Company, 1949) , 141; Metzger, "An Appraisal of Shelburne's Western Policy," 171.

21.   Alvord, "Genesis of the Proclamation of 1763," 32–33; Dickerson, *American Colonial Government,* 348–54.

22.   Alvord, "Genesis of the Proclamation of 1763," 35–51; Robin A. Humphreys, "Lord Shelburne and the Proclamation of 1763," *English Historical Review,* XLIX (April, 1934) , 241–64; Alvord, *Mississippi Valley in British Politics,* I, 172–73, and 202–3; Billington, *Western Expansion,* 137–39; Metzger, "An Appraisal of Shelburne's Western Policy," 180; Sosin, *Whitehall and the Wilderness,* 57–64.

23.   Arthur Herbert Basye, *The Lords Commissioners of Trade and Plantations, Commonly Known as the Board of Trade, 1748–1782* (New Haven: Yale University Press, 1924) , 128; Thomas Perkins Abernethy, *Western Lands and the American Revolution* (New York: Russell and Russell, Inc., 1959) , 20–21; Sosin, *Whitehall and the Wilderness,* 51–64; Dickerson, *American Colonial Government,* 348–49, and 356; Alvord, *Mississippi Valley in British Politics,* I, 175–76, and 188–89; Alvord, "Genesis of the Proclamation of 1763," 51–52.

24.   *Ibid.*

25.   Clarence E. Carter claims that the Board of Trade's ignorance of Florida geography prompted the choice of those first inappropriate limits for East Florida. Carter, "Beginnings of British West Florida," 316; The memorial of James Grant. Whitehall, September 19, 1763, PRO:CO 5/548; The Board of Trade report on Grant's memorial. Whitehall, September 28, 1763, PRO:CO 5/548; Great Britain, *By the King: A Proclamation, October 7, 1763* (Mark Baskett, 1763) ; Clarence Walworth Alvord and Clarence Edwin Carter (eds.) , *The Critical Period, 1763–1765,* British Series. (Springfield: Illinois State Historical Library, 1915) , I, 40; Lawrence Shaw Mayo, *The St. Mary's River, A Boundary* (Privately printed, 1914) , 6–7.

26.   The memorial of James Grant. Whitehall, September 19, 1763, PRO:CO 5/548.

27.   The Board of Trade report on Grant's memorial. Whitehall, September 28, 1763, PRO:CO 5/548.

28.   Mayo, *The St. Mary's River, A Boundary,* 7–9; John Tate Lanning, *The Diplomatic History of Georgia* (Chapel Hill: University of North Carolina Press, 1936) , 14–21; Herbert E. Bolton (ed.) , *Arredondo's Historical Proof of Spain's Title to Georgia* (Berkeley: University of California Press, 1925) , 67–72.

29.   A Florida memorial to Minister Julián de Arriaga. Madrid, June 25, 1755, MS, AGI 58–1–25/19; A letter of Governor Fulgencio García de Solís. St.

Augustine, June 25, 1755, MS, AGI 58-1-33/27; Governor of Florida to the crown. Madrid, June 30, 1755, MS, AGI 86-6-6/9; Mayo, *The St. Mary's River, A Boundary,* 10–11; U.S., *American State Papers: Public Lands* (Washington, D.C.: Gales and Seaton, 1834), I, 51–52; Charles C. Jones, *The History of Georgia* (Boston: Houghton Mifflin Company, 1883), I, 539, and II, 27–28; Allen D. Candler (ed.), *The Colonial Records of the State of Georgia, 1754–1759* (Atlanta: The Franklin-Turner Company, 1906), VII, 547–48; Bolton, *Arredondo's Historical Proof of Spain's Title to Georgia,* 101–6.

30.   U.S., *American State Papers: Public Lands,* I, 51–53; Mayo, *The St. Mary's River, A Boundary,* 10–11; William B. Stevens, *A History of Georgia from Its First Discovery by Europeans to the Adoption of the Present Constitution in MDCCXCVIII* (New York: D. Appleton and Company, 1847), I, 448–49, and II, 459–60; Candler, *The Colonial Records of the State of Georgia,* VII, 333, and 425–27.

31.   U.S., *American State Papers: Public Lands,* I, 51–52.

32.   Mayo, *The St. Mary's River, A Boundary,* 12–15.

33.   *Ibid.;* U.S., *American State Papers: Public Lands,* I, 52–57.

34.   U.S., *American State Papers: Public Lands,* I, 53–57.

35.   *Ibid.,* 53–57; Mayo, *The St. Mary's River, A Boundary,* 16–18.

36.   *Ibid.*

37.   U.S., *American State Papers: Public Lands,* I, 53–57; The memorial of James Grant. Whitehall, September 19, 1763, PRO:CO 5/548; The Board of Trade report on Grant's memorial. Whitehall, September 28, 1763, PRO:CO 5/548; Great Britain, *By the King: A Proclamation, October 7, 1763* (Mark Baskett, 1763); U.S., Congress, *Message from the President of the United States Transmitting Documents Relative to the Boundary Line between Georgia and Florida,* 20th Congress, First Session, March 3, 1828; Francis Harper (ed.), *The Travels of William Bartram, Naturalist's Edition* (New Haven: Yale University Press, 1958), 16–27; Verner W. Crane, "Hints Relative to the Division and Government of the Conquered and Newly Acquired Countries in America," *Mississippi Valley Historical Review,* VIII (March, 1922), 372.

38.   Henry E. Chambers, *West Florida and Its Relation to the Historical Cartography of the United States,* Johns Hopkins University Studies in Historical and Political Science, Series XVI, Number 5 (Baltimore: Johns Hopkins Press, 1898), 18–19; Carter, "Beginnings of British West Florida," 325–26; Gipson, *The Triumphant Empire,* IX, 202–3.

39.   Mowat, "First Campaign of Publicity for Florida," 359–76; *Gentleman's Magazine,* London, November, 1763, 552–54; *Gentleman's Magazine,* London, January, 1767, 21–22; *Scots Magazine,* London, January, 1767, 50.

8   *The Religious Transformation of Florida, 1763–1765*

1.   Governor Feliú to Conde de Ricla. St. Augustine, August 25, 1763, MS, AGI 86-7-11/11; Governor Feliú to Conde de Ricla. St. Augustine, September 12, 1763, MS, AGI 86-7-11/12; Inventory of the Apalache possessions. Apalache, November 3, 1763, MS, AGI 86-7-11/16; Bishop of Santiago, Cuba, to Conde de Ricla. Havana, September 2, 1764, MS, PPC, Legajo 372; Michael V. Gannon,

The Cross in the Sand: The Early Catholic Church in Florida, 1513–1870 (Gainesville: University of Florida Press, 1965), 85.

2.   An edict of the bishop of Santiago, Cuba. Havana, February 6, 1764, MS, PPC, Legajo 372; Inventory of the Florida Church's property. Havana, March 30, 1765, MS, PPC, Legajo 372.

3.   *Ibid.*

4.   Memorial of Don Juan Joseph Solana. Sevilla, April 29, 1759, MS, AGI 86–7–21/1; Inventory of the Florida Church's property. Havana, March 30, 1765, MS, PPC, Legajo 372; Wilbur H. Siebert, "Some Church History of St. Augustine during the Spanish Regime," *Florida Historical Quarterly,* IX (October, 1930), 118–19; James A. Robertson, "Notes on Early Church Government in Spanish Florida," *Catholic Historical Review,* XVII (July, 1931), 159.

5.   Inventory of the Florida Church's property. Havana, March 30, 1765, MS, PPC, Legajo 372.

6.   Bishop of Santiago, Cuba, to Conde de Ricla. Havana, September 2, 1764, MS, PPC, Legajo 372; Conde de Ricla to the bishop of Santiago. Havana, November 5, 1764, MS, PPC, Legajo 372.

7.   *Ibid.;* Memorial of Marqués Justiz de Santa Ana. Havana, January 10, 1765, MS, PPC, Legajo 372; Siebert, "Church History of St. Augustine," 117–18.

8.   Testimony of Don Joseph Solana. Havana, January 10, 1765, MS, PPC, Legajo 372; Memorial of Don Juan Joseph Solana. Sevilla, April 29, 1759, MS, AGI 86–7–21/1.

9.   *Ibid.;* Governor Antonio de Benavides to the crown. St. Augustine, April 24, 1722, November 5, 1725, September 23, 1727, and October 2, 1731, MSS, AGI 58–2–4/35/44/49/57; Governor Montiano to the crown. St. Augustine, March 3, 1738, MS, BNM 19508, folio pages 186–213.

10.   Governor Manuel de Montiano to the crown. St. Augustine, March 3, 1738, MSS, BNM 19508, folio pages 186–213; Memorial of Don Juan Joseph Solana. Sevilla, April 29, 1759, MS, AGI 86–7–21/1; Testimony of Don Juan Joseph Solana. Havana, January 10, 1765, MS, PPC, Legajo 372; Testimony of Don Juan Bernardo de Paredes. Havana, January 11, 1765, MS, PPC, Legajo 372; Siebert, "Church History of St. Augustine," 120–28; Gannon, *Cross in the Sand,* 79.

11.   Royal *cédula* to the bishop of Cuba. Madrid, February 8, 10, and 12, 1719, MSS, AGI 58–1–24/33/39/41; Robertson, "Early Church Government in Spanish Florida," 171–74; John Jay TePaske, *The Governorship of Spanish Florida, 1700–1763* (Durham: Duke University Press, 1964), 159–70.

12.   Memorial of Don Juan Joseph Solana. St. Augustine, April 22, 1759, MS, AGI 86–7–21/1; Testimony of Don Juan Joseph Solana. Havana, January 10, 1765, MS, PPC, Legajo 372.

13.   Memorial of Don Juan Joseph Solana. St. Augustine, April 22, 1759, MS, AGI 86–7–21/1; Testimony of Don Juan Bernardo de Paredes. Havana, January 11, 1765, MS, PPC, Legajo 372.

14.   Testimony of Don Juan Elixio de la Puente. Havana, January 12, 1765, MS, PPC, Legajo 372; Testimony of Don Juan Esteban de Peña. Havana, January 15, 1765, MS, PPC, Legajo 372.

15.   The report of Joseph A. Gelabert. Havana, 1765, MS, PPC, Legajo 372.

16.   Memorial of Don Juan Joseph Solana. St. Augustine, April 22, 1759,

MS, AGI 86–7–21/1; Puente to the governor of Cuba. Havana, March 4, 1772, MS, AGI 86–7–11/24; U.S., Congress, Senate, *Claims of the Catholic Church Pertaining to Certain Properties Held by the United States*, 30th Congress, Second Session, January 30, 1849, Senate Executive Document 21, 27–28; Rev. Michael J. Curley, C.S.S.R., *Church and State in the Spanish Floridas, 1783–1822* (Washington D.C.: Catholic University of America Press, 1940), 21–22; John Gilmary Shea, *The Catholic Church in Colonial Days* (New York: John Gilmary Shea, 1886), II, 90–92.

17.　Memorial of Don Juan Joseph Solana. St. Augustine, April 22, 1759, MS, AGI 86–7–21/1; Puente to the governor of Cuba. Havana, March 4, 1772, MS, AGI 86–7–11/24; U.S., Congress, Senate, *Claims of the Catholic Church*, 27–28; General Gage to Secretary of State Henry Conway. New York, March 28, 1766, Clarence E. Carter (ed.), *The Correspondence of General Thomas Gage with the Secretaries of State and with the War Office and the Treasury, 1763–1775* (New Haven: Yale University Press, 1933), I, 87; Curley, *Church and State in the Spanish Floridas, 1783–1822*, 21–22.

18.　Archbishop of Lepanto to Minister Julián de Arriaga. Madrid, December 23, 1763, MS, AGI 86–7–22/18; Governor Feliú and Don Juan Elixio de la Puente to Minister Julián de Arriaga. Havana, April 16, 1764, MS, AGI 86–6–6/43.

19.　After Spanish authority returned to Cuba, Athares was constructed to supplement the perimeter of land defenses obstructing the ground approach to Havana.

20.　Puente to the governor of Cuba. Havana, January 22, 1764, September 26, 1766, and January 27, 1770, MSS, AGI 87–1–5/3/4, SD 2595; Maynard Geiger, *Biographical Dictionary of the Franciscans in Spanish Florida and Cuba (1528–1841)* (Patterson, New Jersey: St. Anthony Guild Press, 1940), 140.

21.　Acts establishing the Pensacola Indians near Vera Cruz. 1764–66, MSS, AGNM 911, Ramo de Tierras, Legajo 466; Conde de Ricla to Governor Parrilla. November 24, 1763, MSS, AGNM 425, Documents: 14–24, and 60–64; Governor Parrilla to Minister Julián de Arriaga. Havana, November 21 and 24, 1763, MSS, AGI 86–7–11/228; Curley, *Church and State in the Spanish Floridas, 1783–1822,* 22–23; Edgar Legare Pennington, "The Episcopal Church in Florida, 1763–1892," *Historical Magazine of the Protestant Espiscopal Church,* VII (March, 1938), 8–9; Cecil Johnson, *British West Florida, 1763–1783* (New Haven: Yale University Press, 1943), 167–68.

22.　Various obligations of the plaza of St. Augustine. Havana, March 17, 1764, MS, AGI 87–1–5/1, SD 2595; Puente to the governor of Cuba. Havana, January 22, 1764, and January 27, 1770, MSS, AGI 87–1–5/4, SD 2595.

23.　Royal *cédula* to the governor of Florida. Sevilla, May 14, 1732, MS, AGI 58–1–24/247; Royal *cédula* to the provincial of the Order of St. Francis. Sevilla, August 14, 1732, MS, AGI 58–1–24/249; Auxiliary bishop of Florida to the crown. Florida, April 29, 1736, MS, AGI 58–1–25/1; Governor Montiano to the crown. St. Augustine, February 16, 1739, MS, AGI 58–2–17/28; Memorial of Don Juan Joseph Solana. St. Augustine, April 22, 1759, MS, AGI 86–7–21/1; TePaske, *Governorship of Spanish Florida,* 159–92; Robertson, "Early Church Government in Spanish Florida," 158–61; Shea, *Catholic Church in Colonial Days,* I, 471–75.

24.   *Ibid.*

25.   *Ibid.*

26.   *Ibid.;* Geiger, *Biographical Dictionary of the Franciscans in Spanish Florida and Cuba,* 138.

27.   *Ibid.*

28.   Enoch Hawksworth to the secretary of state. St. Augustine, June 25, 1767, PRO:CO 5/548; Pennington, "Episcopal Church in Florida," 4; Edgar Legare Pennington, "The Episcopal Church in South Florida, 1764–1892," *Tequesta,* I (March, 1941), 47–49; Charles L. Mowat, *East Florida as a British Province, 1763–1784* (Berkeley: University of California Press, 1943), 37; Johnson, *British West Florida,* 163–64.

29.   The formation of the East Florida Council. East Florida, November 18, 1764, PRO:CO 5/540; The king's confirmation of the council of East Florida. St. James, June 7, 1771, PRO:CO 5/545; Memorial of William Knox, agent of East Florida. St. Augustine, June 26, 1765, PRO:CO 5/540; Memorial of Jones Read. London, March 29, 1765, PRO:CO 5/540; The recommendation of John Firby for schoolmaster of Pensacola. London, March 18, 1765, PRO:CO 5/548; The recommendation of John Forbes for minister of St. Augustine. London, April 17, 1764, PRO:CO 5/540; Charles L. Mowat, "St. Augustine under the British Flag," *Florida Historical Quarterly,* XX (October, 1941), 147; Johnson, *British West Florida,* 164; Pennington, "Episcopal Church in Florida," 4–6; Edgar Legare Pennington, "John Forbes," *Florida Historical Quarterly,* VIII (January, 1930), 164–68; Wilbur H. Siebert, *Loyalists in East Florida, 1774 to 1785* (De Land, Florida: Florida State Historical Society, 1929), I, 5.

30.   Governor James Grant to the Board of Trade. St. Augustine, January 27, 1772, PRO:CO 5/545; Governor Grant to the Board of Trade. East Florida, March 1, 1765, PRO:CO 5/540; Mowat, "St. Augustine under the British Flag," 137–38; Pennington, "Episcopal Church in Florida," 4–5.

31.   *Ibid.*

32.   Memorial of John Forbes, William Dawson, and Samuel Hart. London, June 19, 1764, PRO:CO 5/540; Pennington, "Episcopal Church in Florida," 6–9; Johnson, *British West Florida,* 164–67.

33.   Major Farmar to the secretary of war. Mobile, August 1, 1764, Dunbar Rowland (ed.), *Mississippi Provincial Archives, 1763–1766: English Dominion* (Nashville: Brandon Printing Company, 1921), I, 119–20.

34.   Governor and Council of West Florida to the Board of Trade. West Florida, November 22, 1766, PRO:CO 5/575.

35.   Necessary furniture for the several churches of Florida. East and West Florida, July 20, 1764, PRO:CO 5/540; Siebert, *Loyalists in East Florida,* I, 5.

36.   Propagating Gospel Society to the Board of Trade. London, March 19, 1764, PRO:CO 5/540.

37.   *Ibid.;* Necessary furniture for the several churches of Florida. East and West Florida, July 20, 1764, PRO:CO 5/540; Charles M. Andrews, *Guide to the Materials for American History, to 1783 in the Public Record Office of Great Britain* (Washington, D.C., Carnegie Institution of Washington, 1914), II, 107; Pennington, "Episcopal Church in Florida," 9–10.

38.   James Pownall to the secretary of the Propagating Gospel Society. Whitehall, March 13 and July 21, 1764, and March 27, 1765, PRO:CO 5/563.

39.   *Ibid.*

40.   Pennington, "'Episcopal Church in Florida," 4-8.

41.   R. W. Pettengill (ed.), *Letters from America, 1776-1779* (New York: Houghton Mifflin Company, 1924), 226; Johnson, *British West Florida,* 164-65; Pennington, "Episcopal Church in Florida," 9, and 13-14; Dunbar Rowland, *History of Mississippi Heart of the South* (Chicago: S. J. Clarke Publishing Company, 1928), I, 264-65.

42.   Memorial of George Chapman. London, August 13, 1773, PRO:CO 3/154; Pennington, "Episcopal Church in Florida," 14.

43.   Pettengill, *Letters from America,* 226; Pennington, "Episcopal Church in Florida," 9, and 13-14.

44.   Mowat, *East Florida as a British Province,* 31; Shea, *Catholic Church in Colonial Days,* II, 92-94; Siebert, *Loyalists in East Florida,* I, 6, and II, 360; Kenneth H. Beeson, Jr. "Fromjadas and Indigo: The Minorcan Colony in Florida" (Master's thesis, University of Florida, 1960), 43-44, and 76-77; Pennington, "Episcopal Church in Florida," 10-12.

45.   Many sources refer to the priest of New Smyrna as Pedro Campos or Peter Camps. Baptismal register of Pedro Camps. New Smyrna, 1768-77 (located in the library of the University of Notre Dame, South Bend, Indiana, and in the microfilm collection of the St. Augustine Historical Society, St. Augustine, Florida); A letter of the archbishop of Valencia concerning the clerical privileges of the New Smyrna clergy. Trascati, August 28, 1771; A letter of resolution to the king of Spain from Cuba. Madrid, September 27, 1770; Bishop of Cuba to Don Pedro Camps. Havana, December 3, 1771; Proceedings of the king's council. Madrid, August 21, 1773; The king to the bishop of Cuba. Madrid, August 4, 1773, A. M. Brooks and Annie Averette (ed. and trans.), *The Unwritten History of Old St. Augustine* (St. Augustine: Record Press Company, 1909?), 191-98, and 210-13; Beeson, "Fromjadas and Indigo: The Minorcan Colony in Florida," 43-44; Curley, *Church and State in the Spanish Floridas, 1783-1822,* 25-26, and 40-49.

46.   A letter of resolution to the king of Spain from Cuba. Madrid, September 27, 1770, Brooks and Averette, *Unwritten History of Old St. Augustine,* 191-97.

47.   *Ibid.*

48.   *Ibid.;* Pennington, "The Episcopal Church in Florida," 8-9; Shea, *Catholic Church in Colonial Days,* II, 91-92.

49.   Bishop of Cuba to the crown. Havana, December 14, 1771; Bishop of Cuba to Pedro Camps. Havana, December 3, 1771; Proceedings of the king's council. Madrid, August 21, 1773, Brooks and Averette, *Unwritten History of Old St. Augustine,* 198-200, and 204-25; Curley, *Church and State in the Spanish Floridas, 1783-1822,* 40-47.

50.   Bishop of Cuba to Pedro Camps. Havana, December 3, 1771, Brooks and Averette, *Unwritten History of Old St. Augustine,* 198-200.

51.   *Ibid.*

52.   Proceedings of the king's council. Madrid, August 21, 1773, Brooks and Averette, *Unwritten History of Old St. Augustine,* 214-25; Beeson, "Fromjadas and Indigo: The Minorcan Colony in Florida," 24-25, and 76-77.

53.   *Ibid.*

54.   The king of Spain to the bishop of Cuba. Madrid, August 4, 1773, Brooks and Averette, *Unwritten History of Old St. Augustine,* 226–28; Beeson, "Fromjadas and Indigo: The Minorcan Colony in Florida," 98–105; Curley, *Church and State in the Spanish Floridas, 1783–1822,* 40–49.

9   *Indian Affairs during the Transfer of Florida from Franco-Spanish to British Rule*

1.   Governor Juan de Ayala Escobar to the crown. St. Augustine, November 19, 1717, MS, AGI 58–1–35/74; The visit of the chief of Cavetas to St. Augustine. St. Augustine, December 15, 1717, MS, AGI 58–1–30/68; Governor Juan de Ayala Escobar to the crown. St. Augustine, December 22, 1717, and February 28, 1718, MSS, AGI 58–1–30/68/73/75; Governor Antonio de Benavides to the crown. St. Augustine, September 30, 1718, MS, AGI 58–1–30/84; Governor Antonio de Benavides to the crown. St. Augustine, October 15, 1723, MS, AGI 58–1–29/59; Royal *cédula* to the governor of Florida. Ildefonso, June 16, 1725, MS, AGI 58–1–24/169; Governor Antonio de Benavides to the crown. St. Augustine, October 15, 1728, MS, AGI 58–1–29/100; John Jay TePaske, *The Governorship of Spanish Florida, 1700–1763* (Durham: Duke University Press, 1959), 193–226; Verne E. Chatelain, *The Defenses of Spanish Florida, 1565–1763* (Washington, D.C.: Carnegie Institution of Washington Publications, 1941), 79–92.

2.   The title Creek is a short name for Ochese or Ocheese Creek Indians. Those Indians residing in the valleys of the Flint and Chattahoochee Rivers were called Lower Creeks. Upper Creeks inhabited the territory surrounding the Coosa, Tallapoosa, and Alabama Rivers. Verner W. Crane, "The Origin of the Name of the Creek Indians," *Mississippi Valley Historical Review,* V (December, 1918), 339–42; Helen L. Shaw, *British Administration of the Southern Indians, 1756–1783* (Lancaster, Pennsylvania: Lancaster Press, 1931), 2; For a careful history and description of the Creek Indians and other southeastern tribes see, John R. Swanton, *Early History of the Creek Indians and Their Neighbors,* Bulletin Number 73, Bureau of American Ethnology, Smithsonian Institution (Washington, D.C.: United States Government Printing Office, 1922); John R. Swanton and J. N. B. Hewitt, "Notes on the Creek Indians," *Anthropological Papers,* Bulletin Number 123, Bureau of American Ethnology, Smithsonian Institution (Washington, D.C.: United States Government Printing Office, 1939), 119–60, and John R. Swanton, *The Indians of the Southeastern United States,* Bulletin Number 137, Bureau of American Ethnology, Smithsonian Institution (Washington, D.C.: United States Government Printing Office, 1946).

3.   Royal officials to the crown. St. Augustine, February 22, 1715, MS, AGI 58–1–30/36; Governor Francisco de Córcoles y Martínez to the crown. St. Augustine, July 5, and November 28, 1715, MSS, AGI 58–1–30/42/44; Governor Francisco de Córcoles y Martínez to the crown. St. Augustine, January 25, 1716, and April 11, 1717, MSS, AGI 58–1–30/55; Memorial of Miguel Duran concerning the construction of the fort at Apalache. Madrid, February 12, 1716, MS, AGI 58–1–30/53; Royal *cédulas* to the governor of Florida. Madrid, February 17 and 18, and April 17, 1716, MSS, AGI 58–1–24/37/44/52; Governor Juan de Ayala Escobar to the crown. St. Augustine, January 28 and 31, and November 22,

1717, and April 28 and August 3, 1718, MSS, AGI 58–1–30/60/66/70/177–178; Governor Benavides to the crown. St. Augustine, March 8, 1723, MSS, AGI 58–2–16/8–9; Governor Benavides to the crown. St. Augustine, May 27, 1726, MS, AGI 58–1–29/73; Governor Francisco del Moral Sánchez to the crown. St. Augustine, May 23 and October 12, 1735, MSS, AGI 87–1–1/18/23; TePaske, *Governorship of Spanish Florida*, 193–315; James G. Johnson, "The Colonial Southeast, 1732–1763: An International Contest for Territorial and Economic Control," *University of Colorado Studies*, XIX (May, 1932), 206, 209, and 213.

4. *Ibid.*

5. Governor Montiano to the president of the Havana Company. St. Augustine, December 16, 1744, MS, AGI 58–2–13/19; Royal *cédula* to the governor of Florida. Madrid, December 12, 1744, MS, AGI 86–7–21/38; Governor Montiano to the crown. St. Augustine, February 17, 1745, and March 6, 1746, MSS, AGI 58–2–13/17/19; Commandant of Apalache to Governor Montiano. Apalache, May 21, 1745, MS, AGI 58–2–12/19; TePaske, *Governorship of Spanish Florida*, 215–25.

6. *Ibid.*

7. Governor Montiano to the crown. St. Augustine, August 3, 1747, MS, AGI 86–7–21/44; Governor Montiano to the crown. St. Augustine, March 15, 1748, MS, AGI 86–6–5/81; Memorial of Governor Montiano. St. Augustine, March 16, 1748, MS, AGI 58–1–32/65; Governor Melchor de Navarrette to the crown. St. Augustine, February 15, 1750, MS, AGI 86–7–21/53; Governor Fulgencio de García Solís to the crown. St. Augustine, July 27, 1754, MS, AGI 58–1–33/41; Letters from the governor of Florida concerning English infiltrations in Spanish Florida. July 17 and 27, 1754, and May 24, July 12, and November 11, 1755, MSS, AGNM 436, Documents 1–8 and 1–5; John Tate Lanning, *The Diplomatic History of Georgia* (Chapel Hill: University of North Carolina Press, 1936), 174–230; TePaske, *Governorship of Spanish Florida*, 218–26.

8. *Ibid.*

9. Governor Alonso Fernández de Heredia to Minister Julián de Arriaga. St. Augustine, October 14, 1757, MS, AGI 87–3–13/23, SD 2659; Governor of Cuba to Minister Julián de Arriaga. Havana, October 26, 1757, MS, AGI 87–3–13/25, SD 2659; Bishop of Cuba to the crown. Havana, March 31, 1758, MS, AGI 86–6–6/11A, SD 2660; Governor Lucas Fernando de Palacio to the crown. St. Augustine, November 1, 1758, MS, AGI 87–3–13/28, SD 2659; Governor Lucas Fernando de Palacio to Minister Julián de Arriaga. St. Augustine, February 17, 1759, MS, AGI 86–6–6/58; Governor Lucas Fernando de Palacio to the crown. St. Augustine, May 27, 1760, MS, AGI 86–6–6/11; Governor Lucas Fernando de Palacio to Minister Julián de Arriaga. St. Augustine, January 11, 1761, MS, AGI 86–7–11/4; Governor Lucas Fernando de Palacio to Minister Julián de Arriaga. St. Augustine, July 15, 1761, MS, AGI 86–6–6/24, SD 2660; William B. Griffen, "Spanish Pensacola, 1700–1763," *Florida Historical Quarterly*, XXXVII (January–April, 1959), 246–61.

10. Governor Feliú to Minister Julián de Arriaga. St. Augustine, February 20, 1763, MS, AGI 86–6–6/88, SD 2542; Governor Feliú to Minister Julián de Arriaga. St. Augustine, February 20, and May 28, 1763, MSS, AGI 87–3–13/30–31.

11.   Governor Feliú to Minister Julián de Arriaga. St. Augustine, April 16, 1764, MS, AGI 86–6–6/43, SD 2543; Major Ogilvie to the Board of Trade. St. Augustine, January 26, 1764, PRO:CO 5/540.

12.   Acts establishing the Pensacola Indians near Vera Cruz. 1764–66, MSS, AGNM 911, Ramo de Tierras, Legajo 466; Governor Feliú and Don Juan Elixio de la Puente to the governor of Cuba. St. Augustine and Havana, January 22, 1764, and January 27, 1770, MSS, AGI 87–1–5/4, SD 2595; Puente to the governor of Cuba. Havana, September 22, 1766, MS, AGI 87–1–5/3, SD 2595.

13.   *Ibid.;* One statistical account shows twenty Indian men as émigrés of St. Augustine, while another report mentions a total of only fourteen male exiles.

14.   *Ibid.*

15.   Captain Díaz to Conde de Ricla. Apalache, November 6, 1763, MS, AGI 86–7–11/16; Captain Díaz to Conde de Ricla. Apalache, January 19, and 21, 1764, MSS, AGI 86–7–11/20.

16.   *Ibid.;* Captain Harries to General Gage. Apalache, May 11, 1764, Mark F. Boyd, "From a Remote Frontier: Letters and Documents Pertaining to San Marcos de Apalache, 1763–1769, During the British Occupation of Florida," *Florida Historical Quarterly,* XIX (January, 1941), 193, 206, 208, and XX (July, 1941), 89.

17.   *Ibid.*

18.   Acts establishing the Pensacola Indians near Vera Cruz. 1764–66, MSS, AGNM 911, Ramo de Tierras, Legajo 466; Lieutenant Amoscotigue to the viceroy of New Spain. San Carlos, February 26, and March 6, 1765, MSS, AGNM 911, Ramo de Tierras, Legajo 466.

19.   *Ibid.*

20.   *Ibid.*

21.   *Ibid.*

22.   *Ibid.;* For additional information concerning the Indian community at San Carlos see, Robert L. Gold, "The Settlement of the Pensacola Indians in New Spain, 1763–1770," *Hispanic American Historical Review,* XLV (November, 1965), 567–76.

23.   Dunbar Rowland and Albert G. Sanders (eds.), *Mississippi Provincial Archives: French Dominion, 1729–1740* (Jackson, Mississippi: Press of the Mississippi Department of Archives and History, 1927), I, 54–126, and *passim;* Dunbar Rowland and Albert G. Sanders (eds.), *Mississippi Provincial Archives: French Dominion, 1701–1729* (Jackson, Mississippi: Press of the Mississippi Department of Archives and History, 1929), II, *passim;* Dunbar Rowland and Albert G. Sanders (eds.), *Mississippi Provincial Archives: French Dominion, 1704–1743* (Jackson, Mississippi: Press of the Mississippi Department of Archives and History, 1932), III, 204–5, 228, 264, 343, 504–15, 622–24, and *passim;* John Francis McDermott (ed.), *The French in the Mississippi Valley* (Urbana: University of Illinois Press, 1965), 103–22; Charles Gayarré, *History of Louisiana: The French Domination* (New York: William J. Widdleton, Publisher, 1866), I, 116, 224–35, 273–74, 396–453, and *passim.*

24.   Rowland and Sanders, *Mississippi Provincial Archives,* I, 146–47, 193, 298–320, 329–98; Gayarré, *History of Louisiana,* I, 456–90 and 497–507; II, 1–92, and *passim.*

25. Rowland and Sanders, *Mississippi Provincial Archives,* I, 71, 110, 255–56, 289, 365, and *passim;* Gayarré, *History of Louisiana,* II, 39–42, 49–51, 70–72.

26. Rowland and Sanders, *Mississippi Provincial Archives,* III, 122, 129–30, 159, 400–402, 594, 606–9, 750, and *passim;* Gayarré, *History of Louisiana,* I, 431–32, 457–58, 500, 514–16; II, 35.

27. N. N. Miller Surrey, *The Commerce of Louisiana during the French Regime, 1699–1763* (New York: Columbia University Press, 1916), 418–30.

28. Gayarré, *History of Louisiana,* II, 83–84.

29. *Ibid.,* 89–91.

30. *Ibid.*

31. *Ibid.,* 95, 99, 104–105; Milo B. Howard, Jr., and Robert R. Rea (eds. and trans.), *The Mémoire Justificatif of the Chevalier Montault de Monberaut: Indian Diplomacy in British West Florida, 1763–1765* (University, Alabama: University of Alabama Press, 1965), 28–29.

32. Governor Kerlérec to Major Farmar. New Orleans, October 2, 1763, Dunbar Rowland (ed.), *Mississippi Provincial Archives, 1763–1766: English Dominion* (Nashville: Brandon Printing Company, 1921), I, 54–58.

33. Council with the Choctaws by Major Farmar and Monsieur d'Abbadie. Mobile, November 14, 1763; Major Farmar to the Alibamons. Mobile, January 24, 1764, Rowland, *Mississippi Provincial Archives,* I, 81–91.

34. Gayarré, *History of Louisiana,* II, 99.

35. *Ibid.,* 102–4.

36. Major Farmar to the secretary of war. Mobile, January 24, 1764, Rowland, *Mississippi Provincial Archives,* I, 113.

37. Major Farmar to Captain de Ville. On board the *Stag,* in Pensacola harbor, October 2, 1763, Rowland, *Mississippi Provincial Archives,* I, 59; Gayarré, *History of Louisiana,* I, 98–99.

38. Creek Congress at Picolata. Picolata, November 15–18, 1765, PRO:CO 5/548; Creek Congress at Pensacola. Pensacola, May 26–June 4, 1765; Chickasaws and Choctaws Congress at Mobile. Mobile, March 20–April 4, 1765; Rowland, *Mississippi Provincial Archives,* I, 188–255; John Richard Alden, *John Stuart and the Southern Colonial Frontier, 1754–1775* (Ann Arbor: University of Michigan Press, 1944), 192–214, and 334–36; Shaw, *British Administration of the Southern Indians,* 31–32, and 37–48.

39. Major Farmar to the secretary of war. Mobile, January 24, 1764, Rowland, *Mississippi Provincial Archives,* I, 8, and 11

40. *Ibid.,* 11.

41. Lieutenant Ford to Major Farmar. Tombecbe, December 3, 1763, Rowland, *Mississippi Provincial Archives,* I, 39.

42. Report of Major William Forbes on Pensacola. Pensacola, January 30, 1764, Rowland, *Mississippi Provincial Archives,* I, 112–15.

43. Lieutenant Colonel Provost to the secretary of war. Fort Pensacola, September 7, 1763; Major Farmar to the secretary of war. Mobile, January 24, 1764; Report of Major Forbes. Pensacola, January 30, 1764, Rowland, *Mississippi Provincial Archives,* I, 8, 11, 112–15, and 136–37; Clarence E. Carter, "The Beginnings of British West Florida, *Mississippi Valley Historical Review,* IV (December, 1917), 321.

44. Report of Major Forbes. Pensacola, January 30, 1764, Rowland, *Mississippi Provincial Archives,* I, 112–15.

45. Major Farmar to the secretary of war. Mobile, March 2, 1764; Major Farmar to the secretary of war. Mobile, August 1, 1764; Major Forbes to the secretary of war. Pensacola, January 29, 1764; Governor Johnstone to the Board of Trade. West Florida, May 30, 1764, Rowland, *Mississippi Provincial Archives,* I, 115, 118–19, 141–43, and 150–51; General Thomas Gage to Lord Halifax. New York, August 10 and November 9, 1764, Clarence E. Carter (ed.), *The Correspondence of General Thomas Gage with the Secretaries of State and with the War Office and the Treasury, 1763–1775* (New Haven: Yale University Press, 1933), I, 33–35, and 41–44; Alden, *John Stuart and the Southern Colonial Frontier,* 194–98.

46. Major Farmar and Governor Jean Jacques Blaise d'Abbadie to the Choctaws. Mobile, November 14, 1763, Rowland, *Mississippi Provincial Archives,* I, 83–91.

47. Major Farmer and Governor d'Abbadie to the Choctaws. Mobile, November 14, 1763; Major Farmar's instructions to commanding officers. Mobile, October 24, 1763; Major Farmar's instructions to James Germany. Mobile, January 10, 1764; Major Farmar addresses the Creeks. Mobile, January 24, 1764; Major Farmar and Governor d'Abbadie to the Indians at Alabama. Mobile, January 24, 1764, Rowland, *Mississippi Provincial Archives,* I, 18, and 80–94.

48. Major Farmar's instructions to commanding officers. Mobile, October 24, 1763, Rowland, *Mississippi Provincial Archives,* I, 92–93.

49. Major Farmar and Governor d'Abbadie to the Choctaws. Mobile, November 14, 1763; Major Farmar's instructions to commanding officers. Mobile, October 24, 1763; Major Farmar's instructions to James Germany. Mobile, January 10, 1764; Major Farmar addresses the Creeks. Mobile, January 24, 1764; Major Farmar and Governor d'Abbadie to the Indians at Alabama. Mobile, January 24, 1764, Rowland, *Mississippi Provincial Archives,* I, 18, and 80–94.

50. Major Farmar addresses the Creeks. Mobile, January 24, 1764, Rowland, *Mississippi Provincial Archives,* I, 80–81.

51. Leonard Woods Labaree (ed.), *Royal Instructions to British Colonial Governors, 1670–1776* (New York: D. Appleton-Century Company, 1935), II, 479.

52. *Ibid.*

53. *Ibid.;* Alden, *John Stuart and the Southern Colonial Frontier,* 199–214; Shaw, *British Administration of the Southern Indians,* 31–37; Charles L. Mowat, *East Florida as a British Province, 1763–1784* (Berkeley: University of California Press, 1943), 20–23; Cecil Johnson, *British West Florida, 1763–1783* (New Haven: Yale University Press, 1943), 41–42.

54. Great Britain, *By the King: A Proclamation, October 7, 1763* (Mark Baskett, 1763); Alden, *John Stuart and the Southern Colonial Frontier,* 207–14; Shaw, *British Administration of the Southern Indians,* 40–42, and 47; Albert T. Volwiler, *George Croghan and the Westward Movement, 1741–1782* (Cleveland: Arthur H. Clark Company, 1926), 172–73.

55. *Ibid.;* Ray Allen Billington, *Western Expansion: A History of the American Frontier* (New York: Macmillan Company, 1949), 141.

56. Stuart's Trade Regulations of 1765 are available in Appendix A of the following history. Alden, *John Stuart and the Southern Colonial Frontier*, 210, and 341–43.

57.   Alden, *John Stuart and the Southern Colonial Frontier*, 210, and 341–43.

58.   General Thomas Gage to Lord Halifax. New York, June 1, 1765, Carter, *Correspondence of General Gage*, I, 58–61; Chickasaws and Choctaws Congress at Mobile. Mobile, March 20–April 4, 1765; Creek Congress at Pensacola. Pensacola, May 26–June 4, 1765, Rowland, *Mississippi Provincial Archives*, I, 188–255; Clinton N. Howard, "The Interval of Military Government in West Florida," *Louisiana Historical Quarterly*, XXII (January, 1938), 6, and 10–11.

59.   Howard and Rea, *Mémoire Justificatif of the Chevalier Montault de Monberaut*, 22–43, 69, 82–91, 108–10, 130–33, 141–54, 171–76.

60.   Chickasaws and Choctaws Congress at Mobile. Mobile, March 20–April 4, 1765, Rowland, *Mississippi Provincial Archives*, I, 215–55; Alden, *John Stuart and the Southern Colonial Frontier*, 204–14.

61.   *Ibid.*

62.   The Chickasaw and Choctaw Treaty. Mobile, April 4, 1765, Rowland, *Mississippi Provincial Archives*, I, 249–55.

63.   *Ibid.*; For a fine study of Anglo-Indian boundaries in Florida during the British Period see, Louis DeVorsey, Jr., *The Indian Boundary in the Southern Colonies, 1763–1775* (Chapel Hill: University of North Carolina Press, 1966), 181–227.

64.   *Ibid.*

65.   The report of Governor George Johnstone and Superintendent John Stuart. Pensacola, June 12, 1765, Rowland, *Mississippi Provincial Archives*, I, 185–86.

66.   *Ibid.*

67.   General Thomas Gage to Lord Halifax. New York, March 10, April 13, and May 12, 1764, Carter, *Correspondence of General Gage*, I, 17–24, and 26–29; The report of Governor Johnstone and John Stuart. Pensacola, June 12, 1765; Creek Congress at Pensacola. Pensacola, May 26–June 4, 1765; Medal ceremony for the Upper and Lower Creeks. Pensacola, June 4, 1765; The Creek Treaty. Pensacola, May 28, 1765, Rowland, *Mississippi Provincial Archives*, I, 184–215.

68.   *Ibid.*

69.   The Creek Treaty. Pensacola, May 28, 1765, Rowland, *Mississippi Provincial Archives*, I, 184–215.

70.   Governor James Grant to the Board of Trade. East Florida, December 9, 1765, PRO:CO 5/540; General Thomas Gage to Lord Halifax. New York, March 10, April 13, and May 12, 1764, Carter, *Correspondence of General Gage*, I, 17–24, and 26–29; The report of Governor Johnstone and Superintendent John Stuart. Pensacola, June 12, 1765; Creek Congress at Pensacola. Pensacola, May 26–June 4, 1765; Medal ceremony for the Upper and Lower Creeks. Pensacola, June 4, 1765; The Creek Treaty. Pensacola, May 28, 1765, Rowland, *Mississippi Provincial Archives*, I, 184–215; Alden, *John Stuart and the Southern Colonial Frontier*, 204–7; Johnson, *British West Florida*, 41–42; Howard, "Interval of Military Government in West Florida," 11; DeVorsey, *Indian Boundary in the Southern Colonies*, 204–7.

71.   The report of Governor George Johnstone and Superintendent John

Stuart. Pensacola, June 12, 1765, Rowland, *Mississippi Provincial Archives*, I, 187.
72. *Ibid.*
73. Governor James Grant to the Board of Trade. East Florida, November 22, 1764, PRO:CO 5/540; Governor James Grant to the Board of Trade. East Florida, March 1, 1765, PRO:CO 5/540.
74. *Ibid.*
75. Governor James Grant to the Board of Trade. East Florida, September 2, 1764, PRO:CO 5/540.
76. Governor James Grant to John Pownall and the Board of Trade. London, July 30, 1763, PRO:CO 5/546.
77. Governor James Grant to John Pownall. London, July 30, 1763, PRO:CO 5/540; Governor Grant to the Board of Trade. East Florida, September 2, 1764, PRO:CO 5/540; Governor Grant to the Board of Trade. East Florida, November 22, 1764, PRO:CO 5/540; Governor Grant to the Board of Trade. East Florida, March 1, 1765, PRO:CO 5/540; The report of Governor George Johnstone and Superintendent John Stuart. Pensacola, June 12, 1765, Rowland, *Mississippi Provincial Archives*, I, 186–87.
78. Assorted presents for a proposed meeting with East Florida Indians in 1766. East Florida, January 13, 1766, PRO:CO 5/540; Governor George Johnstone to the Board of Trade. West Florida, January 29, 1764, PRO:CO 5/547; General account of the receipt and expenditures of the civil establishment of East Florida. East Florida, March 11, 1765, PRO:CO 5/540; Captain Harries to General Gage. Apalache, May 11, 1764, Boyd, "From a Remote Frontier," XX (July, 1941), 89, 204–7; Mowat, *East Florida as a British Province*, 35 and 38; Clinton N. Howard, *The British Development of West Florida, 1763–1769* (Berkeley: University of California Press, 1947), 119–23.
79. *Ibid.*
80. Governor Grant to the Board of Trade. East Florida, September 2, 1764, PRO:CO 5/540; Governor Grant to the Board of Trade. East Florida, December 9, 1765, PRO:CO 5/540; Journal of the Picolata Congress. Picolata, November 15–18, 1765, PRO:CO 5/548; The Picolata Treaty. Picolata, November 18, 1765, PRO:CO 5/548; Alden, *John Stuart and the Southern Colonial Frontier*, 229–33.
81. Governor Grant to the Board of Trade. East Florida, January 13, 1766, PRO:CO 5/540; Journal of the Picolata Congress. Picolata, November 18, 1765, PRO:CO 5/548.
82. Journal of the Picolata Congress. Picolata, November 18, 1765, PRO:CO 5/548; Governor Grant to the Board of Trade. East Florida, December 9, 1765, PRO:CO 5/540.
83. Governor Grant to the Board of Trade. East Florida, December 9, 1765, PRO:CO 5/540.
84. Journal of the Picolata Congress. Picolata, November 18, 1765, PRO:CO 5/548.
85. The Picolata Treaty. Picolata, November 18, 1765, PRO:CO 5/548; DeVorsey, *Indian Boundary in the Southern Colonies*, 181–203.
86. Governor Grant to the Board of Trade. East Florida, December 9, 1765, PRO:CO 5/540; Governor Grant to the Board of Trade. East Florida, January 13, 1766, PRO:CO 5/540.

87.   Governor Grant to the Board of Trade. East Florida, April 26, 1766, PRO:CO 5/541; Governor Grant to the Board of Trade. East Florida, August 5, 1766, PRO:CO 5/541; State of Indian affairs in the southern provinces of America from 1765-66. Florida, August 30, 1766, PRO:CO 5/541; Lord Shelburne to Governor Grant. Whitehall, February 19 and November 14, 1767, PRO:CO 5/548; The Second Picolata Congress. November 21, 1767, PRO:CO 5/549; Governor Grant to Lord Shelburne. East Florida, December 10, 1767, PRO:CO 5/549; Memorial of Governor James Grant of East Florida. London, January, 1772, PRO:CO 5/545; Report of Governor George Johnstone. Pensacola, June 23, 1766, Rowland, *Mississippi Provincial Archives,* I, 511-15; Mr. Pierce Sinnot to John Stuart. Apalache, March 2, 1768, Boyd, "From a Remote Frontier," XXI (October, 1942), 136-37; Johnson, *British West Florida,* 76-82.

88.   Lord Shelburne to Governor Grant. Whitehall, November 14, 1767, PRO:CO 5/548.

89.   Governor Grant to the Board of Trade. East Florida, April 26, 1766, PRO:CO 5/541; Governor Grant to the Board of Trade. St. Augustine, August 5, 1766, PRO:CO 5/541; State of Indian affairs in the southern provinces of America from 1765-66. Florida, August 30, 1766, PRO:CO 5/541; Lord Shelburne to Governor Grant. Whitehall, February 19 and November 14, 1767, PRO:CO 5/548; The Second Picolata Congress. November 21, 1767, PRO:CO 5/549; Governor Grant to Lord Shelburne. East Florida, December 10, 1767, PRO:CO 5/549; Memorial of Governor Grant. London, January, 1772, PRO:CO 5/545; Report of Governor George Johnstone. Pensacola, June 23, 1766, Rowland, *Mississippi Provincial Archives,* I, 511-15; Mr. Pierce Sinnot to John Stuart. Apalache, March 2, 1768, Boyd, "From a Remote Frontier," XXI (October, 1942), 136-37; Johnson, *British West Florida,* 76-82.

90.   General Thomas Gage to Lord Shelburne. New York, April 28, 1767, and April 24, 1768; General Gage to Lord Hillsborough. New York, April 1, 1769, and July 7, 1770, Carter, *The Correspondence of General Thomas Gage,* I, 138, 170, 210, 222, and 262; James W. Covington, "Trade Relations between Southwestern Florida and Cuba, 1600-1840," *Florida Historical Quarterly,* XXXVIII (October, 1959), 116-17.

Bibliography

The majority of primary source materials employed in this manuscript are concentrated in the P. K. Yonge Memorial Library of Florida History. The P. K. Yonge Memorial Library is located at the University of Florida, Gainesville, Florida. In this rich archive of Floridiana, there exists a number of superb collections of photostated and original documents concerning the history of Florida from the sixteenth through the twentieth centuries. The John B. Stetson Collection of Spanish Colonial Papers is outstanding among the extant research materials of the Yonge Memorial Library. It includes literally thousands of photostated documents from the Archivo General de Indias (AGI) in Seville, Spain. The Stetson Papers contain the principal documentation for the history of Florida from 1513 to 1820. These comprehensive sources for the study of Florida have been available since 1954, but unfortunately, only a few scholarly works appear today as evidence of their significance. Perhaps, the numerous subjects of scholarship present in this collection will eventually be examined as "borderlands" history again becomes fashionable.

The P. K. Yonge Memorial Library of Florida History also owns several other bodies of sources relevant to this study. English East and West Florida materials for the period from 1763 to 1784 are totally accessible in this archive. Public Records Office: Colonial Office (PRO:CO) papers exist in microfilm and occasionally transcript form. The Yonge Memorial Library additionally possesses, in approximate order of utility, a number of microfilm reels of the Papeles Procedentes de Cuba (PPC), North Carolina Collection of Spanish Records (NCCSR), and manuscripts from the Biblioteca Nacional de Madrid (BNM). These microfilms appropriately relate to the Spanish Period of Florida history.

Some French materials for West Florida are also present in the Yonge Library. Since the civic records for French Colonial Mobile are apparently missing from the Mobile County depository, this study relies upon the published document collections edited by Dunbar Rowland and Albert G. Sanders and entitled *Mississippi Provincial Archives*. The *Mississippi Provincial Archives: French Dominion* and *English Dominion* certainly offer sufficient documentary sources for French and English Louisiana east of the Mississippi River, 1701-66.

Three other repositories were important to the preparation of this book. In the Archivo General de la Nación, México (AGNM), the documentation for three centuries of Spanish history is available for the viceroyalty of New Spain.

Property papers from this famous archive were examined in reference to the Florida settlement in New Spain. The East Florida Papers (EFP) located in the Library of Congress also provided valuable sources, although this document collection typically concerns the Second Spanish Period of Florida history, 1784–1821. Finally, this work includes documentation from Mark F. Boyd's excellent personal library of late eighteenth-century Florida history.

Public Documents

Florida. Florida Deeds: Town Lots and Lands. 357. Documents: 20 and 28. Field Note Division, Department of Agriculture, Tallahassee, Florida.

———. *Florida Statutes: Helpful and Useful Materials*. III. University of Florida Law Library, Gainesville, Florida.

———. *Spanish Land Grants in Florida, Confirmed Claims*. III and V. United States, WPA Division of Professional and Service Projects, Tallahassee: State Library Board, 1940.

———. *Spanish Land Grants in Florida, Unconfirmed Claims*. I. United States, WPA Division of Professional and Service Projects, Tallahassee: State Library Board, 1940.

Great Britain. *By the King: A Proclamation, October 7, 1763*. Printed by Mark Baskett, 1763. A copy is in the P. K. Yonge Memorial Library of Florida History, Gainesville, Florida.

———. *Par Monsieur Robert Farmar Majeur du 34ᵐᵉ Regiment & Commandant des Troupes de Sa Majesté Britannique, dans la Lousiane*. . . . Chicago: Students of Chicago School of Printing, 1939.

New York. New York Colonial Manuscripts. 84. Document 54. New York State Library, Albany, New York, and Mark F. Boyd Library of Florida History, Tallahassee, Florida.

U.S. *American State Papers: Documents of the Congress of the United States*. IV. Washington, D.C.: Gales and Seaton, 1859.

———. *American State Papers: Public Lands*. I. Washington, D.C.: Gales and Seaton, 1834.

———. Congress. *Message from the President of the United States Transmitting Documents Relative to the Boundary Line between Georgia and Florida*. 20th Congress, First Session, March 3, 1828.

———. Congress, Senate. *Claims of the Catholic Church Pertaining to Certain Properties Held by the United States*. 30th Congress, Second Session, January 30, 1849. Senate Executive Document 21.

Published Document Collections

Alvord, Clarence Walworth, and Carter, Clarence Edwin (eds.). *The Critical Period, 1763–1765*. British Series, I. Springfield: Illinois State Historical Library, 1915.

Andrews, Charles M. *Guide to the Materials for American History to 1783, in the Public Record Office of Great Britain*. II. Washington, D.C.: Carnegie Institution of Washington, 1914.

Brooks, A. M., and Averette, Annie (eds. and trans.). *The Unwritten History of Old St. Augustine*. St. Augustine: Record Press Company, 1909?.

Candler, Allen D. (ed.). *The Colonial Records of the State of Georgia, 1754–1759*. VII. Atlanta: The Franklin-Turner Company, 1906.

Carter, Clarence E. (ed.). *The Correspondence of General Thomas Gage with the Secretaries of State and with the War Office and the Treasury, 1763–1775*. I and II. New Haven: Yale University Press, 1933.

Colección de documentos inéditos relativos al descubrimiento, conquista, y colonización de los posesiones españoles en América y Oceania. XVI. Madrid: 1864–84.

Conner, Jeannette Thurber (trans. and ed.). *The Colonial Records of Spanish Florida, 1570–1580*. I and II. De Land, Florida: Florida Historical Society, 1925 and 1930.

Cumming, William P. *The Southeast in Early Maps*. Princeton: Princeton University Press, 1958.

Davenport, Frances Gardner, and Paullin, Charles Oscar (eds.). *European Treaties Bearing on the History of the United States and Its Dependencies*. IV. Washington, D.C.: Carnegie Institution of Washington, 1937.

Geiger, Maynard. *Biographical Dictionary of the Franciscans in Spanish Florida and Cuba (1528–1841)*. Patterson, New Jersey: St. Anthony Guild Press, 1940.

Giménez Fernández, Manuel. *Las bulas alejandrinas de 1493 referentes á las Indias*. Sevilla: Escuela de Estudios Hispano-Americanos, 1944.

Hansard, T. C. (ed.). *The Parliamentary History of England from the Earliest Period to the Year 1803*. XV. London: T. C. Hansard, 1813.

Harper, Francis (ed.). *The Travels of William Bartram, Naturalist's Edition*. New Haven: Yale University Press, 1958.

Labaree, Leonard Woods (ed.). *Royal Instructions to British Colonial Governors, 1670–1776*. I and II. New York: D. Appleton-Century Company, 1935.

Pettengill, R. W. (ed.). *Letters from America, 1776–1779*. New York: Houghton Mifflin Company, 1924.

Priestley, Herbert I. (trans. and ed.). *The Luna Papers: Documents Relating to the Expedition of Don Tristan de Luna y Arellano for the Conquest of Florida, 1557–1561*. I and II. De Land, Florida: Florida State Historical Society, 1928.

Rowland, Dunbar (ed.). *Mississippi Provincial Archives, 1763–1766: English Dominion*. I. Nashville: Brandon Printing Company, 1921.

Rowland, Dunbar, and Sanders, Albert G. (eds.). *Mississippi Provincial Archives: French Dominion, 1729–1740*. I. Jackson, Mississippi: Press of the Mississippi Department of Archives and History, 1927.

———. *Mississippi Provincial Archives: French Dominion, 1701–1729*. II. Jackson, Mississippi: Press of the Mississippi Department of Archives and History, 1929.

———. *Mississippi Provincial Archives: French Dominion, 1704–1743*. III. Jackson, Mississippi: Press of the Mississippi Department of Archives and History, 1932.

The St. Augustine Expedition of 1740: A Report to the South Carolina General Assembly, Reprinted from the Colonial Records of South Carolina. Columbia: South Carolina Archives Department, 1954.

Tratado definitivo de paz concluido entre el rey nuestro señor y s. m. christiani sima por una parte, y s. m. británica por otra, en Paris á 10. de Febrero de 1763, con sus artículos preliminares y la accesión de s. m. fidelísima á ellos, y al mismo tratado. Madrid: En la Imprenta Real de la Gaceta, 1763.

Walker, Fowler. *The Case of Mr. John Gordon with Respect to Certain Lands in East Florida, Purchased of His Catholic Majesty's Subjects by Him and Mr. Jesse Fish for Themselves and Others, His Britannick Majesty's Subjects: In Conformity to the Twentieth Article of the Last Definitive Treaty of Peace.* London: Printed 1772. Microfilm in the P. K. Yonge Memorial Library of Florida History from the New York City Public Library.

Whitaker, Arthur P. (trans. and ed.). *Documents Relating to the Commercial Policy of Spain in the Floridas with Incidental Reference to Louisiana.* De Land, Florida: Florida State Historical Society, 1931.

Books

A Geographical and Historical Description of the Principal Objects of the Present War in the West Indies, viz. Cartagena, Puerto Bello, La Vera Cruz, The Havana and St. Augustine Shewing Their Situation, Strength, Trade, etc. London: Printed for T. Gardner, 1741.

Abernethy, Thomas Perkins. *Western Lands and the American Revolution.* New York: Russell and Russell, Inc., 1959.

Alden, John R. *John Stuart and the Southern Colonial Frontier, 1754–1775.* Ann Arbor: University of Michigan Press, 1944.

Altamira, Rafael. *A History of Spain,* trans. M. Lee. New York: D. Van Nostrand Company, Inc., 1951.

Alvord, Clarence W. *The Mississippi Valley in British Politics.* I. Cleveland: Arthur H. Clark Company, 1917.

Arnade, Charles W. *Florida on Trial.* Coral Gables, Florida: University of Miami Press, 1959.

———. *The Siege of St. Augustine in 1702.* Gainesville: University of Florida Press, 1959.

Ballesteros y Beretta, Antonio. *Historia de España y su influencia en la historia universal.* I. Barcelona: Salvat Editores, S.A., 1928.

Basye, Arthur Herbert. *The Lords Commissioners of Trade and Plantations, Commonly Known as the Board of Trade, 1748–1782.* New Haven: Yale University Press, 1924.

Beer, George L. *British Colonial Policy, 1754–1765.* New York: Peter Smith, 1933.

Billington, Ray Allen. *Western Expansion: A History of the American Frontier.* New York: Macmillan Company, 1949.

Bolton, Herbert E. *Arredondo's Historical Proof of Spain's Title to Georgia.* Berkeley: University of California Press, 1925.

———. *The Mission as a Frontier Institution in the Spanish American Colonies.* El Paso: Texas Western College Press, 1960.

———. *The Spanish Borderlands, A Chronicle of Old Florida and the Southwest.* New Haven: Yale University Press, 1921.

Bond, Beverley W. *The Quit-Rent System in the American Colonies.* New Haven: Yale University Press, 1919.

Boyd, Mark F., Smith, Hale G., and Griffen, John W. *Here They Once Stood: The Tragic End of the Apalache Missions.* Gainesville: University of Florida Press, 1951.

Carroll, Mary Teresa Austin. *A Catholic History of Alabama and the Floridas.* New York: P. J. Kennedy and Sons, 1908.

Caughey, John Walton. *Bernardo de Gálvez in Louisiana, 1776–1783.* Berkeley: University of California Press, 1934.

Chambers, Henry E. *West Florida and Its Relation to the Historical Cartography of the United States.* Johns Hopkins University Studies in Historical and Political Science, Series XVI, Number 5. Baltimore: Johns Hopkins Press, 1898.

Chatelain, Verne E. *The Defenses of Spanish Florida, 1565–1763.* Washington, D.C.: Carnegie Institution of Washington Publications, 1941.

Conner, Jeannette Thurber (trans.). *Pedro Menéndez de Avilés, Adelantado, Governor and Captain General of Florida: Memorial by Gonzalo Solís de Merás.* De Land, Florida: Florida State Historical Society, 1923.

Curley, Rev. Michael J., C.S.S.R. *Church and State in the Spanish Floridas, 1783–1822.* Washington, D.C.: Catholic University of America Press, 1940.

De Vorsey, Louis Jr. *The Indian Boundary in the Southern Colonies, 1763–1775.* Chapel Hill: University of North Carolina Press, 1966.

De Voto, Bernard A. *The Course of Empire.* Boston: Houghton Mifflin Company, 1952.

Dickerson, Oliver M. *American Colonial Government, 1696–1765.* New York: Russell and Russell, Inc., 1962.

Dovell, J. E. *Florida—Historic, Dramatic, Contemporary.* I. New York: Lewis Historical Publishing Company, Inc., 1952.

Dunn, William E. *Spanish and French Rivalry in the Gulf Region of the United States, 1678–1702.* Austin: University of Texas Bulletin Number 1705, 1917.

Folmer, Henry. *Franco-Spanish Rivalry in North America, 1524–1763.* Glendale, California: Arthur H. Clark Company, 1953.

Ford, Lawrence C. *The Triangular Struggle for Spanish Pensacola, 1689–1739.* Washington, D.C.: Catholic University of America Press, 1939.

Gannon, Michael V. *The Cross in the Sand: The Early Catholic Church in Florida, 1513–1870.* Gainesville: University of Florida Press, 1965.

Gayarré, Charles. *History of Louisiana: The French Domination.* I and II. New York: William J. Widdleton Publisher, 1866.

Geiger, Maynard, O.F.M. *The Franciscan Conquest of Florida, 1573–1618.* Washington, D.C.: Catholic University of America Press, 1931.

Gibson, Charles. *The Aztecs under Spanish Rule: A History of the Indians of the Valley of Mexico, 1519–1810.* Stanford: Stanford University Press, 1964.

Gipson, Lawrence Henry. *The Great War for the Empire: The Victorious Years, VII, The British Empire before the American Revolution.* New York: Alfred A. Knopf, 1956.

———. *The Great War for the Empire: The Culmination, 1760–1763, VIII, The British Empire before the American Revolution.* New York: Alfred A. Knopf, 1954.

————. *The Triumphant Empire: New Responsibilities within the Enlarged Empire, 1763–1766, IX, The British Empire before the American Revolution.* New York: Alfred A. Knopf, 1956.

Haggard, J. Villasana. *Handbook for Translators of Spanish Historical Documents.* Oklahoma City: Semco Color Press, 1941.

Halstead, Murat. *The Story of Cuba.* Akron: Werner Company, 1896.

Hamilton, Peter J. *Colonial Mobile.* New York: Houghton Mifflin Company, 1898.

Haring, Clarence H. *The Spanish Empire in America.* New York: Oxford University Press, 1941.

Hart, Francis Russell. *The Siege of Havana, 1762.* New York: Houghton Mifflin Company, 1931.

Howard, Clinton N. *The British Development of West Florida, 1763–1769.* Berkeley: University of California Press, 1947.

Howard, Milo B., Jr., and Rea, Robert R. (eds. and trans.). *The Mémoire Justificatif of the Chevalier Montault de Monberaut.* University, Alabama: University of Alabama Press, 1954.

Jacobs, Wilbur R. (ed.). *Indians of the Southern Colonial Frontier: The Edmond Atkin Report and Plan of 1755.* Columbia, South Carolina: University of South Carolina Press, 1954.

Johnson, Cecil. *British West Florida, 1763–1783.* New Haven: Yale University Press, 1943.

Jones, Charles C. *The History of Georgia.* I and II. Boston: Houghton Mifflin Company, 1883.

Kerrigan, Anthony (trans.). *Barcia's Chronological History of the Continent of Florida . . . from the Year 1512, in Which Juan Ponce de León Discovered Florida, until the Year 1722.* Gainesville: University of Florida Press, 1951.

Lanning, John Tate. *The Diplomatic History of Georgia.* Chapel Hill: University of North Carolina Press, 1936.

————. *The Spanish Missions of Georgia.* Chapel Hill: University of North Carolina Press, 1935.

Lawson, Edward. *The Discovery of Florida and Its Discoverer Juan Ponce de León.* St. Augustine: By the Author, 1946.

Lecky, William E. H. *A History of England in the Eighteenth Century.* New York: D. Appleton and Company, 1891.

Leonard, Irving A. *The Spanish Approach to Pensacola, 1689–1693.* Albuquerque: Quivira Society, 1939.

Lowery, Woodbury. *The Spanish Settlements within the Present Limits of the United States, 1513–1574.* I and II. New York: G. P. Putnam's Sons, 1905.

Mayo, Lawrence Shaw. *The St. Mary's River, A Boundary.* Privately printed, 1914.

McDermott, John Francis (ed.). *The French in the Mississippi Valley.* Urbana: University of Illinois Press, 1965.

Monette, John W. *Extent of Florida: History of the Discovery and Settlement of the Valley of the Mississippi by the Three Great Powers, Spain, France, and Great Britain and the Subsequent Occupation, Settlement and Extension of Civil Government by the United States up to the Year 1846.* New York: Harper & Brothers, 1846.

Mowat, Charles L. *East Florida as a British Province, 1763–1784.* Berkeley: University of California Press, 1943.

Namier, Louis. *England in the Age of the American Revolution.* New York: St. Martin's Press, Inc., 1961.

Nobbe, George. *The North Briton: A Study in Political Propaganda.* New York: Columbia University Press, 1939.

Parkman, Francis, *A Half-Century of Conflict, Part VI, France and England in North America.* Boston: Little, Brown and Company, 1933.

———. *Montcalm and Wolfe,* III. New York: Charles Scribner's Sons, 1915.

———. *Pioneers of New France.* I. New York: Charles Scribner's Sons, 1915.

Peckham, Howard H. *Pontiac and the Indian Uprising.* Chicago: University of Chicago Press, 1947.

Pittman, Captain Philip. *The Present State of the European Settlements on the Mississippi.* Reprint of original edition, London, 1770. Cleveland: Arthur H. Clark Company, 1906.

Priestley, Herbert I. *Tristan de Luna, Conquistador of the Old South.* Glendale, California: Arthur H. Clark Company, 1936.

Rashed, Zenab Esmat. *The Peace of Paris, 1763.* Liverpool: The University Press, 1951.

Roberts, William. *An Account of the First Discovery and Natural History of Florida with Particular Detail of the Several Expeditions and Descents Made upon that Coast.* London: Printed for T. Jefferys, 1768.

Romans, Bernard. *A Concise Natural History of East and West Florida.* Facsimile Reproduction of 1775 Edition. Gainesville: University of Florida Press, 1962.

Rowland, Dunbar. *History of Mississippi Heart of the South.* Chicago: S. J. Clarke Publishing Company, 1925.

Rudiaz y Caravia, Eugenio. *La Florida: su conquista y colonización por Pedro Menéndez de Avilés.* I and II. Madrid: Hijos de J. A. Garcia, 1893.

Scoville, Joseph A. *The Old Merchants of New York City.* New York: Carleton Company, 1863.

Selley, W. T. *England in the Eighteenth Century.* London: Adam and Charles Black, 1934.

Shaw, Helen L. *British Administration of the Southern Indians, 1756–1783.* Lancaster, Pennsylvania: Lancaster Press, 1931.

Shea, John Gilmary. *The Catholic Church in Colonial Days.* I and II. New York: John Gilmary Shea, 1886.

Siebert, Wilbur H. *Loyalists in East Florida, 1774 to 1785.* I and II. De Land, Florida: Florida State Historical Society, 1929.

Sosin, Jack M. *Whitehall and the Wilderness: The Middle West in British Colonial Policy, 1760–1775.* Lincoln, Nebraska: University of Nebraska Press, 1961.

Stevens, William B. *A History of Georgia from Its First Discovery by Europeans to the Adoption of the Present Constitution in MDCCXVIII.* I and II. New York: D. Appleton and Company, 1847.

Stork, William, M.D. *A Description of East Florida with a Journal Kept by John Bartram of Philadelphia, Botanist to His Majesty for the Floridas: Upon a Journey from St. Augustine to the River St. Johns as Far as the Lakes.* London: W. Nicoll, 1769.

Surrey, N. N. Miller. *The Commerce of Louisiana during the French Regime, 1699–1763*. New York: Columbia University Press, 1916.

Swanton, John R. *Early History of the Creek Indians and Their Neighbors*. Bulletin Number 73, Bureau of American Ethnology, Smithsonian Institution. Washington, D.C.: United States Government Printing Office, 1922.

————. *Indian Tribes of the Lower Mississippi Valley and Adjacent Coast of the Gulf of Mexico*. Bulletin Number 43, Bureau of American Ethnology, Smithsonian Institution. Washington, D.C.: United States Government Printing Office, 1911.

————. *The Indian Tribes of North America*. Bulletin Number 145, Bureau of American Ethnology, Smithsonian Institution. Washington, D.C.: United States Government Printing Office, 1952.

————. *The Indians of the Southeastern United States*. Bulletin Number 137, Bureau of American Ethnology, Smithsonian Institution. Washington, D.C.: United States Government Printing Office, 1946.

Tanner, Helen Hornbeck. *Zéspedes in East Florida, 1784–1790*. Coral Gables. Florida: University of Miami Press, 1963.

TePaske, John Jay. *The Governorship of Spanish Florida, 1700–1763*. Durham: Duke University Press, 1964.

Vargas Ugarte, Rubén, S.J. *Los mártires de Florida, 1566–1572*. Lima: A. Castañeda, 1940.

Volwiler, Albert T. *George Croghan and the Westward Movement, 1741–1782*. Cleveland: Arthur H. Clark Company, 1926.

Walpole, Horace. *Memoirs of the Reign of King George the Third*. I. London: Lawrence and Bullen, 1894.

Wilson, James G. *Memorial History of the City of New York*. New York: 1892–93.

Zubillaga, Felix, S.I. *La Florida: la misión jesuítica, 1566–1572 y la colonización española*. Roma: Institutum Historicum S.I., 1941.

Articles and Periodicals

Aiton, A. S. "Spanish Colonial Reorganization under the Family Compact," *Hispanic American Historical Review*, XII (August, 1932), 269–80.

Alden, John Richard. "The Albany Congress and the Creation of the Indian Superintendencies," *Mississippi Valley Historical Review*, XXVII (September, 1940), 193–210.

Alvord, Clarence W. "The Genesis of the Proclamation of 1763," *Michigan Pioneer and Historical Society*, XXXVI (1908), 20–52.

Arnade, Charles W. "Cattle Raising in Spanish Florida, 1513–1763," *Agricultural History*, XXXV (July, 1961), 116–24.

————. "Florida Keys: English or Spanish in 1763?" *Tequesta*, XV (1955), 41–53.

————. "The Architecture of Spanish St. Augustine," *The Americas*, XVIII (October, 1961), 149–86.

————. "The Avero Story: An Early St. Augustine Family with Many Daughters and Many Houses," *Florida Historical Quarterly*, XXXX (July, 1961), 1–32.

———. "The English Invasion of Spanish Florida, 1700–1706," *Florida Historical Quarterly*, XLI (July, 1962) , 29–38.

———. "The Failure of Spanish Florida," *The Americas*, XVI (January, 1960) , 271–81.

Boyd, Mark F. "Apalache during the British Period: A Description Contained in a Series of Four Reports by Lt. Pittman R. E.," *Florida Historical Quarterly*, XII (October, 1933) , 114–22.

———. "Diego Peña's Expedition to Apalache and Apalachicola in 1716," *Florida Historical Quarterly*, XXVIII (July, 1949) , 1–27.

———. "Enumeration of Florida's Spanish Missions in 1675," *Florida Historical Quarterly*, XXVII (October, 1948) , 181–88.

———. "From a Remote Frontier: Letters and Documents Pertaining to San Marcos de Apalache, 1763–1769, during the British Occupation of Florida," *Florida Historical Quarterly*, XIX (January, 1941) , 179–212; XIX (April, 1941) , 402–12; XX (July, 1941) , 82–92; XX (October, 1941) , 203–9; XXI (October, 1942) , 135–46.

———. "From a Remote Frontier: Letters Passing between Captain Harries in Command at Apalache (St. Marks), 1763–1764 and the Commanders-in-Chief, Amherst and Gage," *Florida Historical Quarterly*, XIX (April, 1941) , 402–12.

———. "From a Remote Frontier: Letters Passing between Captain Harries in Command at Apalache (St. Marks) in 1764 and His Commander-in-Chief, General Gage, in New York," *Florida Historical Quarterly*, XX (July, 1941) , 82–92.

———. "Further Considerations of the Apalache Missions," *The Americas*, IX (April, 1953) , 459–79.

———. (trans.) . "The Siege of St. Augustine by Governor Moore of South Carolina as Reported to the King by Don Joseph de Zúñiga y Zerda, Governor of Florida," *Florida Historical Quarterly*, XXVI (April, 1948) , 345–53.

Carter, Clarence E. "Some Aspects of British Administration in West Florida," *Mississippi Valley Historical Review*, I (December, 1914) , 364–75.

———. "The Beginnings of British West Florida," *Mississippi Valley Historical Review*, IV (December, 1917) , 314–41.

Conner, Jeannette Thurber "Nine Old Wooden Forts of St. Augustine," *Florida Historical Quarterly*, IV (January and April, 1926) , 103–11 and 172–80.

Corbitt, Duvon C. "Spanish Relief Policy and the East Florida Refugees of 1763," *Florida Historical Quarterly*, XXVII (July, 1948) , 67–82.

Covington, James W. "Trade Relations between Southwestern Florida and Cuba, 1600–1840," *Florida Historical Quarterly*, XXXVIII (October, 1959) , 114–28.

Crane, Verner W. "Hints Relative to the Division and Government of the Conquered and Newly Acquired Countries in America," *Mississippi Valley Historical Review*, VIII (March, 1922) , 367–73.

———. "The Origin of the Name of the Creek Indians," *Mississippi Valley Historical Review*, V (December, 1918) , 339–42.

Davis, T. Frederick. "Pioneer Florida: An Interpretation of Spanish Law and Land Titles," *Florida Historical Quarterly*, XXIV (October, 1945) , 113–20.

Dunkle, John R. "Population Change as an Element in the Historical Geography of St. Augustine," *Florida Historical Quarterly,* XXXVII (July, 1958), 3–32.

Gentleman's Magazine. (November, 1763), 552–54.

Gentleman's Magazine. (January, 1767), 21–22.

Georgia Gazette. (April 14, 1763).

Gold, Robert L. "The Departure of Spanish Catholicism from Florida, 1763–1765," *The Americas,* XXII (April, 1966), 377–88.

———. "The East Florida Indians under Spanish and English Control, 1763–1765," *Florida Historical Quarterly,* XXXXIV (August, 1965), 105–20.

———. "The Settlement of the Pensacola Indians in New Spain, 1763–1770," *Hispanic American Historical Review,* XLV (November, 1965), 567–76.

Griffen, William B. "Spanish Pensacola, 1700–1763," *Florida Historical Quarterly,* XXXVII (January–April, 1959), 242–62.

Hanna, Alfred J. "The Beginnings of Florida," *American Heritage,* IV (December, 1952), 62–64.

Howard, Clinton N. "Alleged Spanish Grants in British West Florida," *Florida Historical Quarterly,* XXII (October, 1943), 74–85.

———. "Colonial Pensacola: The British Period," *Florida Historical Quarterly,* XIX (October, 1940), 109–27.

———. "Early Settlers in British West Florida," *Florida Historical Quarterly,* XXIV (July, 1945), 45–55.

———. "Some Economic Aspects of British West Florida, 1763–1768," *Journal of Southern History,* VI (May, 1940), 202–21.

———. "The Interval of Military Government in West Florida," *Louisiana Historical Quarterly,* XXII (January, 1939), 1–15.

———. "The Military Occupation of British West Florida," *Florida Historical Quarterly,* XVII (January, 1939), 181–99.

Humphreys, Robin A. "Lord Shelburne and the Proclamation of 1763," *English Historical Review,* XLIX (April, 1934), 241–64.

Johnson, Cecil. "Expansion in West Florida, 1770–1779," *Mississippi Valley Historical Review,* XX (March, 1934), 481–96.

Johnson, James G. "The Colonial Southeast, 1732–1763: An International Contest for Territorial and Economic Control," *University of Colorado Studies,* XIX (May, 1932).

Lawson, Katherine S. "Luciano de Herrera: Spanish Spy in British St. Augustine," *Florida Historical Quarterly,* XXIII (January, 1945), 170–76.

London Magazine. (March, 1763), 149–58.

Merritt, Webster. "West Florida, Three Centuries under Four Flags, Conquest and Disease," *Journal of the Florida Medical Association,* XXXIX (April, 1953), 749–65.

Metzger, Charles. "An Appraisal of Shelburne's Western Policy," *Mid-America,* XVIII (July, 1957), 169–81.

Mowat, Charles L. "St. Augustine under the British Flag," *Florida Historical Quarterly,* XX (October, 1941), 131–50.

———. "St. Francis Barracks, St. Augustine; A Link with the British Regime," *Florida Historical Quarterly,* XXI (January, 1943), 266–80.

———. "The First Campaign of Publicity for Florida," *Mississippi Valley Historical Review,* XXX (December, 1943), 359–476.

————. "The Land Policy in British East Florida," *Agricultural History*, XIV (April, 1940), 75–77.

Pennington, Edgar Legare. "John Forbes," *Florida Historical Quarterly*, VIII (January, 1930), 164–68.

————. "The Episcopal Church in Florida, 1763–1892," *Historical Magazine of the Protestant Episcopal Church*, VII (March, 1938), 1–77.

————. "The Episcopal Church in South Florida, 1764–1892," *Tequesta*, I (March, 1941), 47–88.

Robertson, James A. "Notes on Early Church Government in Spanish Florida," *Catholic Historical Review*, XVII (July, 1931), 151–74.

Scots Magazine. XXV (November, 1763), 627.

Scots Magazine. XXIX (January, 1767), 50.

Siebert, Wilbur H. "How the Spaniards Evacuated Pensacola in 1763," *Florida Historical Quarterly*, XI (October, 1932), 48–57.

————. "Slavery and White Servitude in East Florida," *Florida Historical Quarterly*, X (July, 1931), 1–23.

————. "Some Church History of St. Augustine during the Spanish Regime," *Florida Historical Quarterly*, IX (October, 1930), 117–23.

————. "The Departure of the Spaniards and Other Groups from East Florida, 1763," *Florida Historical Quarterly*, XIX (October, 1940), 145–54.

————. "The Port of St. Augustine during the British Regime," *Florida Historical Quarterly*, XXIV (April, 1946), 247–65, and XXV (July, 1946), 76–93.

South Carolina Gazette. (June 20, 1757, February 5–12, July 10–23, November 12–19, and December 21, 1763, and November 3–10, 1766).

Stetson, John B., Jr. "Florida as a Field for Historical Research," *Annual Report of the American Historical Association*, I (1922), 191–98.

Tingley, Helen E. B. "Florida under the English Flag, 1763–1783," *The Journal of American History*, XI (January, February, and March, 1917), 66–81.

Vigneras, L. A. "Fortificaciones de la Florida." *Anuario de Estudios Americanos*, XVI (1955), 533–52.

Unpublished Material

Beeson, Kenneth H., Jr. "Fromjadas and Indigo: The Minorcan Colony in Florida." Unpublished Master's thesis, University of Florida, 1960.

Boyd, Mark F. Unpublished two volume history of eighteenth-century Florida and Don Juan Elixio de la Puente—awaiting publication. Mark F. Boyd Library of Florida History. Tallahassee, Florida, 1962.

Dunkle, John R. "St. Augustine, Florida: A Study in Historical Geography." Unpublished Ph.D. dissertation, Clark University, 1957.

Index

Acpuro, Lamas, 151
Adelantados, 30–31
Agriculture: in Spanish Florida, 6
Alabama: Indian conferences, 176–77; mentioned, 108–10
Alabama Fort, 106, 112, 114
Alabama River, 178, 231*n*2
Alachua, 180
Albemarle, Earl of. *See* Keppel, Augustus
Alberja, Lázaro, 55
Alexander VI, 4
Alibamon Indians: British relations, 114, 165–67; French relations, 162, 164–65
Allegheny Mountains: Indian boundaries, 123–24, 188
Altamaha River, 10, 118, 127–28, 130, 188
Amelia Island, 11
American Independence, 16
American Revolutionary War, 48, 140, 150, 210*n*53
Amherst, Jeffrey, 14, 45, 92, 97
Amoscotigui y Bermudo, Pedro: Indian protector, 160–61; mentioned, 55
Anglican Church: employs Spanish buildings, 42, 138–39; Florida organization, 143–48, 151–52, 186
Anglo-Indian Relations: Spanish-Indian relations, 156, 158–59; mentioned, 179, 182
Annibel, Pierre Nicolas

(Chevalier Sieur de Ville), 107, 111–12
Antigua Vera Cruz. *See* José Cardel
Apalache: attacked by Carolina, 8; evacuation, 36, 66, 69, 73, 75, 92–99, 104, 133, 185–86; British occupation, 55, 144, 148, 219*n*55; mentioned, 6–8, 140, 154–55, 208*n*25
Apalachicola Indians, 154, 181
Apalachicola River: Florida boundary, 118; mentioned, 222*n*35
Arkansas, 162
Arriaga, Julián de: exodus correspondence, 90; mentioned, 102, 156–57
Arriola, Andrés de, 10
Atlantic Coast: Florida boundary, 118, 181–82
Audiencias, 31
Avoyelle Indians, 115
Azores, 4

Bahama Channel: Florida exodus, 68–69, 75; mentioned, 4, 24–25, 189
Bahama Islands, 24
Baldías, 33
Baptiste, Jean (Sieur de Bienville) , 61
Barra de la Florida: obstacle to trade, 39–40; mentioned, 36, 90
Barrio de Guadalupe (Havana) , 77
Barrio de San Antonio (Havana) , 85

Baton Rouge, 61
Bayou Lafourche, 165
Bedford, Duke of. *See* Russell, John
Bedfordites, 16
Bermuda, 25–26
Bernet, Joseph: Spanish evacuation, 100–102; mentioned, 55
Bienville, Sieur de. *See* Baptiste, Jean
Biloxi: British occupation, 114; mentioned, 58, 61, 162
Bimini, 3
Blood for Blood: Anglo-Indian relations, 171, 175, 177–78, 181
Board of Trade and Plantations: Florida settlement, vii, 188; Shelburne presidency, 22; Gordon case, 28; Grant correspondence, 52–53, 178–79; Indian policy, 122, 168, 179; Proclamation of 1763, 122–26, 130; Florida boundaries, 125–27, 225*n*25; Gray affair, 128–30; church organization, 144–45; mentioned, 46
Boca de Ratones, 24
Boone, Thomas, 45, 129–30
Borderlands, vii, 11, 125–32
Bouquet, Henry, 114
Bourbon Family Compact, 13, 164–65
Bourbon Kings: Indian alliances, 163; mentioned, 14

INDEX